MW00355489

The Osteology of Infants and Children

NUMBER TWELVE:
TEXAS A&M UNIVERSITY ANTHROPOLOGY SERIES
D. GENTRY STEELE, GENERAL EDITOR

The Osteology *of* Infants and Children

Brenda J. Baker, Tosha L. Dupras, and Matthew W. Tocheri

DRAWINGS BY SANDRA M. WHEELER

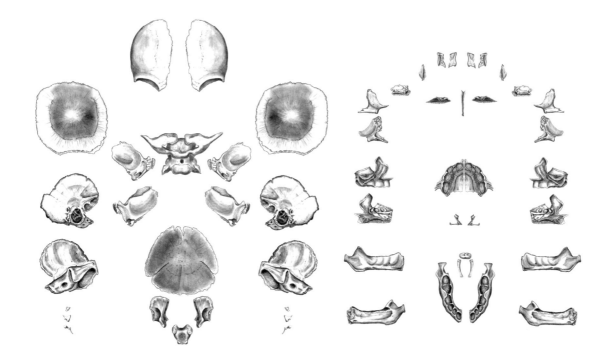

TEXAS A&M UNIVERSITY PRESS ■ *College Station*

Copyright 2005 © by Brenda J. Baker, Tosha L. Dupras,
Matthew W. Tocheri, and Sandra M. Wheeler
Manufactured in the United States of America
All rights reserved
First edition
Second printing, 2010

The paper used in this book meets the minimum requirements
of the American National Standard for Permanence
of Paper for Printed Library Materials, Z39.48-1984.
Binding materials have been chosen for durability. ∞

Library of Congress Cataloging-in-Publication Data

Baker, Brenda J.
    The osteology of infants and children / Brenda J. Baker, Tosha L.
Dupras, and Matthew W. Tocheri ; drawings by Sandra M. Wheeler.—1st ed.
        p. cm.—(Texas A&M University anthropology series ' no. 12)
    Includes bibliographical references and index.
    ISBN 1-58544-428-6 (cloth : alk. paper) — ISBN 1-58544-465-0 (pbk. : alk. paper)
    1. Children—Physiology.   2. Infants—Physiology.   3. Fetus—Physiology.
    4. Human skeleton—Identification.   5. Human remains (Archaeology)
    I. Dupras, Tosha L.   II. Tocheri, Matthew W.   III. title.   IV. Texas A&M
University anthropology series ; no. 12.
        GN63.B35   2005
        930.1—dc22
                                                              2004028032

    ISBN-13: 978-1-58544-465-6

Contents

Chapter 5. The Dentition   **53**

Preface

This book is intended to fill the need for a field and lab manual on subadult osteology and provide a textbook for human osteology courses. Unlike other osteology texts, it focuses on the recovery, identification, and siding of skeletal elements from fetuses, infants, and children, as well as from adolescents who have nearly attained adult morphology. Basic descriptions of each skeletal element at varying stages of development, along with sections on differentiation from other bones and siding tips are provided. The book can serve as a guide to field and lab procedures and will help investigators distinguish human and nonhuman bones, particularly those of fetuses and infants. The book provides many illustrations of juvenile skeletal elements as reference material for those who lack access to a study collection with such remains. These illustrations and descriptions will permit identification of human subadult remains in field and lab settings.

Our work with abundant subadult remains from ancient Egyptian contexts provides a unique opportunity to undertake a book on subadult osteology. We are involved in long-term projects in which we have excavated and analyzed many extremely well-preserved burials of fetuses, infants, and children. This book is derived from our combined experience in working with these remains. We have all contributed significantly, in complementary ways, to this collaboration. The result is a vastly stronger book than any of us could have produced separately.

This book would not have been possible without the support of the respective projects in Egypt. Brenda Baker has been the physical anthropologist for the University of Pennsylvania Museum–Yale University–Institute of Fine Arts, New York University Expedition to Abydos since 1988, and Sandra Wheeler served as an artist for the 2002–2003 field season. Abydos was the site of Early Dynastic royal tombs and funerary enclosures, with cemeteries that have been in use over the past 5,000 years. Codirected by David O'Connor (IFA) and William Kelly Simpson (Yale University), the expedition was initiated in 1967. Special gratitude is owed to David O'Connor and particularly to Matthew Adams (University of Pennsylvania and IFA), associate director, and Janet Richards (University of Michigan), director of the Abydos Middle Cemetery Project, University of Michigan, for their continuing interest in the human remains and incorporation of bioarchaeology in their respective projects at Abydos. The many subadult burials that have been carefully excavated during the fieldwork directed by Adams and Richards in the North Cemetery, Middle Cemetery, and settlement site have been invaluable in creating this book. All photographs of Abydos material are the property of Brenda Baker and are published with the permission of the University of Pennsylvania Museum–Yale University–Institute of Fine Arts, New York University Expedition to Abydos.

Tosha Dupras has been a member of the physical anthropology team of the Dakhleh Oasis Project since 1995, and Matthew Tocheri joined the team in 1998. The mandate of the Dakhleh Oasis Project is the study of human adaptation to the harsh Saharan environment. This international multidisciplinary project began in 1978 under the auspices of the Royal Ontario Museum and the directorship of Anthony Mills. The physical anthropology team is directed by El Molto (University of Western Ontario). The subadult remains from this project are associated with two cemeteries of the village of Kellis and span the Ptolemaic through Christian periods. The analysis of these burials has also proved indispensable to the production of this book.

Many other individuals have contributed to this work through participation in field projects in which the remains that form the basis of the book were excavated or analyzed. We are indebted to all of them. We especially thank Scott Haddow, Jaime Ullinger, Lana Williams, and Melissa Zabecki for their assistance. Matthew Adams, Scott Burnett, and Rebecca Hill reviewed drafts of certain chapters and provided helpful comments that have improved the book, as did the two anonymous reviewers. We also thank our families for their support of our endeavors.

PART ONE
The Bare Bones of Subadult Skeletons

In this section, the basics of studying the skeletal remains of fetuses, infants, and children are addressed. Students who take a course in human osteology often receive little or no training in the recognition of such remains. Thus, skeletal material from children, and particularly from fetuses and infants, is often confused with animal bone during archaeological fieldwork. Certain skeletal elements may be overlooked because the archaeologist or bioarchaeologist conducting the fieldwork does not have a framework for identifying the remains or is using excavation techniques that are not suited to recovery of small bones or growth centers that are just beginning to ossify.

In the first chapter, therefore, the importance of recognizing subadult remains and including them in studies concerning bioarchaeology, osteology, and paleopathology is delineated. Recognition of subadult skeletal remains relies on an understanding of skeletal development and the anatomical terminology needed to identify and side specific elements. The second chapter is devoted to recovery and storage of subadult remains and procedural recommendations that differ from strategies generally employed for adult burials.

Chapter **1** Studying the Bones of Children

■ The field of human osteology typically emphasizes the bones of the adult skeleton, yet the burials of subadults often represent up to half of the remains in many mortuary sites. It is, therefore, crucial to include them in bioarchaeological investigations. The skeletons of subadults at varying stages of development differ in the number of skeletal elements present and in their appearance, complicating their identification. For this reason, it is important to develop a basic understanding of bone growth and development from the fetal through adolescent stages to aid in identification of the bones that are present in a given skeleton or in a set of commingled remains. The ability to identify and side specific bones at each of these stages relies on standard anatomical terminology that is defined in this chapter.

Why Are Skeletal Remains of Subadults Important for Interpreting the Archaeological Record?

Burials of fetuses, infants, and children are overlooked in many investigations. Their exclusion arises partly from the perception that subadult skeletal material is poorly preserved in comparison to that of adults (Guy et al., 1997; Mays, 1998), but also from a lack of recognition and inadequate excavation techniques. Recovery and investigation of subadult skeletons are hampered by sparse coverage in most human osteology courses and textbooks. General human osteology texts (e.g., Bass, 1995; Steele and Bramblett, 1988; White, 2000) emphasize the adult skeleton and have few illustrations of subadult skeletal elements. Study collections of subadult material are usually very small or unavailable at most universities. As a result, students of human osteology generally do not become well acquainted with the range of age-based variation until they have several years of experience and have delved into specialized texts such as Fazekas and Kósa's (1978) long out-of-print work *Forensic Fetal Osteology* or Scheuer and Black's (2000) treatise *Developmental Juvenile Osteology*. Even then, many choose to avoid working with subadult remains because they may be perceived as too difficult and time-consuming to deal with or not worthwhile in terms of information gained. This perception is likely rooted in unfamiliarity. However, there is still no reliable method of determining the sex of preadolescents, so why should we worry about remains if we cannot distinguish males and females with confidence? On the other hand, we can more accurately and precisely age subadult versus adult remains, so why not include children in our studies? The sheer numbers of subadult skeletons in archaeological settings and the need to identify them in forensic contexts makes it increasingly necessary to counter their neglect in osteological training and research. Subadult osteology is vital for understanding the range of modern human skeletal variation in bioarchaeological and forensic contexts, and is also imperative in paleoanthropology for fossil fragments of hominid subadults to be more readily recognized.

Skeletons of fetuses, infants, and children can provide a wealth of information on the populations from which they come. Whenever skeletal remains are recovered, estimating the age at death of the individual is often a critical first step for further investigation. In forensic and occasionally historic archaeological cases, establishing the age at death is important for positive identification of the deceased. In archaeological samples, age estimates are important for a variety of reasons depending on the specific research objectives. For instance, if a researcher is interested in how different environments have affected the growth and development of two or more past human populations, the age at death of each subadult included in the sample needs to be estimated. Another instance might involve trying to understand the burial practices of a past population by determining at what age subadults receive treatment similar to adults. Determining the demographic structure and overall health status of the population also relies heavily on accurate estimations of subadult age at death.

Studying the patterns and processes of growth in prehistoric skeletal samples is perhaps the most typical component of a research design that involves subadult skeletons. Variations in the timing and trajectory of skeletal and dental development are known to exist within and between populations for many reasons. These include differences due to genetic, environmental, nutritional, and socioeconomic factors. Such growth-related studies typically include the goal of investigating general aspects of health and well-being in prehistoric populations (e.g., Johnston and Zimmer, 1989; Saunders and Hoppa, 1993). Humphrey (2000) and Saunders (2000) provide excellent syntheses of growth-related studies in physical anthropology. Data derived from these studies often form a baseline for further studies of paleodemography and paleopathology.

Paleodemography, which is the study of past populations' age and sex composition, birth and mortality rates, and other population statistics, relies on analyses of representative skeletal samples. The inclusion of subadult remains in such samples is critical for accurate reconstructions of population size and structure, mortality and survivorship rates, life expectancies at birth, and population fertility and birth rates. A large body of literature in physical anthropology is associated with paleodemography. For more detailed information on this area of research, we suggest the following overviews and the references within them: Hoppa and Vaupel (2002); Konigsberg and Frankenberg (1994); Milner et al. (2000); and Paine (1997).

Despite the onset of many diseases in childhood (e.g., nutritional deficiencies like rickets and scurvy, and infections like tuberculosis and yaws), research in paleopathology, the study of disease in past populations, is often limited to adults. The incorporation of subadults in paleopathology serves to broaden our understanding of disease prevalence, transmission, susceptibility, age-of-onset, and differential diagnosis. The prevalence of conditions such as porotic hyperostosis (pitting on the skull vault) and cribra orbitalia (lesions on the roof of the eye orbits, fig. 1.1) attest to nutritional adequacy and health status, as do disruptions in the formation of tooth enamel

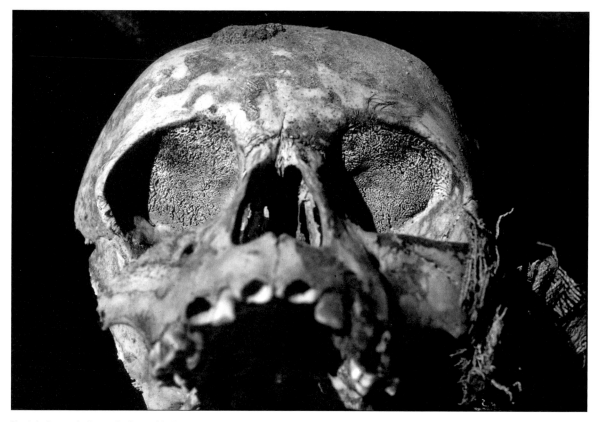

Fig. 1.1 Severe lesions of cribra orbitalia were active at the time of death in a young child, 1 to 4 years old, from the Abydos Middle Cemetery in Egypt (AMC1999.35). The pathology in this child is indicative of anemia, arising from inadequate nutrition, malabsorption of iron due to a heavy parasite load, diarrheal diseases, or a combination of these factors. *Photograph by Brenda Baker*

(hypoplasias) during childhood. Patterns of trauma elucidate the risks of childhood and, potentially, even child abuse (Walker et al., 1997). Congenital abnormalities or developmental defects in subadult and adult remains can shed light on the prevalence of both symptomatic and asymptomatic abnormalities in past populations. Major treatises on paleopathology include Aufderheide and Rodríguez-Martín (1998) and Ortner (2003). For a general overview of nonspecific stress indicators, as well as infectious disease, see Larsen (1997) and Mays (1998). Lewis (2000) specifically addresses issues in nonadult paleopathology and provides many references for those interested in investigating past disease in subadult skeletons.

The primary books devoted to the osteology of subadult remains (Fazekas and Kósa, 1978; Scheuer and Black, 2000, 2004) are invaluable resources on the embryological and fetal development of the human skeleton. A principal goal of these books is the determination of age. Scheuer and Black (2000) also delineate many developmental anomalies and their formation during growth. While they devote some attention to the differentiation of similar bones and siding techniques, these sections are brief and pertain mainly to perinatal elements. In this book, means of distinguishing skeletal elements from those with similar morphology and techniques for determining which side of the body is represented are priorities.

Techniques used to identify and side adult bones do not always apply to fetal, infant, or juvenile remains. Hence, the approach taken in subsequent chapters is to provide descriptions of bones at various stages of development with methods used to identify, side, and differentiate them from bones of similar appearance at these stages. In some cases, the techniques used pertain to adult bones as well. The information provided should improve the ability to identify and side bones from fetal, infant, and juvenile skeletons easily and promote their inclusion in future research. Excellent casts of subadult material of varying ages (including bones from a neonate, an infant 0.5–1.5 years, and children 1–2 years and 7.5–8.5 years, as well as dental development casts) are available from France Casting (www.francecasts.com/home) to supplement study collections and the illustrations in this book. In addition, the mini-osteometric board developed by Jim Kondrat of Paleo-tech Concepts (www.paleotech.com) greatly facilitates measurements of subadult bones.

The present volume relies considerably on Fazekas and Kósa (1978), Scheuer and Black (2000), and other standard osteological (Bass, 1995; Schwartz, 1995; Steele and Bramblett, 1988; White, 2000), anatomical (e.g., Gray, 1977), and radiological (e.g., Garn et al., 1967; Greulich and Pyle, 1959; MacKay, 1961; Tanner and Whitehouse, 1959) references for the age of appearance and fusion of ossification centers. While some knowledge of adult osteology is helpful, it is not a prerequisite for using this book. The basic mechanisms of bone growth and development, as well as anatomical terminology used in the descriptions of skeletal elements, are included in this chapter to provide a complete reference manual for use in the field or lab.

The Developing Skeleton: A Framework for Understanding How Bones Grow

Bone is a dynamic tissue that serves multiple functions: it protects and supports soft tissue; it anchors muscles, tendons, and ligaments, and acts as levers to produce movement; and it provides centers for the production of blood cells and storage of fat and minerals. Bone is comprised of an inorganic or mineral component, as well as an organic or protein component. In adults, the organic portion comprises 24% of the dry weight of cortical (dense) bone, while the inorganic portion constitutes 76% (Baker, 1992). In children, the organic portion forms a larger proportion than in adults. The organic material is composed principally of the protein collagen, which imparts elasticity, flexibility, and tensile strength. The inorganic component (hydroxyapatite) provides rigidity, hardness, and strength in compression. In infants and children, some of the skeleton is still cartilaginous or membranous, resulting in greater elasticity and flexibility than adult bone. Therefore, it is no surprise that young children can perform amazing feats of agility and break bones infrequently in comparison to older individuals exposed to similar stresses.

In the developing fetus, bone replaces models preformed in cartilage or connective tissue membrane. Thus, ossification proceeds in two ways: endochondral (based on a cartilage template) or intramembranous (within dermal or membranous precursors). In some cases, bones develop from a combination of these processes. The initial bone that forms is referred to as woven, or immature, bone. Woven bone develops rapidly and is less organized than the lamellar, or mature, bone that gradually replaces it. Lamellar bone has two forms. One is the dense compact or cortical bone that comprises the shafts of the tubular bones of the appendages and the outer surface (cortex) of most other bones (e.g., the ilium, scapula, cranial bones). The other type of lamellar bone is formed from a network of spicules called trabeculae and resembles a sponge. For this reason it is often called spongy bone, but it is more correctly termed cancellous or trabecular bone.

This type of bone is found in the ends of tubular bones, the bones of the wrist (carpals) and ankle (tarsals), vertebral centra (the bodies in adults), and the interior regions of flat bones such as the ilium, scapula, and ribs.

The initial site of ossification is referred to as the primary center. Most primary centers appear during fetal development, although some, such as most of the carpals and tarsals, appear after birth. Secondary centers appear in many bones after the primary center has developed. These can coalesce quickly with the primary center or develop as separate elements known as epiphyses. Epiphyses fuse to the main body of the bone at later stages of development, typically in adolescence. At birth, approximately 450 separate ossification centers or elements are present. These gradually enlarge throughout childhood and fuse together to form the typical 206 bones of the adult human skeleton.

The complex process of ossification and bone growth is delineated in many texts. The following discussion is simplified to provide a basic understanding of bone growth. Readers should consult Scheuer and Black (2000) for a more detailed account. Most human osteology textbooks describe the process of bone development for the long bones of the arms and legs, with little attention paid to bones that ossify from only a single center or to the growth of epiphyses. While similar, there are some differences in the growth pattern. In all cases, growth arises from a combination of bone formation (apposition) and removal (resorption) that relies upon the adequate supply of nutrients from blood vessels (vascularization). This combination of apposition and resorption is called modeling in an immature bone, while in the mature bone it is referred to as remodeling.

In long bones, the primary center of ossification forms the diaphysis, or shaft. Bone apposition begins in an area of vascularity that invades the cartilaginous template, with one vessel eventually predominating. This vessel is the nutrient artery, which enters the diaphysis through a nutrient foramen. Osteoblasts are bone-forming cells that deposit osteoid, which is the organic matrix of bone. The osteoid is rapidly mineralized in the midshaft area, forming a shell of woven bone. Encasing this newly formed bone is the periosteum, which continues to be osteogenic (bone-producing) throughout life. After the primary center of ossification forms, a highly vascularized cartilaginous region develops at each end of the bone, which is known as the growth plate. At the ends of the diaphysis, in the areas known as metaphyses, vascular loops arranged perpendicular to the growth plate extend from the bone into the zone of ossification. In this zone, cartilage cells become mineralized and are replaced by osteoblasts. Once the secondary centers begin to ossify, the disk-shaped growth plate separates the epiphysis from metaphysis and permits the bone to continue growing in length. The end of the metaphysis generally displays a furrowed or billowy surface where it eventually joins with the epiphysis. This surface is referred to as the epiphyseal surface since it faces the epiphysis. An epiphysis has a similar roughened or furrowed surface that eventually fuses to the shaft and is termed the metaphyseal surface. The side opposite the metaphyseal surface is articular if part of a joint (e.g., the femoral head) or nonarticular if not at a joint (e.g., the greater trochanter).

The metaphysis also plays a role in transverse growth of the bone. As it is laid down, new bone is reorganized through resorption by osteoclasts (bone-removing cells). New bone is deposited along the margins of the metaphysis and growth plate, permitting the width of the bone to expand as it grows in length. Subperiosteal bone apposition continues along the diaphysis, while it is resorbed at the inner margin, or endosteal surface, which is also osteogenic. This process allows the entire length of the bone to increase in width and permits the formation of the medullary or marrow cavity in the bone's interior. As the diaphysis continues to grow and the epiphysis (which also has a growth plate) ossifies and enlarges, the expansion of the cartilaginous growth plate slows and bone formation eventually outpaces the formation of cartilage. The growth plates of the diaphysis and epiphysis eventually meet and the cartilage plate thins and is pierced by blood vessels. The periosteum then extends over the abutting growth plates and, as bone is formed along the vascular channels, bridges begin to connect the epiphysis with the diaphysis. The process of epiphyseal fusion is gradual. Upon completion of epiphyseal union, longitudinal growth ceases.

Epiphyses, as well as bones that form from a single, primary center (e.g., carpals, tarsals, vertebral centra) are also dependent upon endochondral ossification and vascularization. The many vascular foramina encountered in developing epiphyses and nonarticular areas of largely trabecular bone like the carpals, tarsals, or vertebral centra attest to the invasion of blood vessels via cartilage canals. Cartilage begins to calcify in the vascularized areas and is replaced by osteoid. Due to the highly vascularized nature, the bone is cancellous, or filled with spaces to permit the passage of the blood vessels. The growth plate in these elements is spherical. Thus, bone continues to replace cartilage in a radiating pattern. As with long bones, growth stops when the pace of cartilage formation falls behind that of bone apposition and the zone of ossification makes contact with the perichondrium (outer covering of the cartilage template). Intramembranous ossification of the periosteum then occurs and the modeling process ends. The bones subsequently continue to change through the process of remodeling.

Intramembranous ossification in the fetus is a simpler process and occurs earlier than endochondral ossification.

It involves the direct mineralization of the membranous template. Osteoid is deposited in the matrix as vascularization occurs, forming a center of ossification. This type of ossification characterizes many of the flat bones of the skull vault and bones of the face. New bone continues to be deposited on the surface, permitting expansion of the ossification center.

Anatomical Terms and Directions

For reference purposes, the adult human skeleton is typically oriented in a standing posture with no bone crossing over another. Thus, the legs are together with the toes pointing forward and the arms are at the sides with the palms facing forward. This orientation is known as standard anatomical position. While it feels awkward for most of us to stand with our palms facing forward rather than toward the legs, this position ensures that the bones of the forearm are not crossed. It is important to remember the hand position in reference to directional terms relating to anatomical features that permit identification of the side of the body from which a bone comes. While standard anatomical position is based on the adult skeleton, it pertains to any child who has begun to walk. For fetuses and infants who have not yet begun to walk, the body can be envisioned in a supine position (on the back), with the toes pointing up and the palms facing up along the sides of the body. This position is essentially the equivalent of an adult body in anatomical position that has been tipped over onto its back.

A human body or skeleton oriented in standard anatomical position is typically divided into three planes of reference—the sagittal, coronal or frontal, and the transverse planes (fig. 1.2). These planes form the basis of many of the directional terms used in anatomy. The sagittal plane divides the body into right and left halves along a midline that begins at the top of the skull and continues downward between the legs and feet. Medial is toward the midline, while lateral is away from the midline. In the forearm, the ulna is the medial bone and the radius is the lateral bone in anatomical position. Paired bones (those that appear on both the right and left sides) have medial and lateral portions. Many students become confused if they attempt to divide each appendage along its center instead of referring to the plane dividing the body as a whole. Thus, in the tibia, the medial side of the bone is on the inside of the leg (toward the midline of the body), while lateral is toward the fibula or outside of the leg. Anatomical landmarks on a given bone are typically described as medial or lateral to other features as well. For example, the head of a femur is medial to its neck and the greater trochanter is lateral to both.

The coronal or frontal plane begins at the crown of the head and divides the body into front and rear halves. The front part is referred to as ventral or anterior. The rear part is termed dorsal or posterior. Some bones, therefore, lie in the anterior part of the body (e.g., the sternum and clavicles), while others lie in the posterior half (e.g., vertebrae and scapulae). Bones also have anterior (ventral) and posterior (dorsal) sides and anatomical features are described in relation to each other based on these relationships (e.g., the tibial tuberosity is on the anterior part of the tibia; the spinous process of a thoracic vertebra is posterior to the transverse processes).

The transverse plane is perpendicular to the sagittal and frontal planes. It divides the body into upper and lower halves. Bones from the upper portion of the body are cranial (toward the head) or superior (on top), while bones from the lower portion are caudal (toward the tail) or inferior (beneath). The prefixes "supra" and "infra" are also used to indicate the superior and inferior directions. Bones also have superior and inferior (or cranial and caudal) aspects. A vertebral body, for example, has a superior surface and an inferior surface. The glenoid cavity of a scapula is inferior to the coracoid and acromion processes, but it is superior to the axillary margin and the inferior angle.

Other directional terminology derives from the relationship of major divisions of the body. The skeleton is often divided at the neck, with bones of the skull referred to as cranial and all bones below the skull referred to as infracranial (under or beneath the skull). In quadrupeds, where the body is behind the skull, the terms cranial and postcranial are used. The latter terminology technically pertains to crawling infants as well. The axial skeleton forms the trunk of the body (the skull, thorax, and pelvic girdle), while the appendicular skeleton refers to the appendages or limbs (bones of the arms and legs). Proximal and distal are directional terms used in relation to these divisions (fig. 1.3). Proximal refers to a bone or part of a bone that is closest to the trunk or axial skeleton, while distal is a bone or portion of a bone that is farthest from the trunk. Thus, the humerus is proximal to the radius and ulna, but the trochlea and olecranon fossa are features on the distal end of the bone. The medial and lateral epicondyles, however, are proximal to the trochlea and capitulum.

Special terms are used for the hands and feet. Dorsal refers to the back of the hand (as it lies in standard anatomical position), but it also refers to the top of the foot. The opposite side or sole of the foot is its plantar surface, while the opposite side of the hand is the palmar,

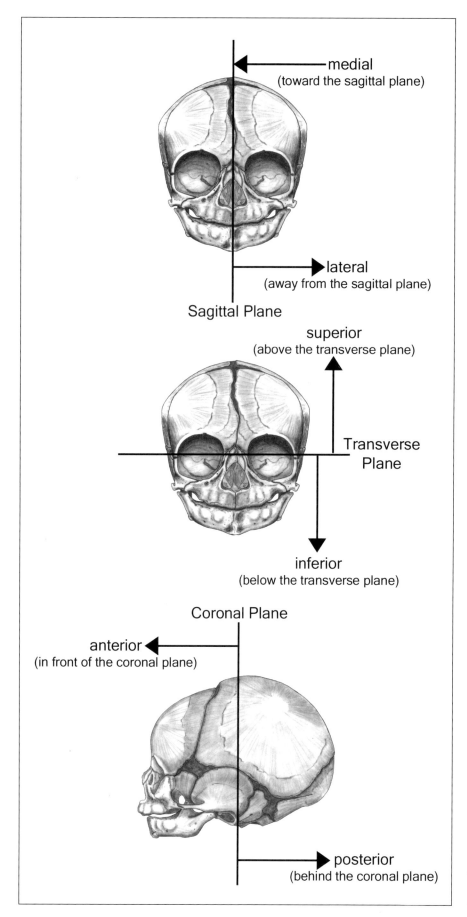

Fig. 1.2 Three anatomical planes of reference divide the skeleton into left and right halves (sagittal), upper and lower halves (transverse), and front and back halves (coronal). Anatomical directions pertaining to each plane are used to describe relationships between features on each bone and are demonstrated on a neonatal skull.

or volar, surface (see chap. 9). Other terms are particular to the dentition (see chap. 5). In both the upper and lower jaws, mesial is toward the point on the midline where the central incisors meet, and distal is away from that point. Thus, the mesial surface of a canine is next to the distal surface of the second (or lateral) incisor. Teeth also have a buccal (toward the cheek) or labial (toward the lip) side that is opposite the lingual side, which is toward the tongue. The biting portion of the anterior teeth is referred to as the incisal edge, while the grinding portion of molars and premolars is known as the occlusal surface. Interproximal refers to spaces between adjacent teeth, and is easily remembered as the areas where you put your dental floss.

Bones themselves are often categorized by their shapes. Long bones are large, tubular bones of the limbs with articular ends. Short bones are small versions of long bones and include the metacarpals, metatarsals, and phalanges of the hands and feet, along with the clavicle. Many bones of the cranial vault are classified as flat bones because they lack the tubularity of long and short bones and are, instead, thin and wide. Flat bones also include the ribs, ilia (os coxae in adults), scapulae, and sternebrae. Bones that do not fit into these categories are termed irregular bones because of their odd shapes. These tend to be blocky bones such as those comprising the vertebral column, as well as the carpals, tarsals, patellae, and some cranial bones (e.g., the sphenoid).

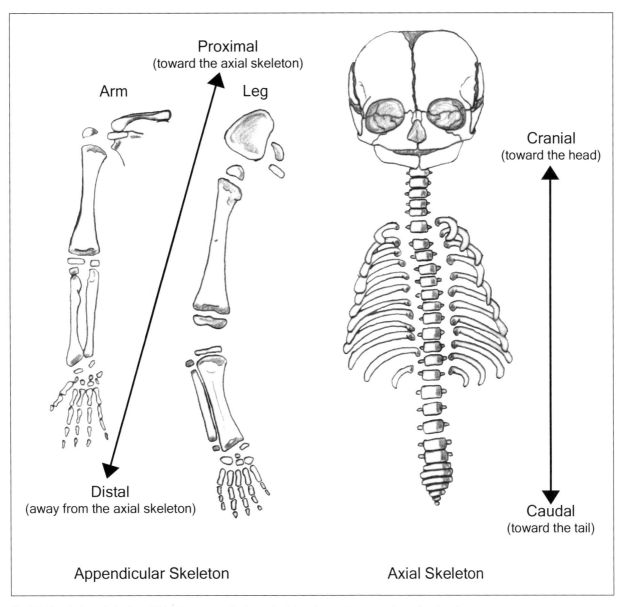

Fig. 1.3 The skeleton is further divided into appendicular and axial sections with concomitant directional terms.

When faced with a bone to identify, it is easiest to begin by determining whether it is cranial or infracranial. Infracranial bones should then be classified by their shape to narrow the possibilities (e.g., if it is a flat bone then all the long and short bones can be eliminated from consideration). Proper identification of a bone necessitates knowledge of its morphology and anatomical features at various stages of development. In this book, the appearance of each bone is described at key stages of development to aid in its identification at different ages. The section on differentiation from other bones points out distinguishing features at each stage in relation to bones of similar shape. Once a bone is identified, the side of the body it comes from must be determined if it is a paired bone (e.g., the femur, ribs, etc.). Many siding techniques rely on positioning the bone in standard anatomical position and then looking for distinguishing anatomical features. In addition to these techniques, we also provide alternative ways of siding bones that do not require orientation in anatomical position. Some of these tricks are quick and easy means of determining a bone's side that often help you remember its most distinctive features.

Placing Subadult Skeletons in Age and Sex Categories

Many different terms are employed to describe individuals who are not yet considered mature adults. In fact, there is no agreement on exactly when an individual becomes adult. In many textbooks, the division occurs at age 18 or 20. In others, adulthood is perceived to be slightly earlier, at the end of puberty or adolescence (i.e., after sexual maturity is achieved and the adolescent growth spurt is complete). All those younger than adults can be referred to as subadults. Some osteologists prefer to label these individuals as nonadults. Additional terms used in this volume are fetus, perinate, neonate, infant, child or juvenile, and adolescent.

Fetus applies to any skeleton that is less than full term. This 9-month gestational period is divided into trimesters or 3-month intervals. Perinatal refers to the time just before or after birth. In practice, it is often difficult to separate a late-term fetus from a newborn. In this situation, the term perinate may be the most accurate. Neonate refers specifically to a newborn in its first month of life, while infant encompasses the period from birth to one year of age. A child is an individual over age 1 and up to puberty. Juvenile has been used interchangeably with child in this book, but often refers to older children in whom the permanent dentition has begun to erupt. This distinction can also be used to divide childhood into early and late stages, so that young childhood extends from age 1 to 6 and older childhood from about 7 to 12 years. Puberty begins as early as age 10 in females and 12 in males and marks the onset of adolescence. Adolescence extends through the period of growth, generally culminating around age 14 in females and 16 in males. Adolescents are typically included in the child or juvenile grouping because they are not yet mature. The period from the beginning of ossification in the fetus through adolescent bone development forms the focus of this book. The templates and tables in chapter 10 summarize the general developmental stages of bone growth for placement in the age categories we have defined.

Determining the sex of the fetal and juvenile skeleton is a difficult endeavor given that most of the morphological features related to sexual differences in human skeletal remains are not present until after the onset of puberty. In most cases, researchers agree that determining the sex of subadult skeletal remains cannot be accomplished with much accuracy. Research on sexing fetal and juvenile remains has concentrated on potential sexual morphological and metric differences in the pelvis (Boucher, 1955; 1957; Holcomb and Konigsberg, 1995; Hunt, 1990; Mittler and Sheridan, 1992; Rogers and Saunders, 1994; Schutkowski, 1987; 1993; Weaver, 1980), mandible (Loth and Henneberg, 2001; Schutkowski, 1987; 1993; Scheuer, 2002) and dentition (Black, 1978; DeVito and Saunders, 1990; Hunt and Gleiser, 1955). Generally, morphological characteristics have been found to be more reliable than metric techniques.

Among the various methods advanced for determining sex of juvenile remains, males have been found to classify at a higher rate of accuracy than females. Many of the proposed methods, however, have not been tested further on documented samples of known sex. Those that have been tested on another sample tend to produce much lower accuracy than originally reported (e.g., Scheuer, 2002). Because no method for sexing juvenile remains is currently widely accepted, we have chosen not to describe such techniques more fully in this book. Consult Sutter (2003) and Scheuer and Black (2000) for further discussion of this issue.

Chapter 2   Excavating the Remains of Fetuses, Infants, and Children

■ The burials of children, especially those of fetuses and infants, are sometimes missed or ignored in archaeological excavations and are, thus, poorly represented in many extant skeletal collections. Ubelaker (1999:2) suggests that "skeletal collections in museums often contain only adults because it was previously believed that little could be learned from immature individuals." Extant samples, therefore, are often biased, skewing observations of mortality and health status. Other factors that contribute to the underrepresentation of subadults include differential mortuary treatment, differential preservation, and inadequate excavation techniques.

Recognition and Preservation

In any mortuary program, age is often a criterion for differential treatment of the dead. Children may be buried in the same location as adult family members (fig. 2.1), but they are often interred in separate areas reserved specifically for children. Burials of children in many societies are often separated from those of adults, particularly if they were stillborn or did not survive long after birth. Socioeconomic status is frequently a factor in determining the disposition of a child's body. For example, remains of infants and young children are often found under house floors of ancient Egyptian settlement sites (fig. 2.2), while others are located in formal cemeteries amid the burials of adults (fig. 2.3). In this case, burials from the cemetery context alone are not representative of the living population, since subadults would be underenumerated. Burials may also be found in midden contexts. Sample bias is, thus, often a reflection of the area excavated. Archaeological research designs should take such potential bias into account. Osteologists analyzing any collection must also learn as much as possible about the excavation and burial context to avoid misinterpretations due to potential sample bias. For example, infanticide is sometimes suggested as a cause of infant underenumeration in skeletal samples (e.g., Mays, 1993; Smith and Kahila, 1992); however, more probabilistic approaches to skeletal aging suggest that the observed peaks in perinatal mortality are more likely a consequence of differential burial treatment for stillbirths and premature babies unable to survive without modern medical intervention (Gowland and Chamberlain, 2002; Tocheri et al., 2005).

Differential preservation is another factor contributing to underrepresentation of subadult burials (Gordon and Buikstra, 1981; Guy et al., 1997; Mays, 1998). Bones of children are small and may just be starting to ossify. Because they are not as well mineralized as the bones of adults, they are more subject to diagenesis and may suffer greater postmortem degradation. The small size of baby bones and ossification centers that are just beginning to form makes them more likely to be displaced by bioturbation or disturbance by animals. In some cases, however, the bones of children may be better preserved than those of adults due to differential mortuary treatment (e.g., interment in pottery vessels) or even taboos concerning their disturbance. Because of their small size, however, it is much more likely that burials of infants and children will be missed in test excavations or any sampling procedure. It is also much more likely that they will be inadvertently destroyed by backhoes or misplaced shovels because the burial features are small and not as obvious as those of adults.

Fig. 2.1 An infant interred next to the legs of its mother from the Kellis 2 cemetery (Roman period) at Dakhleh Oasis. *Photograph by Tosha Dupras*

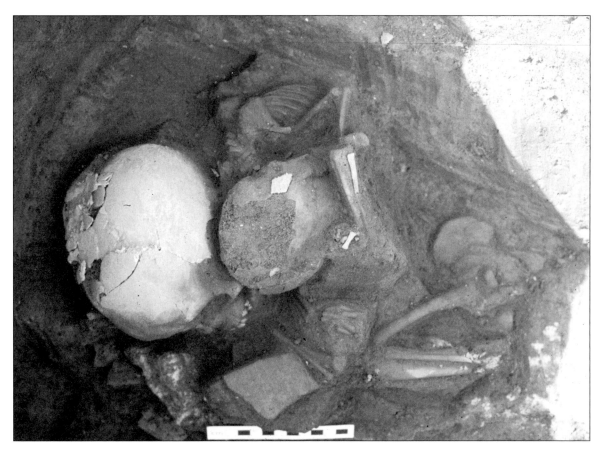

Fig. 2.2 A perinate and a child, 16 to 18 months old, were interred together under a house floor at the Abydos Settlement Site (ASS91, Burials 1A and 1B). An overturned bowl dating to the First Intermediate Period (c. 2181–2040 B.C.) covered the bodies. The water table in this area is high due to the proximity of cultivation, and the burials were moist and began to dry out as excavation proceeded. *Photograph by Brenda Baker*

Fig. 2.3 An area of burials in the Abydos North Cemetery (ANC88, E840N780, Burials 9–13) consists of two small wooden coffins containing infants to the left of a group of three anthropoid coffins of adults. *Photograph by Brenda Baker*

Excavation procedures are, therefore, crucial to the recovery of subadult burials. It is critical to perform careful recovery and documentation in the field. To do so requires some knowledge of subadult osteology, particularly when remains are poorly preserved. Archaeologists who lack osteological training, and even those who have taken osteology courses but have no experience with subadult bones, sometimes do not recognize such remains as human. Lack of recognition is particularly problem-atic for fetal and infant skeletons (figs. 2.4 and 2.5). Because the bones have not developed adult morphology and are very small, they are easily mistaken for bones of small mammals like rodents. The descriptions that follow in chapters 2 through 9 should help alleviate this predicament. Special excavation and laboratory processes are needed to ensure these burials are available for osteological analyses.

How to Excavate Subadult Burials

Excellent discussions of the procedures required to excavate, document, and prepare human burials are found in Brothwell (1981), Ubelaker (1999), and White (2000). The latter two are replete with photographs and should be consulted for general steps to be taken in any burial excavation. Subadult burials, however, are not addressed

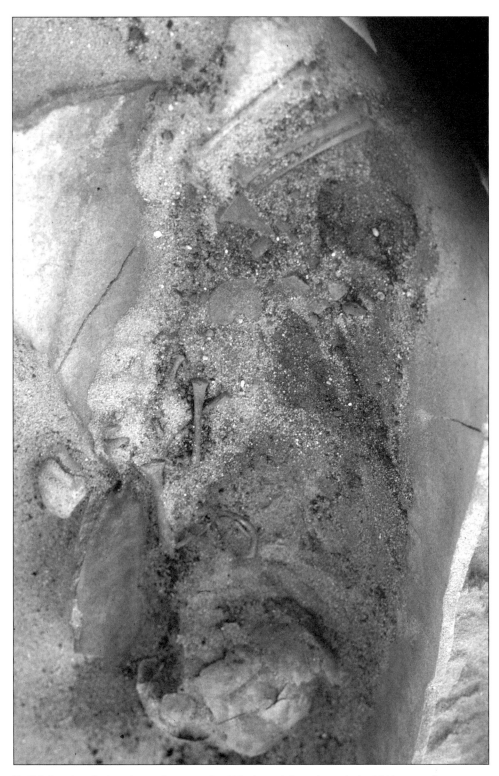

Fig. 2.4 Remains of a fetus (approximate age, 6 to 7 fetal months) are shown in the initial stages of exposure. The pot in which the fetus was interred, which is badly damaged, was located in the midst of a concentration of broken animal bones in the Abydos North Cemetery. Part of the skull and bones of the arms and legs are evident but could easily be mistaken for those of a small animal. *Photograph by Brenda Baker*

Fig. 2.5 The skeleton (ANC2002.53) is more fully exposed and recognizable, showing the fetus in fig. 2.4 positioned on its back with the skull toward the bottom of the photo and the legs slightly flexed at the top of the photo. *Photograph by Jody Waldron*

specifically in these works. Because these burials require additional measures to ensure optimal recovery and curation, they must be treated somewhat differently at all stages. We limit our discussion to general techniques and guidelines that are useful in excavating subadult burials in most situations.

The fragility and size of bones in subadult burials require more delicate tools and a gentler touch than are necessary in excavation of adult burials (fig. 2.6). Use of a 2-inch paintbrush on an infant burial, for instance, will dislodge most of the bones. Once near bone level, trowels are also likely to inflict damage, as it is easy to remove too much dirt or damage bone surfaces with the metal edge. Metal implements (e.g., dental picks) should also be avoided for this reason, unless extremely hard and compact soil conditions necessitate their use. Bamboo picks, wooden skewers, or soft wooden or bamboo sculpture tools should be used because they are softer than bone and will not damage it. A range of small, soft artist's brushes and paintbrushes up to ½-inch are most suitable for exposing fetal and infant skeletons, while somewhat larger brushes (e.g., 1-inch) are useful on skeletons of older children. The key factor is that the brushes should be soft so they do not inflict damage on the bone (fig. 2.7). Stiff brushes may scrape the cortex away from infant bones or even break them if too much pressure is applied during soil removal.

Small scoops or spoons facilitate removal of soil from subadult burials. Sets of wooden or plastic scoops and measuring spoons available at kitchen and department stores are perfect for burial excavation. These are small enough to use in tight spots within the grave of an infant or child or to remove soil from infants interred in small coffins or in pots.

As in any burial excavation, all soil must be screened to ensure complete recovery. Normally, screens used in general excavation have ¼-inch mesh (c. 6 mm), and those employed in burial excavation are typically ⅛-inch mesh (about 3 mm). While these are sufficient for adult burials, finer screens must be used for subadult burials to ensure recovery of epiphyses, developing teeth, carpals, tarsals, or fragments. Window screen with 1/16-inch mesh (or about 1.5 mm) is adequate for most subadult burials, but even finer screen (e.g., 1 mm) is necessary for fetal or neonatal burials. Graduated sieves, such as those used by geologists and for flotation, are ideal. These small, round screens are an appropriate size and come in U.S. Bureau of Standards mesh sizes (e.g., no. 10 is 2-mm and no. 18 is 1-mm mesh). These can be combined to facilitate the screening process (e.g., a 2-mm sieve placed above a 1-mm sieve permits rapid identification of larger elements in the first screen and smaller items in the second screen (fig. 2.8). This type of sieve is available through such outlets as Forestry Suppliers (www.forestry-suppliers.com).

Although it takes longer to screen through fine mesh, the reward is recovery of such items as tiny tooth buds or barely formed carpals that permit a precise age estimate.

Patience is a prerequisite for excavating subadult remains. Removing soil too quickly or removing too much can cause small bones to disarticulate. Often, a domino effect ensues. Soil conditions determine how much matrix should be removed from the bones. While full exposure of the skeleton is preferred for mapping and photographs, it is sometimes necessary to expose only the tops of the bones to avoid collapse. Excavators who have little familiarity with subadult burials should err on the side of caution and ask for assistance from someone with more experience. Once the small bones of the hands and feet or epiphyses are removed from their original position, they can be extremely difficult or even impossible to identify correctly in a fetus or neonate.

During and after the careful exposure of the skeleton, a form specific to burial recovery should be completed and standard information on position and orientation of the body, context, soil conditions, associated artifacts, and measurements of the burial facility recorded. A drawing should show the major bones and their relationship to pit or coffin edges, as well as any associated artifacts. When permitted, photographs are indispensable for documentation. Many Native American groups currently prohibit photographs of human remains. If photos are not permitted at the site, it is imperative to document the burials with detailed drawings and descriptions (figs. 2.9 and 2.10). A visual record of the bone presence or absence, along with observations of unusual features or damage, can be made on a standard homunculus of an infant or child (fig. 2.11) or on other drawings included in chapter 10. Additional forms and drawings of this nature are found in Buikstra and Ubelaker (1994).

Once the burial has been thoroughly documented, several bags should be labeled with the project and site number, burial number, and the bones the bag will contain, along with the side of the body from which they are taken. For example, separate bags should be labeled for the right and left ribs, right and left arms, and so forth. Care should be taken to observe the position of all epiphyses or small bones just starting to ossify. These elements should be put in separate bags with explicit labels if the morphology is not obvious (e.g., the right leg bag of an infant should clearly differentiate the distal femoral epiphysis from the proximal tibial epiphysis, as these are otherwise indistinguishable at this stage of development). Bones of the skull can be bagged together if the cranium is intact. The mandible should be separated. Be careful not to turn the maxillae or mandible upside down before bagging. If you must do so, be sure to have the bones over the bag in which they will be placed or over a fine-mesh screen so any developing tooth crowns are not lost.

Fig. 2.6 Soft brushes and a bamboo pick are used by Laurel Bestock to expose a child's legs. This child, age 3 to 5 years, was interred in a subsidiary grave of a Dynasty 1 royal funerary enclosure (c. 3100 B.C.) in the North Cemetery at Abydos (ANC2002.36). Plastic bags for artifacts and bone fragments are also evident. *Photograph by Brenda Baker*

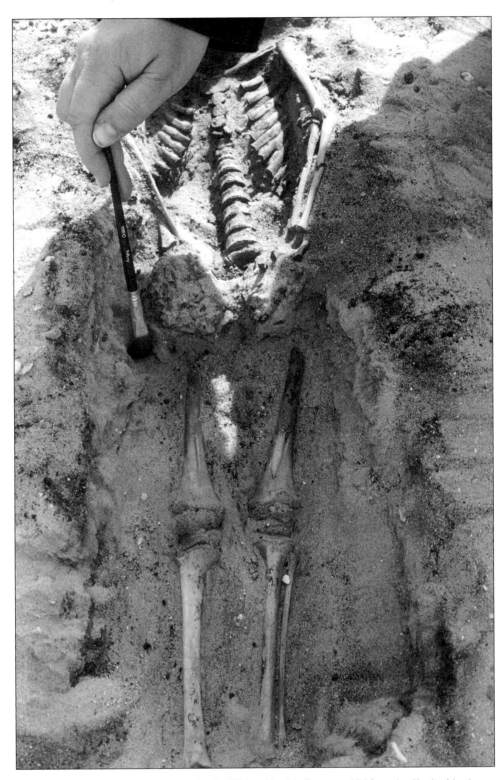

Fig. 2.7 Exposure of a Middle Kingdom (c. 2040–1786 B.C.) burial of a young child from the Abydos North Cemetery (ANC2002.51). Using a small brush, sand is removed from the thorax and pushed toward the legs for removal. The hands, lying over the pelvis and upper legs, and feet are the last areas exposed, ensuring that the tiny bones are not dislodged as the burial is excavated. *Photograph by Brenda Baker*

If the skull is fragmentary, pieces from specific bones should be bagged separately where possible. Because the metacarpals, metatarsals, and phalanges do not develop distinctive features until childhood, it is difficult to identify and side them in the lab. Thus, bones of the hands and feet should be separated not only by side but also by ray (the bones that form each digit), if possible. The additional time taken to remove each ray and bag it separately in the field is far less than the time required to sort them out in the lab. The same can be said for vertebral elements. Bagging all these parts separately ensures that no information is lost between the field and the lab.

Bones should then be removed individually by gradually undercutting the remaining soil on which they rest. The bones that are uppermost should be taken out first, with those underlying them remaining until they are easily accessible (fig. 2.12). For example, in a burial that is flexed on its right side, the skull, left arm, and left leg are generally the highest parts of the skeleton and are re-

moved first. The left ribs and the bones of the left hip are usually accessible once the arm has been bagged. Bones of the vertebral column and the right side are removed last. In a burial that is supine and extended, the bones of the vertebral column and pelvis are usually the last to be removed. Light brushing of the bones to remove the bulk of adhering dirt can be done in the field if the bones are well preserved. Generally, however, it is best simply to bag the bones for cleaning in the lab with the soil still attached.

Because they are less dense, the bones of infants and young children often break or are crushed under the weight of the overlying soil. Some consolidation may, therefore, be necessary in the field. Consolidants should never be used to treat all bone; instead, they should be judiciously applied only to bones that would otherwise crumble during removal and only when permitted by agreements with descendant groups. Only chemicals with demonstrated stability and reversibility should be used to

Fig. 2.8 Brenda Baker uses graduated sieves as she excavates a neonate interred in a pot found under a house floor of the Abydos Settlement Site (ASS91, Burial 3). The First Intermediate Period pot was removed from the field to the lab intact, where the infant's bones were discovered as the project botanist scooped soil out of the vessel for analysis. *Photograph by Leslie Hammond*

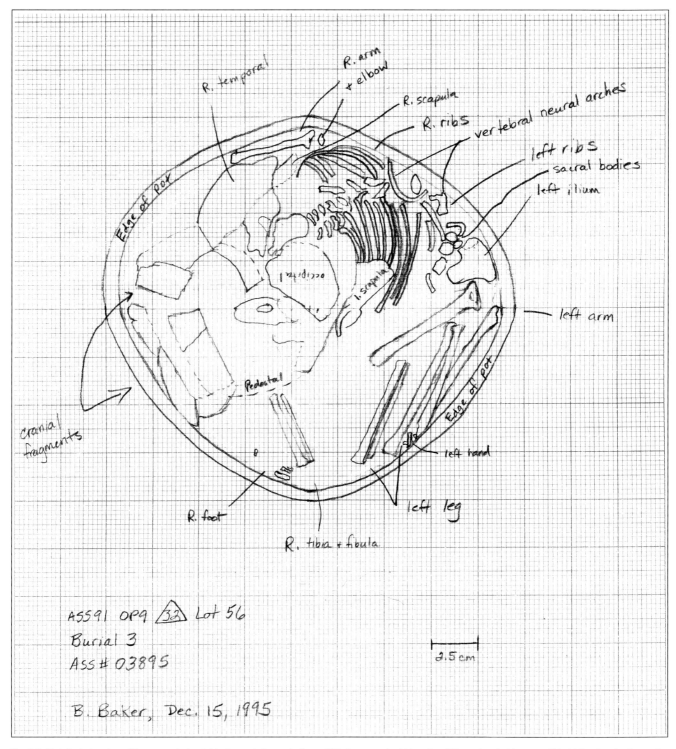

Fig. 2.9 Detailed drawing of the neonate burial in the pot shown in figure 2.8. *Courtesy the University of Pennsylvania Museum—Yale University—Institute of Fine Arts, New York University Expedition*

stabilize the bones so they can be removed intact (Johansson, 1987; Kres and Lovell, 1995). Use of reversible consolidants ensures that any dirt still adhering to the bone during treatment in the field can later be removed during cleaning and reconstruction in the lab.

A variety of material has been used by conservators as adhesives and consolidants (Elder et al., 1997; this leaflet can be viewed by clicking on **Publications** at www.spnhc.org). New consolidants are always being developed, including those intended specifically for organic materials, such as Passivation Polymers (Smith, 2002). These materials can be obtained through chemical or conservation suppliers (Horie, 1987). Excellent sources of links to chemical and conservation supply companies in the United States and the UK are found at www.spnhc.org

(click on **Sources**) and http://palimpsest.stanford.edu/bytopic/suppliers.

Some common consolidants and their usage are discussed by Brothwell (1981:10). A few materials frequently used in the past, such as shellac and cellulose nitrate (sold as Duco and UHU), are no longer recommended for long-term conservation. Shellac darkens considerably and is very difficult to remove. Cellulose nitrate typically becomes brittle over time and can crack or peel off the bone, sometimes causing damage to the surface on which it was applied. Alvar is a polyvinyl acetal that has been widely used. It can also darken considerably over time. While it is soluble in acetone, personal experience has found it difficult to remove without damaging the bone. The cortex often comes off along with

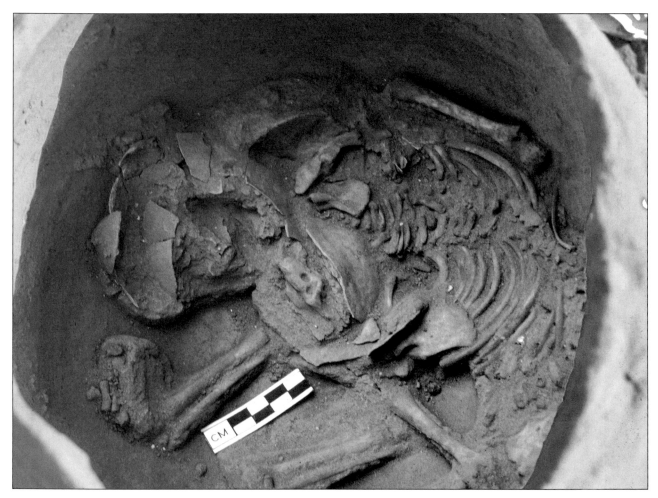

Fig. 2.10 Photograph of the fully exposed skeleton (ASS91, Burial 3) from figure 2.8. Both the drawing (fig. 2.9) and the photograph document the position of the baby's body, which was probably initially placed in a seated position in the vessel. The head and torso have slumped to the right and onto the floor of the vessel. The right humerus is evident against the side of the pot (*top right*), while the left humerus crosses over the left leg (*bottom right*). The right leg (*bottom left*) is stretched out near the skull. *Photograph by Brenda Baker*

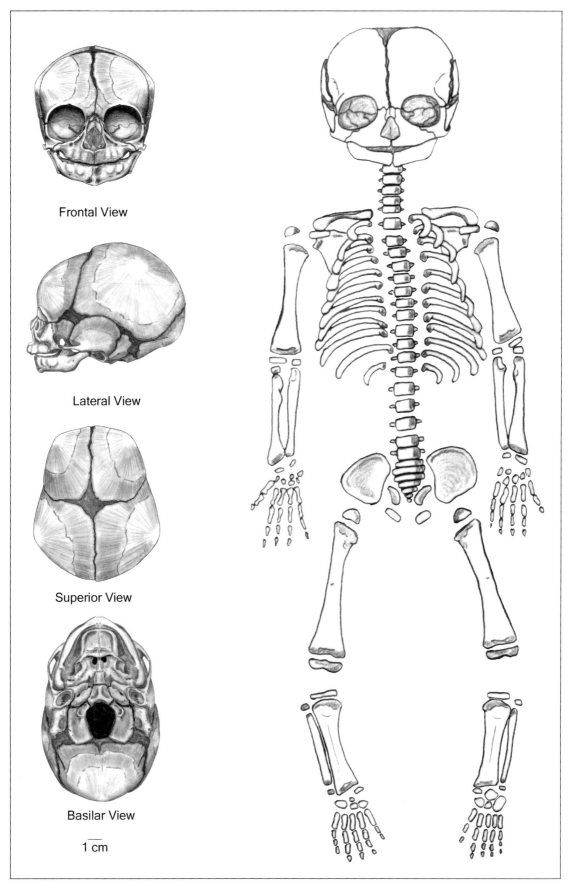

Frontal View

Lateral View

Superior View

Basilar View

1 cm

Fig. 2.11 A generalized homunculus of an infant/child skeleton and views of a neonatal skull for use in burial recovery and inventory forms.

the preservative. Although epoxies may be used as consolidants, they are not easily soluble and they discolor with time.

One of the consolidants most often used in the field is polyvinyl acetate (PVA), as it has good stability and does not discolor. It also comes in many different viscosities, allowing for consolidation of materials of different densi-

ties. A consolidant preferred over PVA by many conservators is Acryloid B72, which has very good durability and does not discolor. In higher concentrations, it is an excellent adhesive for repairing breaks. Polyvinyl alcohol (PVAL) is another effective consolidant. It is only soluble in water, and it can be applied to wet bone (very helpful in some archaeological contexts). Cyclododecane, a low-

Fig. 2.12 Removal of a burial begins with the uppermost bones and requires many labeled bags to separate parts of the skeleton. Jaime Ullinger is excavating ANC2002.51, also shown in fig. 2.7. *Photograph by Brenda Baker*

melting wax that sublimates over time without leaving a residue, is also a useful, temporary stabilizer (Sanchita Balachandran, personal communication).

In the past, bones were commonly treated in the lab with consolidants such as PVA even when they were in excellent condition. Such treatment was thought to enhance long-term preservation. One of the potential problems with using consolidants, however, is the long-term effects they have on bone composition (McGowan and LaRoche, 1996). DNA and stable isotope analyses can be adversely affected by the use of consolidants on bone (Cooper et al., 1994; Johnson, 1994; Sease, 1994). For instance, glues derived from organic substances are known to introduce contaminant DNA to treated bone samples (Nicholson et al., 2002). If such analyses may be performed in the future, we recommend that some bone not be treated with consolidants. We advocate the use of consolidants only when necessary to extract poorly preserved remains from the field and for use as adhesives to reconstruct skeletal elements when required for analysis.

The assistance of a conservator is often indispensable, as in the case of a small child buried in a subsidiary grave of a royal First Dynasty funerary enclosure at Abydos (fig. 2.13). The lower half of the body was still in situ in the grave, though it had been crushed in some places by roof-fall. Application of B72 and placement of rice paper strips over the badly damaged areas ensured that each bone of this very significant burial could be taken out and transported to the lab in one piece, where it could then be cleaned and repaired for study.

In some cases, it is best to remove burials of fetuses or infants in blocks so trained personnel can excavate them from the matrix in a lab setting. Removal in blocks or partial blocks is also necessary for subadult burials that are damp or waterlogged, as they are easily damaged even by bamboo or wooden picks (see fig. 2.2). Once dry, soil can be more easily removed under controlled lab conditions (fig. 2.14). Block removal is much less difficult for baby burials than it is for adults. Thin boards (often even legal-size clipboards) are suitable for slipping under the skeleton as a burial is undercut. The soil surrounding the bone must be firm and compact for block removal to be considered. Otherwise, the block can collapse and cause considerable breakage or crumbling of fragile bones. Where necessary, jacketing in plaster can be employed to stabilize the block (see Ubelaker, 1999; White, 2000).

Bones should be packaged in a box or basket for transport to the laboratory with plenty of padding to ensure they do not break. Never pack a subadult skeleton with that of an adult because the small bones will be crushed by those of the adult. As for adult burials, it is best to place the largest, heaviest bones on the bottom (e.g., long bones) and lighter or more fragile bones (e.g., separate cranial bones, ribs, scapulae, hands, and feet) on the top. Air in the bags helps protect the bones for transport.

Laboratory Treatment and Curation of Subadult Remains

Once a burial is back in the lab, any moisture in the bones should be allowed to escape by opening the bags, especially if they are plastic. If wet, the bones should be allowed to dry gradually and should not be placed under lamps to hasten the process. In arid climates like that of the Egyptian desert or American Southwest, it is often most important to make sure that skeletal remains are stored out of direct sunlight, which causes rapid drying and bleaching and often leads to warping and cracking in a very short period of time. Bones of subadults should be cleaned initially by dry brushing only to remove adhering soil. In cases where the bones are extremely well preserved, they can be washed with water, but they should never be soaked or placed under a running tap. It is far safer to use a soft brush dipped in water for the cleaning process.

Any bone that has been stabilized in the field may require removal of consolidants and special care in cleaning and piecing it back together. Once most bones are cleaned, breaks can be mended by joining the pieces together with B72 or some other stable, reversible adhesive.

If the descendant group prohibits use of adhesives, care should be taken to ensure that all fragments of a bone are kept together for examination. This procedure is particularly important for subadult burials in which bone fragments are not easily identifiable. When permitted, and in any case where long-term storage of the skeletons ensues, all bones large enough should be labeled in small print with indelible ink. Labels should contain identifying information (project/site and burial designations) so that individuals are not confused during subsequent inventory or study (fig. 2.15). Writing directly on the bone is sometimes possible, but a thin layer of B72 solution may be required to provide a smooth surface for the label and prevent the ink from soaking into porous bone.

Ideally, skeletal inventory forms should be specific to adults and subadults. Presence or absence of separate ossification centers (e.g., epiphyses) should be noted, as these are integral in age estimation. Separate elements of bones like the occipital should be recorded individually (e.g., left lateral portion present, right absent, squamous portion fragmentary, etc.). Simply indicating that an occipital is

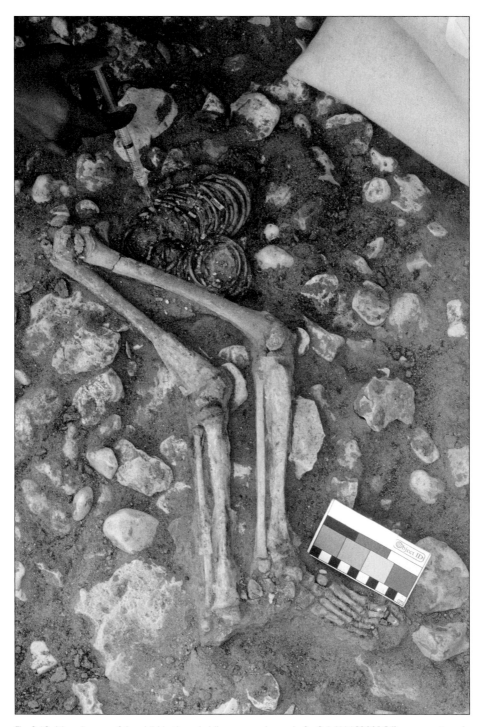

Fig. 2.13 Many bones of the child in the subsidiary grave shown in fig. 2.6 (ANC2002.36) were scattered and crushed by roof-fall. The lower half of the body and a cache of ivory bracelets near the right thigh remained in situ on the cobble floor, but the bones were broken in several places. Stabilization required application of B72 and rice-paper strips to hold the bones together during removal. *Photograph by Brenda Baker*

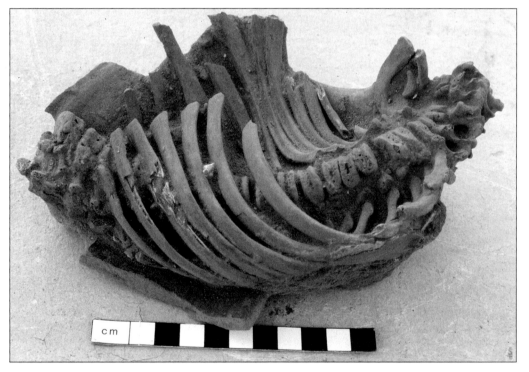

Fig. 2.14 The double burial shown in fig. 2.2 was removed in a series of blocks to limit damage to the bones. *Above,* the thorax block from the child (ASS91, Burial 1A), age 16 to 18 months, after it has dried and before removal of the silt; *below,* the thorax after removal of the silt in the lab shows full definition of the ribs and vertebrae. Attempting such exposure in the field would have caused substantial damage to the soft, wet bones. *Photographs by Brenda Baker*

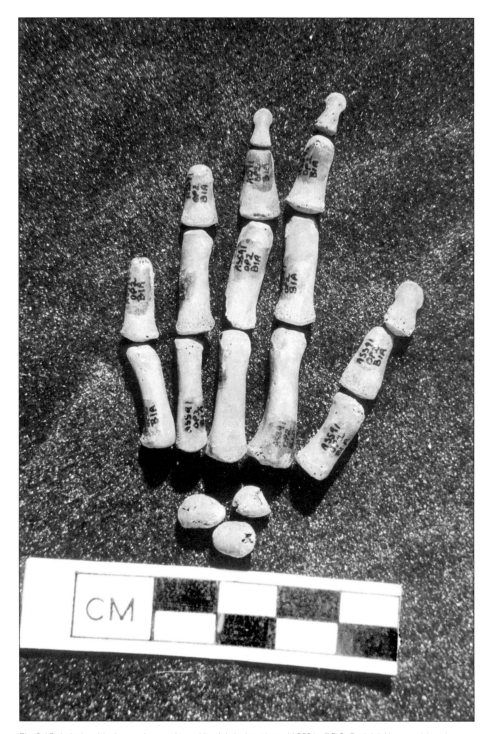

Fig. 2.15 Labels with the project, unit, and burial designations (ASS91, OP 2, Burial 1A) are evident in this dorsal view of the left hand bones of the child in the double burial from the Abydos Settlement Site (fig. 2.2). Note the small, nearly featureless carpals present at this stage, about 16 to 18 months. *Photograph by Brenda Baker*

present or fragmentary may be suitable in an adult, but it is not particularly informative in subadults for whom the ossification centers have not yet united. The descriptions of each bone of the skull and infracranial skeleton and the techniques for rapid determination of an age category that follow in chapters 3 through 10 should be consulted for additional information on identification and siding of each element. Visual recording forms (e.g., fig. 2.11 and templates in chap. 10) can be used to assist in documentation of the skeleton.

Once the bones have been cataloged for each individual, they should preferably be placed in archival storage media for long-term curation. Like adhesives, archival packaging material can be purchased through conservation suppliers. Boxes should be sturdy, and light boxes should always be placed above heavy boxes if they must be stacked. If adult-size storage boxes are used, the skeletons of two or more subadults can be stored together so the bones do not slide around when the box is moved. The burials must each be clearly labeled in separate bags so they do not get mixed together, and each should be indicated on the exterior box label. If a subadult burial is stored separately and takes up only a small portion of the box, extra bags filled with air or some other padding material (e.g., archival foam or tissue) should be used to cushion the bones and prevent them from slamming into the sides of the box whenever it is moved. Following these excavation and lab procedures and precautions will ensure that subadult burials are well represented in a skeletal collection and are available for research.

PART TWO
The Skull and Teeth

The adult skull is comprised of twenty-eight bones that form the cranial vault, the face, and the jaws. Another bone, the hyoid, is suspended from the skull base and is included in this section. Many of these twenty-nine bones ossify from multiple centers, so that a typical newborn has at least thirty-nine separate elements. Some bones in a neonate, therefore, have more than one component, while other centers have not yet begun to ossify.

The development of the bones encasing the brain is delineated in chapter 3. The bones comprising the face, which contribute to the eye orbits, nasal cavity, hard palate, and jaws, are the subject of chapter 4. Chapter 5 is devoted to the deciduous and permanent dentition.

Chapter 3   The Bones of the Cranial Vault

■ The bones of the cranial vault are those that surround and form a protective cocoon for the brain. They consist of the frontal, the parietals, the occipital, the temporal bones, and the sphenoid. Although they do not contribute to the cranial vault, the auditory ossicles are included in this chapter due to their anatomical location within the temporal bones. The majority of bones discussed in this chapter are categorized as flat bones (frontal, parietals, temporals, occipital) or irregular bones (sphenoid and auditory ossicles). Most of these bones ossify from separate centers that eventually fuse together to form the adult bone. Thus, in fetuses, infants, and children, one must be able to identify the separate parts of each bone.

The Frontal

Description at Major Stages

The frontal bone (fig. 3.1) is located on the anterior portion of the cranium and makes up the superior part of the face (i.e., the forehead and roof of the eye sockets). It articulates with twelve other bones: the sphenoid, ethmoid, parietals, nasal bones, maxillae, lacrimals, and zygomatics. The frontal initially develops as a pair of right and left bones that eventually fuse together medially at the metopic suture (fig. 3.1a). Each half of the frontal bone ossifies intramembranously, typically beginning by the end of the eighth fetal week. This portion of the skull quickly develops the morphology that characterizes the adult bone.

Frontal bone morphology is usually described in two sections. The first of these refers to the portions of the bone associated with the eye orbits (fig. 3.1b) while the second refers to portions associated with the forehead or frontal squama (fig. 3.1c). Fusion of the metopic suture is variable throughout human populations. Typically, the right and left halves of the frontal bone partly or completely fuse in the first year of life, although it sometimes takes up to four years for complete fusion. In some cases, the metopic suture persists throughout life.

In fetuses and neonates, the right and left halves of the frontal bone are completely separate. Each half consists of a thin, curved squamous portion that has a long, straight edge on one side and a curved contour around the rest of its perimeter that gives the bone a D shape.

The straight edge is the slightly serrated metopic suture, while the curved aspect is the coronal suture (fig. 3.1d). The rounded protuberance in the middle of the bone is the frontal eminence (fig. 3.1e). Internally, the squamous portion is slightly cupped and striated. A thin sheet of bone extending at a right angle to the anterior edge of the squama is the orbital plate. The orbit is smooth on the anterior aspect and somewhat convex on the back or internal aspect of the cranium. The upper edge, where the orbital roof joins the frontal squama, is known as the supraorbital margin (fig. 3.1f). It is marked by a notch or foramen, even in early stages of development. At its lateral edge, the supraorbital margin thickens into the zygomatic process (fig. 3.1g), marked by a suture where it articulates with the zygomatic or cheekbone.

In older infants and children, the two halves of the frontal bone fuse together and some of the adult morphology becomes observable at this stage. At the midline, on the anterior portion of the internal frontal squama, a sharp ridge known as the frontal crest develops, along with the foramen cecum—a tiny hole at its root. The back of the orbital plate becomes bumpy, differentiating internal aspect from the smooth orbital surface. The orbits are divided by the ethmoidal notch, in which the ethmoid bone is situated, and small cells for the ethmoidal air sinuses line its perimeter. Larger openings for the frontal sinuses expand in early childhood.

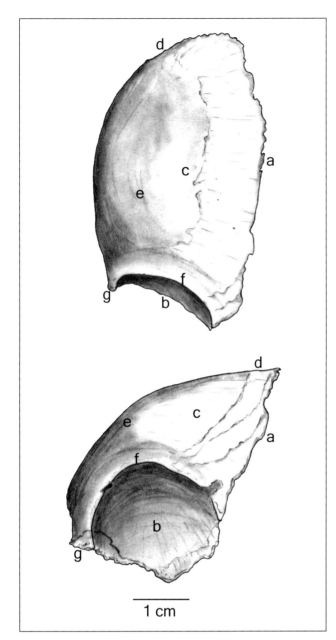

Fig. 3.1 Right frontal from an infant, top = anterior, bottom = inferior: *a*, metopic suture; *b*, orbit; *c*, squama; *d*, coronal suture; *e*, frontal eminence; *f*, supraorbital margin; *g*, zygomatic process.

Differentiation from Other Bones

Unless fragmentary, the frontal bone is distinct enough to prevent confusion with other cranial bones from fetal development onward. In particular, the orbital portions are unique and can help differentiate even badly frag-

mented frontal elements. When fragmentary, however, the frontal squama can be confused with squamous portions of the parietals, temporals, and even the occipital. For unfused right and left halves, the internal morphology is not well developed but the small size of the bone and roughly **D** shape help distinguish it. Noting that one edge (for the metopic suture) is straight (fig. 3.1a), while the other sutural edge is curved (fig. 3.1d) from its posterior juncture with the metopic suture, aids in identifying a neonatal frontal squama. The primary distinction between various squamal elements in children and adults lies in the internal morphology. In the frontal bone, the posterior midline has a groove for the sagittal sinus, anterior to which lies the frontal crest and foramen cecum. Small vessel impressions may also be present near the coronal suture.

Siding Techniques

For a fetus or neonate, the separate halves of the frontal must be sided. If a complete bone is present, place the concave surface down, the convex squamal surface up (fig. 3.1c), and the orbit facing away from you (fig. 3.1b). The straighter border for the metopic suture (fig. 3.1a) is medial, while the curved coronal suture (fig. 3.1d) marks the side to which the bone belongs. Note also that the lateral corner of the orbit is thickened, while the medial border projects farther away from you. Thus, the thickened corner of the bone, the zygomatic process (fig. 3.1g), is on the side from which the bone comes, which is helpful in identifying many fragmentary frontals. Another siding technique for a complete right or left frontal is to orient the bone with the convex squamal surface toward you and the orbital portion pointing to the floor. In this view, the straight border for the metopic suture is on the side to which the bone belongs.

In cases where the orbital plate is broken off and only a squamous portion is present, orient the fragment with the cupped internal aspect down and the tapered end toward you. The broadest part of the squama faces away from you where it would join the orbital plate. Thus, the curved margin again reflects the side from which the bone comes. For fragmentary orbital portions, siding can be accomplished by identifying the orbital plate and the zygomatic process (fig. 3.1b, g). If you place the zygomatic process away from you with the orbital plate pointing toward the floor, the internal side of the orbital plate projects toward the side to which the bone belongs.

The Parietal

Description at Major Stages

The right and left parietal bones (fig. 3.2) make up the top and upper sides of the cranial vault. Each articulates

with the opposite parietal bone, the frontal bone, the sphenoid, temporal, and occipital (fig. 3.2a–e). The parietal originates from an intramembranous precursor. Ossification begins at the inferior and central portion of the bone, and slowly moves superiorly, with the bone taking on an elliptical shape by 5 months in gestation. After this point the borders of the parietal start to devlop their characteristic shapes and the center of the bone becomes quite prominent. This rounded prominence on the external aspect is known as the parietal eminence or boss (fig. 3.2f) and marks the point toward the back of the vault where the bone curves from the top to the side of the skull. The parietal eminences are very pronounced in infants and young children.

The longest border of the bone is the most superior, located along the midline at the top of the cranium. This serrated margin is the sagittal suture (fig. 3.2b) and articulates with the opposite parietal. As the bone develops, a shallow groove known as the sagittal sulcus becomes evident along this suture. The shortest, relatively straight, border is located anteriorly, where it will fuse with the frontal bone along the coronal suture (fig. 3.2a). Although not readily observable in neonates, grooves for the meningeal vessels mark the internal surface of the bone in older infants and children. The deepest and widest meningeal groove runs along the coronal suture and terminates laterally where the bone juts outward to meet the sphenoid bone (fig. 3.2e). Just posterior to this flange, on the most lateral and inferior border of the parietal, is a curved and somewhat beveled squamosal suture for the articulation with the temporal bone (fig. 3.2d). Posterior to the squamosal suture is a short curve or angle that marks the parietomastoid suture, where the parietal bone articulates with the mastoid portion of the developing temporal bone. This portion is the thickest part of the bone, even in infants and small children, and flares slightly upward. It is also characterized on the internal table by a slight depression for the sigmoid or transverse sulcus that becomes more obvious throughout childhood. The posterior border of the parietal is irregular compared to the other borders for its articulation with the squamous portion of the occipital. Known as the lambdoidal suture (fig. 3.2c), this border is generally thicker and more deeply serrated than the other sutures as the bone develops.

Differentiation from Other Bones

If complete, even a fetal parietal can be distinguished from squamous portions of other cranial bones because it is more uniform and lacks distinct features, such as the orbital plates of the frontal, the suture pattern of the occipital, and the zygomatic process of the temporal bone. During fetal and infant development, however, the parietal is a very thin, fragile bone, and in the burial environment it is not unusual for it to be fragmented. In fragmentary condition, it may be very difficult to distinguish parietal fragments from squamous fragments of other vault bones since the development of interior features such as the sulci and meningeal grooves may not be readily apparent until after the first year of life. Identification of parietal fragments in neonates and infants, therefore, depends mainly upon the parietal eminence (fig. 3.2f) and the finely serrated borders. Because the parietal is larger than the squamous portions of the other vault bones, large fragments are more likely to be identifiable at this stage. Once past infancy, the internal features that characterize the parietal bone aid in its recognition.

Siding Techniques

For a complete fetal or neonatal parietal, determining which side the bone is from necessitates identification of the superior, anterior, inferior, and posterior borders. To orient the bone in standard anatomical position, place the parietal with concave surface down and the parietal eminence (fig. 3.2f) facing up, and locate the very short, curved and beveled squamosal suture (fig. 3.2d). When oriented properly, the flange of bone (fig. 3.2e) between the squamosal suture and the short and slightly concave border will be at the anterolateral corner (away from you) and the thicker corner that flares slightly upward will be at the posterolateral corner (toward you). In this position, the curved squamosal suture indicates the side to which the bone belongs. In older infants and in children, check for the presence of the deep meningeal groove that runs along the coronal suture at the front of the bone and the depression for the sigmoid sulcus at the posterolateral corner. Doing so will ensure you have oriented the bone correctly so that the squamosal suture determines the side to which the bone belongs.

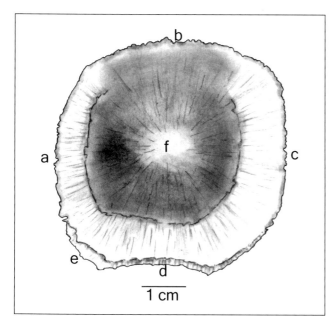

Fig. 3.2 Left parietal from an infant, external view: *a*, coronal suture; *b*, sagittal suture; *c*, lambdoidal suture; *d*, squamosal suture; *e*, sphenoid articulation; *f*, parietal eminence.

A siding technique that does not rely on orienting the bone in anatomical position is to place the concave surface down with the parietal eminence up. Then place the longest, straight border for the sagittal suture (fig. 3.2b) away from you. The side that has an indentation (for articulation with the frontal) will be the side from which the bone comes.

Parietal fragments are more difficult to side and may not be distinguishable in fetal and infant remains due to the lack of diagnostic features. In children, as in adults, siding fragments relies upon the internal features such as the sigmoid sulcus, the sagittal sulcus, and the meningeal grooves. Again, note that the deepest and straightest meningeal groove is parallel to the coronal suture at the front of the bone. The other meningeal grooves fan out from the anterolateral corner of the bone, therefore running up and toward the back of the bone. The pattern will follow that of your hand when placed upon your own parietal, with the side of the hand and little finger running parallel to the coronal suture and the other fingers spreading out to the sagittal and lambdoidal sutures—in other words, up and toward the back of your head.

The Occipital

Description at Major Stages

The occipital (figs. 3.3 and 3.4) forms the posterior and most inferior portion of the cranial vault and articulates with both parietals along the lambdoidal suture (fig. 3.3a), with the temporals at the occipitomastoid sutures (fig. 3.3b) and with the sphenoid at the basilar or spheno-occipital synchondrosis (fig. 3.3c). The inferior part of the occipital also articulates with the first cervical vertebra or atlas via the occipital condyles.

During early prenatal development, the human occipital bone consists of five separate elements: the basilar part or basiocciput, two lateral parts, the squama or interparietal part, below which is the supraoccipital part (fig. 3.3d–g). Ossification of these elements is complex and occurs both intramembranously and endochondrally. The supraoccipital, basilar, and lateral parts are all preformed in cartilage, whereas only the interparietal part of the squama ossifies directly from membrane. Fusion of these elements occurs in sequence, beginning posteriorly and continuing anteriorly, usually ending by age 6, but sometimes as late as 8 years.

By the fifth fetal month, the interparietal and supraoccipital parts begin to fuse together at the center, forming a united squama. The external occipital protuberance is the bulge that forms at the point of union of these elements on the exterior surface of the bone. The interparietal and supraoccipital parts remain divided laterally by the mendosal suture (fig. 3.3h). This suture generally fuses completely in the first year, but sometimes persists into adulthood. At birth, therefore, the occipital is comprised of four separate pieces—the squama, two lateral parts, and the basilar part.

The two lateral parts appear as small, bladelike pieces of bone that display two small projections on one edge, known as the condylar and jugular limbs (fig. 3.4i, j). These limbs, which eventually form the hypoglossal canal, begin development early in fetal life. The jugular tubercle (fig. 3.4k) is a bump situated at the base of the jugular limb on the internal surface, while the poste-

rior portions of the occipital condyles (fig. 3.4l) are smooth ovals located on the inferior (external) surface of the condylar limb. The lateral parts generally fuse to the supraoccipital part of the squama at the posterior interoccipital suture by age 4. While persistence of this suture into adulthood is not as well documented as the mendosal suture, it has been observed in several human populations.

The basilar part forms from one or occasionally two endochondral ossification centers that appear during the first trimester of pregnancy. This part of the immature occipital is small and thick. Its diagnostic features include the smooth, scooped-out curve that marks the anterior edge of the foramen magnum (fig. 3.4m) and small articular facets that form the anterior portion of the occipital condyles. Opposite the curved border of the foramen magnum is a straight border with a rough, porous surface that abuts the body of the sphenoid. The basilar part begins to assume its diagnostic Y form by the end of the twentieth fetal week. The posterolateral borders of the bone display two facets. The more posterior facet (fig. 3.4n) articulates with the condylar limb of the lateral part, while the more anterior facet (fig. 3.4o) articulates with the jugular limb. Fusion of the basilar part to the lateral parts usually occurs by age 7. The anterior portion of the bone generally does not completely fuse to the base of the sphenoid until early adulthood, but may begin to fuse around puberty.

Differentiation from Other Bones

A separate basilar part can sometimes be confused with the manubrium of the sternum. The characteristic adult shape of the manubrium, however, is not present until well after the basilar part is no longer a separate element. In infants, the manubrium is a thin, flat disk. In the case of commingled juvenile remains, it is best to remember that the basilar part displays portions of the occipital condyles as well as a smooth, U-shaped notch for the foramen magnum between the condylar facets (fig. 3.4l).

A lateral part, when unfused, is most commonly mistaken for a scapula. It might also be confused with a first rib or even a vertebral element because of its slightly curved, bladelike appearance. A key to correct identification of the lateral parts is recognition of the portions of the occipital condyles that are located on one of the bony projections or limbs (fig. 3.4i, l). Another identifying feature is the jugular tubercle (fig. 3.4k), where the jugular limb joins the body of the bone. Also, the morphology of the hypoglossal canal, which is formed as a result of the condylar and jugular limbs (fig. 3.4i, j) fusing to one another, is a key characteristic of the lateral parts in young children. Recognition of the developing hypoglossal canal ensures proper identification of this element even in badly damaged specimens. Another feature to look for is the smooth and curved edge that represents the border of the foramen magnum (fig. 3.4p). In contrast, a scapula from the same individual will be much larger in size with a larger and thinner blade that curves more gradually than the border of a lateral part. A first rib or developing ver-

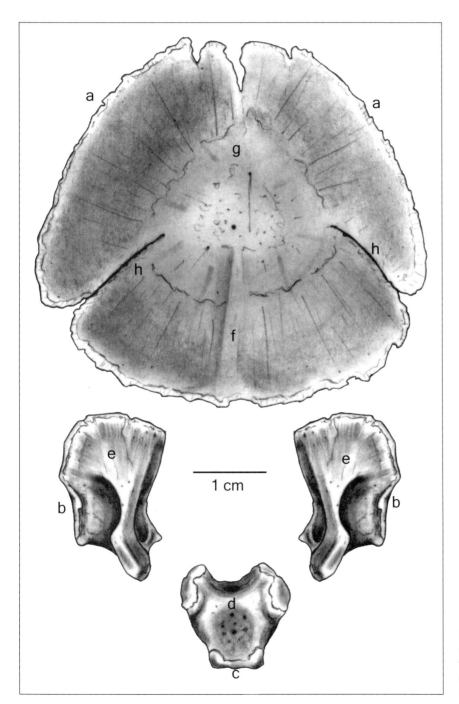

Fig. 3.3 Internal view of the occipital from a neonate: *a*, lambdoidal suture; *b*, occipitomastoid suture; *c*, spheno-occipital synchondrosis; *d*, basilar part; *e*, lateral part; *f*, supraoccipital part; *g*, interparietal part; *h*, mendosal suture.

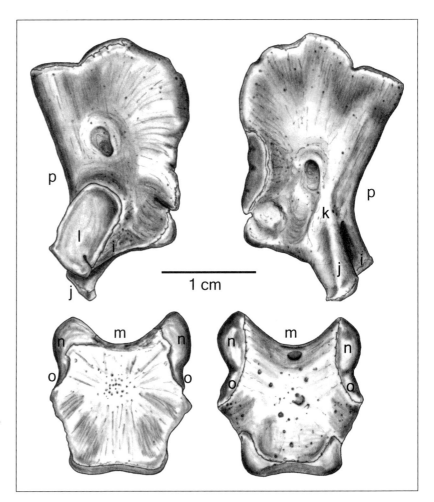

Fig. 3.4 Right lateral part (*top*) and basilar part (*bottom*) of a neonatal occipital, left side = external, right side = internal: *i*, condylar limb; *j*, jugular limb; *k*, jugular tubercle; *l*, occipital condyle; *m*, anterior border of foramen magnum; *n*, articulation for condylar limb; *o*, articulation for jugular limb; *p*, border of foramen magnum.

tebral neural arch has only one articular head, in contrast to the two limbs of a lateral part.

Unless fragmentary, the squamous portion of the occipital is distinct enough to prevent confusion with other cranial bones from late fetal development onward. The bulge of the external occipital protuberance, along with the winglike projections of the interparietal part above the mendosal suture (fig. 3.3h), permits identification. When fragmentary, however, a fetal or neonatal occipital can be confused with squamal portions of the parietals, temporals, and possibly the frontal. Even in these early stages of development, however, the occipital squama will be slightly thicker with deep serrations on its borders.

In older children, where the separate components of the occipital are fused, the whole bone is quite distinctive with its occipital condyles and large opening for the foramen magnum. As the bone develops and takes on its adult morphology, the primary distinction between squamal fragments of the cranial bones can be made on the concave or internal surfaces. The occipital lacks the meningeal grooves found on other vault bones and is easily identified by its cross-shaped internal aspect that divides the bone into four depressions for the occipital lobes and cerebellar hemispheres of the brain. The prominent inter-

nal occipital protuberance is located in the center of the cross, opposite the bulge of the external occipital protuberance on the outside of the bone. On the internal aspect of the squama, a groove for the sagittal sulcus is located in the midline above the protuberance. A ridge of bone known as the internal occipital crest extends from the protuberance to the foramen magnum. The groove running horizontally across the bone is the transverse sulcus. The depressions adjacent to all these features help distinguish occipital fragments from the other vault bones.

Siding Techniques

For a fetal or neonatal occipital, only the lateral parts must be sided before they fuse to the squama. Place the flatter surface on the table and the projections or limbs (fig. 3.4i, j) facing up and toward you (the rounded blade-like surface should be facing away from you). The limbs and the medial border of the foramen magnum (fig. 3.4p) are toward the side to which the bone belongs. Alternatively, place the more uneven surface down with the limbs and occipital condyle (fig. 3.4l) toward you and the broader portion of the bone away from you. In this external view of the bone, the lateral part of the bone curves outward and is on the side from which the bone comes.

The Temporal

Description at Major Stages

The temporal bones (fig. 3.5) are located laterally on the cranium and contain the auditory ossicles (malleus, incus, and stapes; see fig. 3.6). Each temporal articulates with the occipital (at the occipitomastoid suture), the parietal (at the squamous and parietomastoid sutures), the sphenoid (at the sphenosquamous suture), the zygomatic (at the zygomaticotemporal suture), and the mandible (at the temporomandibular joint). The temporal bone ossifies both intramembranously and endochondrally, like the occipital. During early prenatal development and up to birth, the human temporal bone consists of three separate elements: the squama, the petrous portion, and the tympanic portion (fig. 3.5a–c). As with the other bones of the cranial vault, the squamous portion develops intramembranously. The tympanic portion also develops intramembranously, while the petrous portion is preformed in cartilage prior to ossification.

The tympanic portion is initially recognizable as a small, thin semicircle of bone by the middle of fetal development (fig. 3.5c). By late fetal stages, it is generally a more complete ring and is usually fused to the squama at birth. Fusion of the tympanic ring and squama has been suggested as evidence of the viability of the fetus.

The squamous part of the temporal begins to ossify in the seventh or eighth fetal week. It is flat and progressively becomes more circular in shape. A morphological feature that is present very early in fetal development is the projection for the zygomatic process (fig. 3.5d) on the external, inferior aspect of the squama. The small cup

at the root of this process is the mandibular fossa, for articulation with the mandible (fig. 3.5e).

The petrous portion contains the otic capsule for the ear. It appears by the middle of fetal development as a small, irregularly shaped bone with one broad end and the other tapered and more rounded. By late fetal life, the broader end becomes rounded with the additional ossification of the mastoid region, while the tapered end becomes more pointed. The internal auditory meatus (fig. 3.5f) or inner opening of the ear canal is a prominent feature of this bulky bone at all stages. It lies inferior and medial to the subarcuate fossa (fig. 3.5g)—a fissure under the bony enclosure of the superior semicircular canal (fig. 3.5h). During the first postnatal year, the petrous portion fuses to the already joined squama and tympanic portions. Between ages 1 and 5, the triangular mastoid process at the posterior and inferior aspect of the bone develops and the tympanic plate continues to grow. A noticeable opening, known as the foramen of Huschke, forms as the external auditory meatus (outer ear canal; fig. 3.5i) narrows and becomes defined. The foramen of Huschke slowly disappears by about age 5, although a small opening known as the tympanic dehiscence can persist into adulthood.

Differentiation from Other Bones

Before the three main elements of the temporal have fused and developed much of the adult morphology, the temporal squama (fig. 3.5a) is probably the most easily confused with other bones. These include the squamous

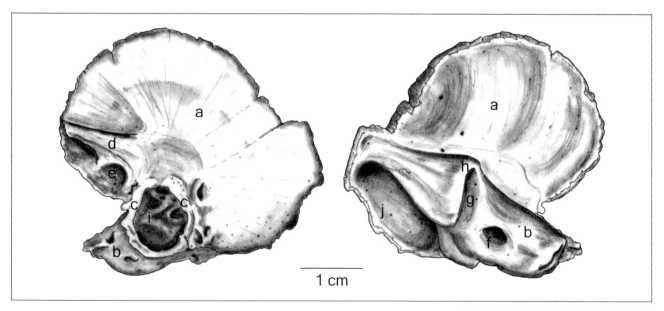

1 cm

Fig. 3.5 Left temporal of an infant, left = external, right = internal: *a*, squama; *b*, petrous portion; *c*, tympanic portion; *d*, zygomatic process; *e*, mandibular fossa; *f*, internal auditory meatus; *g*, subarcuate fossa; *h*, bony enclosure for semicircular canal; *i*, external auditory meatus; *j*, sigmoid sulcus.

portions of the frontal, parietal, and occipital. A key morphological feature that distinguishes the temporal squama from other squamous elements is the bony projection for the zygomatic arch (fig. 3.5d). This process is present and easily distinguishable by the fourth fetal month and possibly as early as the third. Fragments of the squamous part of the temporal are difficult to distinguish from fragments of other vault bones early in fetal development. An unfused tympanic portion appears as a thin piece of bone that almost forms a circle or is semicircular (fig. 3.5c). When still unfused (e.g., less than 8 fetal months), it is unlike any other human bone and is easily mistaken for a faunal bone. The petrous portion assumes its characteristic shape early in fetal development and should not be confused with any other human element due to its blocky nature and large opening for the internal auditory meatus (fig. 3.5f).

A fused squamosal-tympanic part remains distinctive due to the round, flat squama with its complete tympanic ring and straight, narrow zygomatic process on the inferior, external aspects. Once the petrous portion (fig. 3.5b) has also fused, the temporal is much like its adult form and is easily recognized. Fragments of the squamous portion at this stage can be distinguished from those of other vault bones by the interior beveled suture for the parietal bone and the pronounced sigmoid sulcus (fig. 3.5j) at the posteroinferior corner. Meningeal grooves also develop on the internal aspect of the temporal squama, making it more difficult to distinguish small pieces from parietal fragments than other vault bones.

Siding Techniques

For fetal remains that are 7 months in gestation or younger, the temporal bone is likely to be present as three separate elements. In this case it is possible to side the squamous and petrous portions (fig. 3.5a, b). To side the squama, place the flattened or slightly concave surface on a table with the rounded edge away from you. The projection for the zygomatic process (fig. 3.5d) points in the direction from which the bone comes. In many cases, the thin process is broken. The root of the process is thickened and should show a break, making it possible to determine which way it would project if complete. To side the petrous portion, hold the tapered end of the bone toward you and the rounded bulge (fig. 3.5h) enclosing the middle ear up. In this view, the opening for the internal auditory meatus (fig. 3.5f) is on the side to which the bone belongs.

If a complete temporal bone is present (e.g., in older infants and juveniles), the convex squamal surface represents the external aspect of the temporal (i.e., lateral) while the concave surface represents the internal aspect (i.e., medial). Place the concave internal surface on the table with the petrous portion and external auditory meatus (fig. 3.5i) facing toward you. The zygomatic process points to the side from which the bone comes. For fragmentary temporals from children, the bone often breaks into squamous and petrous portions. The directions for fetal temporals are still useful in siding these components.

The Auditory Ossicles

Description at Major Stages

The auditory ossicles (fig. 3.6) are located within the petrous portion of the temporal bone. These three bones, the malleus (hammer), incus (anvil), and stapes (stirrup), are the smallest bones in the human skeleton. When excavating human remains, the auditory ossicles are often missed or lost if fine enough screens are not used. The auditory ossicles are present and take on their characteristic adult shape and size between 9 and 15 fetal weeks.

The malleus or hammer is the most lateral of the ear ossicles and abuts the tympanic membrane or eardrum. It is a slender bone with a rounded head and long handle or manubrium (fig. 3.6a, b). The other main feature is the anterior process extending from the handle at a right angle (fig. 3.6c). A thicker protrusion, known as the lateral process, is located just under the constricted neck of the bone.

The incus, thought to have the shape of an anvil, is the most robust of the three ossicles and has somewhat of a U shape. It has three main components—the body and the long and short processes (fig. 3.6d–f). The lenticular process is a tiny bump located at the end of the long process. The articular surface for the malleus (fig. 3.6g) extends between the long and short processes.

The stapes, aptly named for its stirruplike appearance, is the smallest and most fragile of the ossicles. It contains a flat base, called the footplate (fig. 3.6h), and an arch consisting of an anterior and posterior crus (fig. 3.6i, j), joined at the top by a small protrusion called the head (fig. 3.6k). The anterior crus is slightly longer and straighter than the posterior crus.

Differentiation from Other Bones

Each of the auditory ossicles is very distinct and should not be confused with one another. No other bones in the human skeleton are as small as the auditory ossicles nor are any similar in shape.

Siding Techniques

Due to their small size the auditory ossicles are difficult to side. However, if it is necessary to side them, it is possible based on their characteristic morphology. Be sure

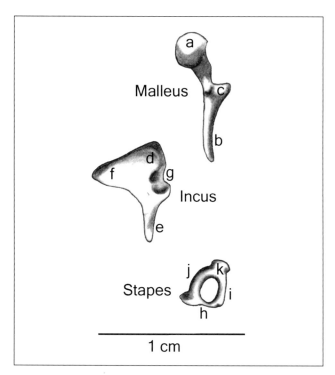

Fig. 3.6 Left auditory ossicles, with the malleus and incus in medial view and the stapes in superior view: *a*, head; *b*, long process; *c*, anterior process; *d*, body; *e*, long process; *f*, short process; *g*, articular surface; *h*, footplate; *i*, anterior crus; *j*, posterior crus; *k*, head.

with the largest part of the articular process for the incus facing you (a small spur is visible at its base). The small lateral process points to the side from which the bone comes. Another option is to hold the malleus by the handle with the head (fig. 3.6a) pointing away from you so the bone is oriented in standard anatomical position. The head inclines upward toward the side to which the bone belongs when properly oriented (Greiner and Walker, 1999), as shown in figure 3.6.

The incus can be sided most easily by holding the bone by the long process (fig. 3.6e) between your thumb and index finger with the articular surface (fig. 3.6g) facing you. The articular surface slants toward the opposite side, while the lenticular process points to the side from which the bone comes. Another option is the method preferred by Scheuer and Black (2000). With the short process (fig. 3.6f) up and oriented horizontally, the long process down, and the superior part of the articular surface for the malleus visible, the short process points to the side to which the bone belongs (as in fig. 3.6).

The stapes is much more difficult to side because it is difficult to distinguish the anterior crus from the posterior crus (fig. 3.6i, j). With the head (fig. 3.6k) up, footplate (fig. 3.6h) down, and the shorter, more curved posterior crus toward you, the head leans toward the side to which the bone belongs. To double-check, put the stapes on a table with the head away from you, the footplate toward you, and the flatter surface of the footplate down. The more rounded aspect of the footplate should be up. In this view, the more curved posterior crus is on the side the bone is from, while the straighter anterior crus is opposite the side to which the bone belongs (as in fig. 3.6). Note also the head tilts in this orientation toward the anterior crus.

to hold the bones over a table when attempting to side them, as they are difficult to hold and are easily dropped and lost if you are not careful.

The malleus can be sided by holding the bone by the handle (fig. 3.6b) between your thumb and index finger

The Sphenoid

Description at Major Stages

The majority of the sphenoid (fig. 3.7) is internal, with only small portions visible externally in the orbits and along the sides and base of the cranium. It articulates with twelve bones of the face and cranial vault (the vomer, ethmoid, frontal, occipital and both parietals, temporals, zygomatics, and palatines). The sphenoid develops through intramembranous and endochondral ossification processes. The name sphenoid means "wedgelike," which reflects its adult shape and position in the skull. The bone is divided into three main components during development: the body and the lesser and greater wings (fig. 3.7a–c). The body is formed endochondrally from the presphenoid and postsphenoid portions. The anterior portion of the body is formed by the presphenoid portion, a small Y-shaped bone that eventually forms the medial walls of the optic canals (fig. 3.7d). The posterior

portion of the body is formed by the postsphenoid, a rectangular block with a superior indentation that forms the hypophyseal fossa (fig. 3.7e). Two small, winglike projections, the alar processes (fig. 3.7f), are located along each side of postsphenoid. The presphenoid and the postsphenoid fuse together shortly before birth to form the body, which at this time starts to resemble its adult morphology.

The right and left lesser wings of the sphenoid (fig. 3.7b) are also preformed in cartilage. They are recognizable as small V-shaped bones after 4 months of gestation and rapidly fuse to the presphenoid portion of the body to form the optic canals (fig. 3.7d). At birth, the sphenoid is represented by either three or four components: the presphenoid fused with the lesser wings and sometimes fused with the postsphenoid body, and the right and left greater wings. Although there is some variation in the order and timing of fusion, generally between

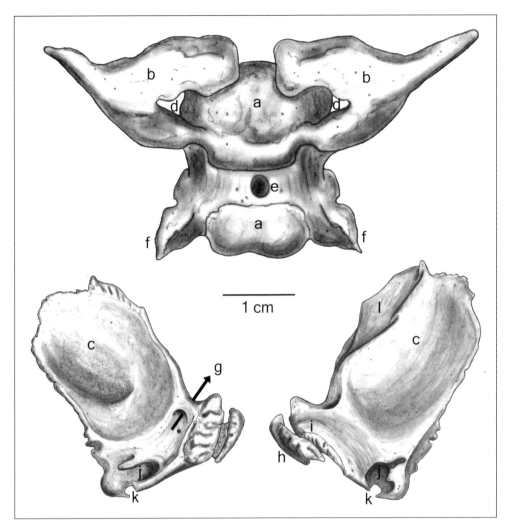

Fig. 3.7 Sphenoid of a neonate with fused body and lesser wings (*top*) and unfused left greater wing (*bottom*), left = internal, right = external: *a*, body; *b*, lesser wings; *c*, greater wings; *d*, optic canals; *e*, hypophyseal fossa; *f*, alar processes; *g*, foramen rotundum; *h*, medial pterygoid plate; *i*, lateral pterygoid plate; *j*, foramen ovale; *k*, foramen spinosum; *l*, orbital surface.

8 fetal months and soon after birth, the presphenoid and lesser wings fuse with the postsphenoid and develop the recognizable appearance of a small butterfly or bat.

The right and left greater wings (fig. 3.7c) form from both endochondral and intramembranous ossification centers and are recognizable as cupped, wing-shaped bones. The lateral portions of the greater wings develop intramembranously, while the medial portion around the foramen rotundum (fig. 3.7g)—a small, round opening —forms from a cartilaginous precursor. Between 6 and 8 fetal months the medial and lateral pterygoid plates (fig. 3.7h, i) fuse to the greater wings. These thin plates of bone attach at the medial, inferior aspect of the greater wings. Lateral to this edge of the bone is a large opening for the incomplete foramen ovale (fig. 3.7j). This oval opening often does not close until late in fetal development or during the first year. Lateral to foramen ovale, the

tiny, round opening for the foramen spinosum (fig. 3.7k) is usually not complete until the second year. At birth, the right and left greater wings are still separate from the body. They fuse to the postsphenoid portion of the conjoined body during the first year to form the bone's adult morphology.

Differentiation from Other Bones

In its full adult morphological state the sphenoid is unique, resembling a great horned owl or a bat, and it is not likely to be confused with other bones. During development, however, some of the small components may be confused with other bones. The shape of the postsphenoid portion of the body is similar in appearance to the basilar part of the occipital. The hypophyseal fossa (fig. 3.7e) of the postsphenoid portion distinguishes it from the basilar occipital, as do the lateral projections forming the alar processes (fig. 3.7f). Some of the smaller components, such as unfused lesser wings and the presphenoid, may initially appear unrecognizable and may be mistaken for nonhuman bones. The lesser wings (fig. 3.7b) are thin and V-shaped when unfused, with a deep notch marking the roof of the optic canal (fig. 3.7d). When joined to the presphenoid, the united lesser wings resemble a small moth or butterfly. The cup shape of the greater wing, with the serrated suture at one end and foramina at the opposite end, helps identify it. When the pterygoid plates (fig. 3.7h, i) are also fused to the greater wing, the inferior part of the bone can stand flat on a table with the wing extending upward.

Siding Techniques

Fetal sphenoid remains consist of multiple elements, and the lesser and greater wings have right and left components. To side unfused lesser wings, place the bone with the larger, flat surface on the table and the top of the V (fig. 3.7d) away from you. The small projection or the lateral tip is on the side from which the bone comes. With the flatter side up and the straight edge of the broader arm of the V away from you, the apex of the V (the lateral tip) points toward the side to which the bone belongs.

To side unfused greater wings (or fragmented sphenoids in which the greater wing has broken off the body), place the flatter surface away from you and the concave surface toward you, with the serrated edge up and the foramina down (similar to the orientation shown in fig. 3.7, bottom left). The large oval opening for the foramen ovale (fig. 3.7j) is on the side to which the bone belongs. Another method is to place the concave surface on the table and the convex surface up, with the long, irregular border facing you and the long, straight border facing away from you. The border with the foramen rotundum and the forming foramen ovale (fig. 3.7g, j) indicates the side from which the bone comes. If the wing is broken off just above the foramina and conjoining pterygoid plates (fig. 3.7h, i) and lacks these features, it can still be sided. Hold the concave surface toward you and the serrated edge up, as oriented on the bottom left side of figure 3.7. The small, flat surface that abuts the temporal bone is on the side to which the bone belongs.

Chapter 4   The Bones of the Face

■ The bones discussed in this chapter are those that make up the most anterior portion of the skull, or the face. These bones comprise parts of the eye orbits, the nasal cavity, and the hard palate. The ethmoid, inferior nasal conchae, vomer, nasal bones, lacrimals, zygomatics, palatines, maxillae, and mandible are included, as well as the hyoid, which is found in the neck.

The Ethmoid

Description at Major Stages

The ethmoid (fig. 4.1) is located at the top of the nasal cavity, inside the skull. It lies between the frontal portion of the orbits and forms part of the medial orbital walls. The ethmoid articulates with thirteen bones—more than any other bone in the skull. The articulations include the frontal, sphenoid, vomer, inferior nasal conchae, nasal bones, lacrimals, maxillae, and palatines.

The ethmoid ossifies endochondrally during fetal development but remains mostly cartilaginous until after the first postnatal year, when it begins to develop more of the adult morphology. At birth, it is comprised of a thin plate of cartilage with two irregularly shaped concentrations of bone on either side known as lateral masses or labyrinths (fig. 4.1). These two masses begin to ossify as early as the fifth fetal month and are filled with air cells. The lateral masses include the superior and middle nasal conchae (fig. 4.1a, b), which are puffy in appearance. The lateral aspects of the superior conchae are smooth and flat, forming the ethmoid's contributions to the orbital wall (fig. 4.1c). During the first year of life, the cribriform plate, a sievelike, horizontal part of the bone that forms the roof of the nasal cavity, rapidly ossifies. This development is accompanied by ossification of the crista galli, a superior projection of bone that marks the top of the flat perpendicular plate. Between 1 and 3 years of age, the crista galli and cribriform plate fuse to the lateral masses or labyrinths. Ossification of the perpendicular plate is slow, continuing throughout childhood.

Differentiation from Other Bones

It is rare to find an isolated ethmoid that is not damaged. Typically, parts of the ethmoid are attached to other cranial bones with which it articulates. To differentiate the ethmoid or fragments of it, try to identify some of its unique morphological characteristics, such as the perpendicular plate, cribriform plate, and crista galli. When badly fragmented, the ethmoid, particularly portions of the superior and middle nasal conchae (fig. 4.1a, b), appear as small shavings of bone. The orbital surface (fig. 4.1c) helps identify fragments of these lateral masses. In older children, fragments of the cribriform plate and crista galli are more likely to be encountered, as they are less fragile

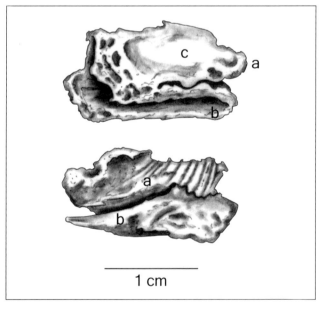

1 cm

Fig. 4.1 Left lateral mass of a neonatal ethmoid, top = lateral, bottom = medial: *a*, superior nasal concha; *b*, middle nasal concha; *c*, orbital surface.

parts of the ethmoid. The crista galli is named for its resemblance to a rooster's comb or crest, and it normally adheres to part of the cribriform plate with its numerous perforations. Ethmoid fragments including these features are easily identifiable.

Siding Techniques

In older fetuses and infants, the lateral masses (fig. 4.1) are unfused and separated into right and left halves. It is difficult to side separate lateral masses. To do so, orient the bone in standard anatomical position by placing the straighter edge with the free ends of the nasal conchae (fig. 4.1a, b) down and the orbital surface (fig. 4.1c) oriented above them. In this position, note that the anterior aspect is more rounded, while the posterior aspects of both nasal conchae come to points. Thus, position the rounder end away from you and the points toward you. Now that the bone is in anatomical position, the thin, bumpy surfaces of the superior and middle nasal conchae are medial, while the smooth and flat orbital surface is lateral, or on the side to which the bone belongs.

The Inferior Nasal Concha

Description at Major Stages

The inferior nasal conchae (fig. 4.2) are located inside the nasal cavity inferior to the ethmoid. These scroll-shaped bones form part of the lateral walls of the nasal cavity and articulate with the ethmoid, lacrimal, maxilla, and palatine. Each inferior nasal concha undergoes endochondral ossification during fetal development and assumes the adult morphological condition by birth or shortly thereafter. The longest, straight edge of the bone represents the inferior border (fig. 4.2a), which ends in a sharp point in one direction (posterior) and blunt point in the other (anterior). The posterior point provides the articulation for the palatine (fig. 4.2b), while the anterior point provides the articulation for the maxilla (fig. 4.2c). Two bony projections are present along the superior border. The more anterior projection (i.e., closer to the maxillary articulation) articulates with the lacrimals (fig. 4.2d), while the more posterior projection (i.e., closer to the palatine articulation) articulates with the ethmoid and maxilla (fig. 4.2e, f). The inferior portion of the bone hangs free.

Differentiation from Other Bones

When complete, an inferior nasal concha is distinct from other skeletal elements as a thin, curved bone with a puffy appearance. When fragmentary, the four bony projections (fig. 4.2b–d) described above distinguish inferior nasal conchae from ethmoidal or other facial fragments. The lack of an orbital surface on an inferior nasal concha differentiates it from the ethmoid. The curvature and irregular surface also help separate it from the smooth, straight perpendicular plate of the vomer and many other bones of the face, which are relatively thin and flat.

Siding Techniques

Because of the fragility of the thin bony labyrinth of the inferior nasal concha, this bone is not commonly found isolated in a complete and undamaged form. It often adheres to the maxilla or other bones with which it articulates. Siding a complete, inferior nasal concha can be done by placing it in standard anatomical position (fig. 4.2, bottom view). Hold the bone so the small, smooth part that curves over is on top (fig. 4.2f) and the long, straight border is down (fig. 4.2a). Place the blunt end (fig. 4.2c) away from you and the sharply pointed end (fig. 4.2b) toward you. The bone is akin to a scroll that curls. The medial (puffy) part is convex, while the smooth, thin part at the top attaches laterally to the ethmoid and maxilla (fig. 4.2e, f), thus indicating the side to which the bone belongs. Another option is to hold the bone with the smooth, concave, lateral surface toward you and the long, straight border (fig. 4.2a) facing down (oriented as shown in the top view of fig. 4.2). The wider, blunt end (fig. 4.2c) is on the side from which the bone comes.

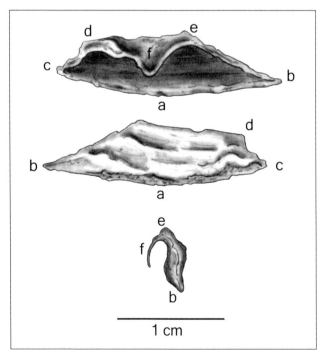

Fig. 4.2 Left inferior nasal concha of a neonate, top = lateral, middle = medial, bottom = posterior: *a,* inferior border; *b,* posterior point for the palatine; *c,* anterior point for the maxilla; *d,* lacrimal process; *e,* ethmoidal process; *f,* maxillary process.

The Vomer

Description at Major Stages

The vomer (fig. 4.3) is located below the ethmoid, essentially dividing the nasal cavity into two equal halves. It articulates with six bones—the sphenoid, ethmoid, maxillae, and palatines. Developing intramembranously, the majority of the vomer ossifies during childhood and is not likely to be identifiable in the fetal skeleton.

At birth, the vomer is a narrow wedge of bone with a superior furrow, known as the vomerine groove (fig. 4.3a), running its length and terminating posteriorly in two projections or alae (fig. 4.3b). When fully ossified, the vomer is a thin, flat bone that is shaped like a scalene triangle (no equal sides). The shortest border is marked by the two posterosuperior alae that flare laterally from the central groove. Inferior to the vomerine groove is the thin perpendicular plate. The longer, somewhat irregular border is inferior and articulates with the maxillae and palatines. The medium-length border is superior and articulates with the perpendicular plate of the ethmoid.

Differentiation from Other Bones

The thin, flat nature of the perpendicular plate of the vomer makes it very susceptible to damage. Even when fragmentary, the vomer is usually recognizable because of the presence of the alae (fig. 4.3b), divided by the vomerine groove (fig. 4.3a), to which at least part of the perpendicular plate (when ossified) usually adheres. This portion is the most robust and commonly found piece. Fragments of the perpendicular plate are easily confused with the perpendicular plate of the ethmoid. Vomer fragments may also be mistaken for inferior nasal conchae or lacrimal fragments. In this case, the nasopalatine grooves, which are faint impressions of nerves and blood vessels on both sides of the perpendicular plate, can help identify it as a vomer fragment.

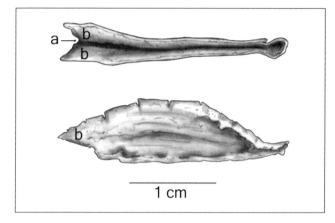

Fig. 4.3 Vomer of a neonate, top = superior, bottom = right lateral: *a*, vomerine groove; *b*, alae.

The Nasal Bone

Description at Major Stages

The left and right nasal bones (fig. 4.4) articulate with each other medially at the finely serrated internasal suture (fig. 4.4a) and, together, form the bridge of the nose. Each nasal bone also articulates with the frontal (at the nasofrontal suture), the maxilla (at the nasomaxillary suture), and the ethmoid. The nasal bones ossify intramembranously early in fetal development. Even in early stages they are easily identifiable because they possess certain adult characteristics, although they have slightly different proportions.

The fetal nasal bone has four smooth edges. The longest border, for the nasomaxillary suture, is lateral (fig. 4.4b) and the next longest border, for the internasal suture, is medial (fig. 4.4a). A short, straight superior border articulates with the frontal bone at the nasofrontal suture (fig. 4.4c). The nonarticular inferior border

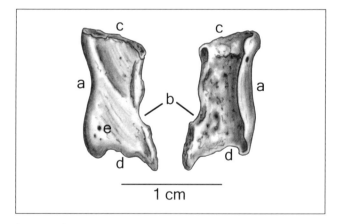

Fig. 4.4 Left nasal of a neonate, left = external, right = internal: *a*, internasal suture/medial border; *b*, nasomaxillary suture/lateral border; *c*, nasofrontal suture/superior border; *d*, inferior border; *e*, nasal foramen.

(fig. 4.4d) is slightly wider than the superior margin, but it is curved and bears a small notch near its midpoint. The internal surface is concave and rough in comparison to the smooth, external (anterior or facial) surface of the bone. At birth or shortly thereafter, the opening for the nasal foramen is evident on the external surface (fig. 4.4e). After 3 years of age, the sutures of the nasal bones become serrated and assist in identification and siding.

Differentiation from Other Bones

Complete nasal bones are usually recognizable because they possess similar morphology to the adult bones even during late fetal development. A nasal bone might be mistaken for the vomer, lacrimal, or possibly fragmentary portions of some of the other flat, thin facial bones. A nasal bone is generally smaller than the vomer, and can be distinguished by the three articular borders (fig. 4.4a–c) and the lack of alae. The lacrimal bones are also distinguishable from the nasals because, although they are both small, lacrimals are thinner and have a groove for the lacrimal gland and a small projection called the hamulus.

Nasals are more likely to be found intact and separate than these other bones because they are slightly thicker. Fragments of the vomer and lacrimals are more likely to adhere to bones with which they articulate.

Siding Techniques

Siding complete fetal or neonate nasal bones is easily accomplished by considering the curvature of the bone and the border length. The concave surface of the nasal bone is the internal surface. To side in standard anatomical position, orient the bone with the rougher, concave internal surface toward you and the smooth side away from you, as shown in figure 4.4 (right). Place the shortest articular border (fig. 4.4c) up and the curved nonarticular border with its slight notch down (fig. 4.4d). The longest border is lateral (fig. 4.4b) and on the side to which the bone belongs. Another way to side a nasal bone is to place the concave internal surface on a table and point the nonarticular, notched border (fig. 4.4d) away from you. The longest border is again on the side from which the bone comes.

The Lacrimal

Description at Major Stages

The lacrimals (fig. 4.5) are small, thin, rectangular bones located anteriorly on the medial part of the eye orbits. They ossify intramembranously and articulate with

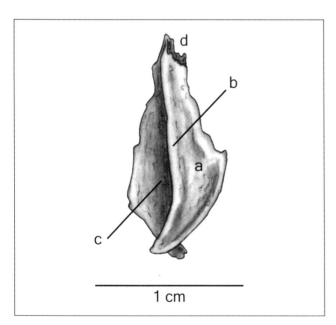

Fig. 4.5 Left lacrimal of a neonate, posterior view with superior end at top: *a*, orbital surface; *b*, posterior lacrimal crest; *c*, lacrimal groove; *d*, frontal suture.

the frontal, ethmoid, inferior nasal concha, and maxilla. At birth, the smooth orbital surface (fig. 4.5a) is very small and lateral to a crest that forms the posterior border of the tear duct or lacrimal canal. This feature is, therefore, known as the posterior lacrimal crest (fig. 4.5b). The medial nasal surface is irregular and bumpy in comparison to the orbital surface as the bone develops. The lacrimals develop recognizable adult morphology, characterized by the lacrimal groove (fig. 4.5c) and the hamulus at the inferior aspect, by approximately 2 to 3 years of age.

Differentiation from Other Bones

The lacrimals are usually found attached to other bones with which they articulate. When fragmentary, the lacrimals are difficult to differentiate from other fragmentary cranial bones such as the ethmoid, particularly if only the orbital surface (fig. 4.5a) is present. When whole, however, a separate lacrimal is not hard to distinguish because of its small, rectangular shape and diagnostic features of the orbital surface, posterior lacrimal crest, lacrimal groove (fig. 4.5a–c), and hamulus. When slightly damaged, the parts most likely to break off are the orbital part and the hamulus. However, the crest (fig. 4.5b) and adjacent lacrimal groove (fig. 4.5c) distinguish it from all but a very small fragment of the frontal process of a maxilla. The latter is generally identifiable by its curvature and larger size. Although the lacrimal bones in fetuses and infants are similar in size to the nasal bones, they are much thinner and their architecture is different enough that they should not be misidentified. In older children, the lacrimals are smaller and more rectangular than the nasal bones.

Siding Techniques

At birth, the lacrimals do not have all the adult characteristics; however, the posterior lacrimal crest (fig. 4.5b) and an adjacent groove or slight concavity for the lacrimal canal (fig. 4.5c) are distinct. With the crest facing you, and the pointed, tapered end facing up, as shown in figure 4.5, the indentation for the lacrimal groove is on the side from which the bone comes.

After 2 to 3 years of age, the lacrimals possess adult morphology and can be sided easily using the hooked projection or hamulus. Place the bone with the hamulus facing up and toward you. The hamulus points to the side from which the bone comes. In cases where the hamulus is broken off, place the small suture or tapered end (fig. 4.5d) up with the orbital surface (fig. 4.5a) toward you. Note that the lacrimal groove is anterior to the crest in standard anatomical position, so it is on the side of the crest from which the bone comes. Thus, if you are looking at the smooth orbital surface with the groove to the right of the crest, the bone is a right lacrimal.

The Zygomatic

Description at Major Stages

Also known as the malars or zygomas, the right and left zygomatic bones (fig. 4.6) make up the cheek region of the face. Each zygomatic articulates with the frontal, sphenoid, maxilla, and temporal. The zygomatics acquire recognizable adult morphology by 4 to 5 fetal months. The bone begins as a squamous portion with the temporal process developing first, followed by the development of the frontal and maxillary processes. In late fetal and infant stages, zygomatic bones display three projections emanating from the central body. The narrowest of these projections is the temporal process (fig. 4.6a), which articulates laterally with the zygomatic process of the temporal bone. The broadest projection or frontal process (fig. 4.6b) is superior, and the remaining medial projection is the maxillary process (fig. 4.6c). The smooth, curved surface extending from the medial edge of the frontal process along the superior part of the maxillary process is the orbital surface (fig. 4.6d). This part of the zygomatic forms the anterolateral rim of the eye orbit. Inferior to the orbit on the external or facial surface of the body is the opening for the zygomaticofacial foramen (fig. 4.6e). There may be only a single foramen or multiple foramina in this area.

As the zygomatic develops in early childhood, features of the adult bone become more useful in identifying and siding the bone. The inferior aspect becomes more robust as the malar tubercle becomes a prominent feature. In neonates, this feature appears as a point directly under the frontal process, adjacent to a notch that separates the maxillary and temporal processes from each other (fig. 4.6f). As the bone develops, the temporal process widens so that it is broader than the frontal process in the adult.

Differentiation from Other Bones

The zygomatic has a characteristic triangular shape with three radiating processes (fig. 4.6a–c) and its curved orbital rim by the middle of fetal development. Zygo-

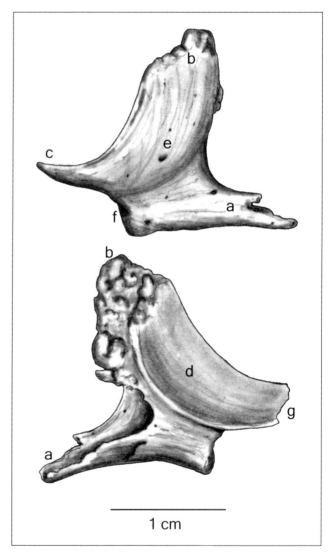

Fig. 4.6 Left zygomatic of a neonate, top = external, bottom = internal: *a*, temporal process; *b*, frontal process; *c*, maxillary process; *d*, orbital surface; *e*, zygomaticofacial foramen; *f*, inferior notch/malar tubercle; *g*, zygomaticomaxillary suture.

matics are usually easily identifiable because they are relatively stout compared with many other cranial bones and often remain intact. When complete, they should not be mistaken for other bones.

If the zygomatics are found in a fragmentary condition, the processes may be confused with projections on other cranial bones, such as the zygomatic process of the temporal and the frontal process of the maxilla. The frontal and temporal processes of a zygomatic (fig. 4.6b, c) usually have adhering portions of the orbital surface that help distinguish them. The lesser wing of the sphenoid could be mistaken for a zygomatic fragment, but it is much thinner and flatter. For broken zygomatics from children, the presence of the zygomaticofacial foramen and the malar tubercle (fig. 4.6e, f) are identifying features. The latter is often the best-preserved part of the bone in older children because it is the most robust portion.

Siding Techniques

Siding complete zygomatic bones of almost any age can be accomplished by recognizing the specific processes. The external surface of the zygomatic is somewhat convex and smooth, while the internal surface is concave and has a ridge. To side the bone in roughly standard anatomical position, hold it with the smooth external surface away from you and the internal ridge toward you (as in fig. 4.6, bottom). In fetal and neonatal bones, point the longer border with a notch in it toward the floor and the broad frontal process upward (fig. 4.6b). The orbital surface is medial (fig. 4.6d), or opposite the side to which the bone belongs, while the long, pointed temporal process is lateral (fig. 4.6a) and points to the side from which the bone comes.

In older children, the malar tubercle (fig. 4.6f) is developed and replaces the inferior notch. Note also that the temporal process (fig. 4.6a) becomes much thicker as the bone grows in early childhood. Thus, when held in anatomical position, with the rough malar tubercle toward the floor, the thickest and widest process is the temporal process and it is on the side to which the bone belongs. The smooth, curved orbital surface is medial (fig. 4.6d), or opposite the side from which the bone comes. Alternatively, place the internal surface on a table with the frontal process pointing away from you (fig. 4.6, top). The orbital surface and the zygomaticomaxillary suture (fig. 4.6d, g) are on the side from which the bone comes. This last method works for all stages of development.

The Palatine

Description at Major Stages

The left and right palatine bones (fig. 4.7) form the posterior aspect of the hard palate, as well as the floor of the nasal cavity via the horizontal plate (fig. 4.7a) and the lateral aspects of the inferior nasal cavity via the perpendicular plate (fig. 4.7b). Each articulates with the opposite palatine, the maxilla, sphenoid, ethmoid, inferior nasal concha, and vomer. The palatine begins to ossify in membrane early in fetal development and is recognizable by the middle of gestation. At this stage, the bone has developed many of its distinctive features but it differs in proportions and does not attain its adult size and morphology until puberty.

Each mature palatine is L shaped. In fetal and infant remains, the horizontal and perpendicular plates are roughly equal in size, while the pyramidal process (fig. 4.7c) at the posterior, inferior aspect of the perpendicular plate is proportionately large compared to that of older individuals. After 3 years, the perpendicular plate grows rapidly, so that it is twice as long as the horizontal plate by adolescence.

The perpendicular plate is irregular, with a combination of processes and crests for articulation with other bones. The orbital process (fig. 4.7d) is the most superior aspect of the palatine, articulating with the ethmoid (medially), sphenoid (posteriorly), and maxilla (anteriorly), while also contributing to the orbital surface. The sphenopalatine notch or foramen (fig. 4.7e) lies just inferior to the ethmoidal crest (fig. 4.7f), where the bone articulates with the ethmoid. The orbital process frequently breaks off at this junction. A small rounded area projecting posteromedially from the ethmoidal crest is the sphenoidal process (fig. 4.7g) that articulates with the sphenoid. Moving down the perpendicular plate, one encounters the maxillary process projecting anteriorly for

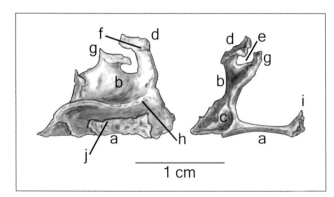

Fig. 4.7 Left palatine of a neonate, left = medial, right = posterior: *a,* horizontal plate; *b,* perpendicular plate; *c,* pyramidal process; *d,* orbital process; *e,* sphenopalatine notch or foramen; *f,* ethmoidal crest; *g,* sphenoidal process; *h,* conchal crest; *i,* posterior nasal spine; *j,* interpalatine suture.

articulation with the maxilla, and the conchal crest (fig. 4.7h), running across the plate for articulation with the inferior nasal concha. Inferior to the conchal crest, on the posterolateral aspect of the perpendicular plate, the bone articulates with the medial pterygoid plate of the sphenoid at the pyramidal process (fig. 4.7c), which resembles a tall pyramid in its shape. This part of the bone is considerably thicker than the thin and fragile portion of the perpendicular plate that lies superior to the conchal crest. As a result, the part most frequently encountered in archaeological remains is that portion inferior to the conchal crest, along with the horizontal plate. In fetal and neonatal remains, the pyramidal process projects almost as far from the horizontal plate as the orbital process. The ethmoidal crest is very close to the horizontal plate, whereas it is nearly halfway up the perpendicular plate in adults. The divergence of the maxillary and orbital processes helps distinguish the perpendicular plate from the flat, rectangular horizontal plate.

The horizontal plate is smooth and flat on the superior or nasal surface, while the inferior surface forming the roof of the palate is marked by ridges. The anterior edge joins with the maxilla at the transverse palatine (or palatomaxillary) suture and the medial border articulates with the opposite palatine at the posterior median palatine (or interpalatine) suture. The posterior aspect of the horizontal plate is nonarticular and concave. The posterior nasal spine (fig. 4.7i) projects upward from the superior surface on the most medial and posterior aspect of the horizontal plate. On the inferior surface of the horizontal plate, two foramina are notable. These are the greater and lesser palatine foramina found at the juncture of the horizontal and vertical plates, where the bone abuts the maxilla.

Differentiation from Other Bones

The palatine has many unique features that distinguish it from other bones to which it frequently adheres. It is not commonly found separate, but parts of it are typically attached to the maxilla or the sphenoid. When fragments are separated from these other bones, it may be difficult to distinguish the perpendicular plate from aspects of other bones contributing to the nasal cavity. The sphenopalatine notch (fig. 4.7e) and the conchal crest (fig. 4.7h) identify such fragments. The perpendicular plates of the vomer and ethmoid bones are much smoother and flatter than the surface of the perpendicular plate of a palatine. When a complete or nearly complete palatine is found, its distinctive L shape and the features of the pyramidal process and horizontal plate (fig. 4.7a, c) make it easy to identify.

Siding Techniques

Techniques for siding a separate palatine or fragments thereof are similar regardless of developmental stage. This bone is easy to position in standard anatomical position because the rougher surface of the horizontal plate (fig. 4.7a) faces down and the perpendicular plate, or any portion of it still remaining (fig. 4.7b), projects upward, with the smooth, concave nonarticular border and pyramidal process (fig. 4.7c) facing you and pointing downward. In this position (fig. 4.7, right), the perpendicular plate and the pyramidal process are on the side to which the bone belongs. Thus, if the perpendicular plate is fragmentary, any remnant of the pyramidal process allows you to side the bone. For example, if it lies to the right of the nonarticular edge of the horizontal plate, then it is a right palatine. If only part of the horizontal plate remains, note that the small projection for the posterior nasal spine (fig. 4.7i) is posterior and medial, or opposite the side to which the bone belongs.

Taking the bone out of standard anatomical position provides another method of siding a whole palatine. Orient the horizontal plate such that the posterior median palatine (or interpalatine) suture (fig. 4.7j) faces you and the perpendicular plate is away from you and points upward (fig. 4.7, left). The pyramidal process (fig. 4.7c) is on the side to which the bone belongs. The nonarticular edge of the horizontal plate also indicates the side to which the bone belongs in this orientation.

The Maxilla

Description at Major Stages

The right and left maxillae (fig. 4.8) form most of the nasal aperture and floor, most of the hard palate, and part of the eye orbit. The maxilla also functions to hold the upper dentition and contributes to the zygomatic arch laterally. In addition, the maxillary sinus is a large air cavity within each maxilla that is inferior to the orbital floor and superior to the part in which the teeth are held (alveolar process). Each maxilla articulates with nine other bones: the opposite maxilla, palatine, vomer, inferior nasal concha, lacrimal, ethmoid, zygomatic, nasal, and frontal.

The maxilla begins to achieve a characteristic shape during early fetal development and by birth shares many features of the adult bone. Like many other forming bones, however, it differs in its proportions. The majority of these features are apparent from the second trimester onward. At this stage, the projections of the frontal process superiorly (fig. 4.8a) and the zygomatic process laterally (fig. 4.8b) are evident, and tooth germs are forming in the thin, bulging tooth crypts (fig. 4.8c) of the alveolar process (fig. 4.8d). The tooth crypts for all deciduous teeth are formed by 17 to 18 fetal weeks. The

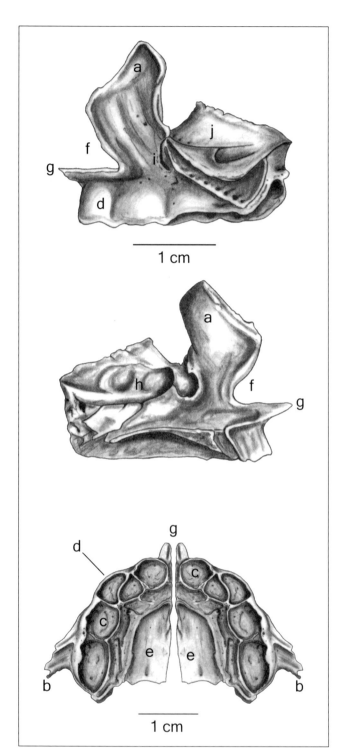

Fig. 4.8 Maxilla of a neonate, top = left lateral, middle = left medial, bottom = right and left inferior: *a*, frontal process; *b*, zygomatic process; *c*, tooth crypts; *d*, alveolar process; *e*, palatine process; *f*, nasal cavity; *g*, anterior nasal spine; *h*, maxillary sinus; *i*, infraorbital suture; *j*, orbital surface.

that in which the deciduous canines and molars develop. By birth, the palatine process forms the roof of the mouth and floor of the nasal cavity (fig. 4.8f) and consists of a small, thin plate of bone. Projecting from the midline of the nasal cavity at the front of the bone is a small anterior nasal spine (fig. 4.8g). The maxilla looks squat in a neonate in comparison to the adult bone. Most of the inferior aspect displays open crypts or cavities where the tooth buds are forming. The maxillary sinus (fig. 4.8h) in a newborn is a small triangle superior to the tooth crypts of the alveolar process and posterior to the frontal process. The frontal process of a neonate is short, due to the small size of the face. Just lateral to the frontal process and inferior to the rim of the orbital surface is a large opening known as the infraorbital foramen (fig. 4.8i). This foramen is the external opening of the infraorbital canal, which continues as the infraorbital sulcus or groove on the posterior part of the orbital surface. The zygomatic process (fig. 4.8b) flares laterally from the orbital rim to articulate with the zygomatic. The maxilla undergoes continual remodeling throughout infancy and childhood as both the deciduous and permanent teeth calcify, emerge, and finally erupt from their crypts. During this time, the bone grows in size, and the maxillary sinus enlarges, becoming a more obvious feature of the bone in older children.

Differentiation from Other Bones

The presence of tooth crypts in late-term fetuses and neonates or erupting teeth in infants and children makes it difficult to confuse the maxilla with other skeletal elements. The only other bone with teeth is the mandible but, even in fetuses, these bones are easy to differentiate. Unlike the mandible, the maxilla contributes to the palate (fig. 4.8e), which joins the two halves of the maxilla together and results in the tooth rows being connected by a floor of bone. Maxillary fragments are thin and light due to the presence of the maxillary sinus (fig. 4.8h) and the orbital surface (fig. 4.8j). The mandible, even in fetal remains, is more robust.

Fragments of the maxilla may be difficult to distinguish from pieces of other bones that comprise parts of the orbit or nasal cavity, especially the zygomatic, lacrimal, and sphenoid. The orbital surface of the maxilla (fig. 4.8j) is most easily identified by the presence of the infraorbital sulcus and the infraorbital foramen (fig. 4.8i) on the external surface of the bone. Fragments of the frontal process are most often confused with the lacrimal due to the presence of the anterior lacrimal crest and anterior portion of the lacrimal duct. Note that the lacrimal bone is flatter and thinner and has both a smooth orbital surface and a projecting hamulus. The frontal process of the maxilla (fig. 4.8a), in contrast, lacks these features and has more curvature. The presence of the maxillary sinus is especially useful in distinguishing maxilla fragments from

palatine process (fig. 4.8e) at this point is not yet complete but is divided into premaxillary and maxillary parts. The premaxilla is the portion anterior to the incisive suture, which separates the area holding the incisors from

most other bones in older children. The only other bones with large sinuses are the frontal and sphenoid, and those of the frontal are much smaller and are surrounded by thicker bone than the maxilla. The sphenoidal sinus is usually attached to identifiable fragments of the sphenoid body and often includes parts of the lesser wings and optic canal. Remember that the maxilla is the only bone that has tooth crypts, a sinus, and an orbital surface (fig. 4.8c, h, j).

Siding Techniques

Techniques for siding a complete maxilla or fragments thereof are similar regardless of developmental stage. To orient the bone in standard anatomical position, hold it with the tooth crypts or erupted teeth down (fig. 4.8c) and the frontal process pointing up (fig. 4.8a). The nasal cavity (fig. 4.8f) should point away from you and the back of the palate and the orbital surface (fig. 4.8j) toward you. In this position, the orbital surface is lateral to the frontal process, or toward the side to which the bone belongs. The external aspect of the bone flares laterally at the zygomatic process (fig. 4.8b), which also indicates the side from which the bone comes.

Another method is to place the maxilla such that the tooth crypts are facing you and the anterior nasal spine (fig. 4.8g) and the incisor crypts are pointing up. Note that the bony palate (fig. 4.8e) has a straight medial edge. In this view, the straight edge is on the side to which the bone belongs (see fig. 4.8, bottom view).

The Mandible

Description at Major Stages

The mandible (fig. 4.9) functions to hold the lower dentition. It articulates with both temporal bones via the mandibular condyles (fig. 4.9a). The mandible begins to attain its characteristic shape during the third fetal month. At this stage, it consists of two symmetrical halves (i.e., a left and right) that continue to arise via endochondral ossification processes. These two halves articulate at the mandibular symphysis (fig. 4.9b), which is anterior and oriented superoinferiorly between the left and right first (or central) incisor crypts. The symphysis typically fuses during the first year. Each half displays morphological features that distinguish the adult mandible, such as the ascending ramus (fig. 4.9c), which terminates superiorly in the condyle at its posterior margin and the thin coronoid process (fig. 4.9d) at its anterior. The internal aspect of the ascending ramus has a large opening known as the mandibular foramen (fig. 4.9e), at the edge of which is a small spine called the lingula (fig. 4.9f). During fetal and infant growth, the superior aspect of the mandibular body (fig. 4.9g), or its alveolar process, displays open crypts (fig. 4.9h) where the tooth buds form. In older infants and children, the mental eminence or chin (fig. 4.9i) is located in the midline of the fused mandible and is generally very pronounced. To either side of the mental eminence are large openings for the mental foramina (fig. 4.9j). The mandible undergoes continual remodeling throughout development as both the deciduous and permanent teeth calcify, emerge, and finally erupt from their crypts.

Differentiation from Other Bones

The presence of tooth crypts in late-term fetuses and neonates, and emerging or erupting teeth in older infants and children, makes it difficult to confuse the mandible with other skeletal elements. The only other bone containing tooth crypts and developing teeth is the maxilla. Unlike the maxilla, the mandible does not have a palate extending from the alveolar process and lacks orbital and nasal components. In unfused mandibles, the symphysis is a roughened but flat area at the midline (fig. 4.9b). In fused mandibles, the mental eminence (fig. 4.9i) helps distinguish it from the maxilla. Fragments of the ascending ramus (fig. 4.9c) may be difficult to identify when separated from the body, but characteristic features such as the condyle, coronoid process, or the mandibular foramen aid in identification (fig. 4.9a, d, e).

Siding Techniques

Until the two halves of the mandible fuse together, it is necessary to side them. These techniques also work with mandibular fragments. Place the tooth crypts (fig. 4.9h) or teeth, if present, facing up with the mandibular condyle (fig. 4.9a) toward you. Orient the mandibular symphysis (fig. 4.9b) so it runs parallel to an imaginary straight line (see fig. 4.9, bottom view). The tooth crypts and ascending ramus (fig. 4.9c, h) curve around toward the side to which the bone belongs. Thus, if the tooth crypts, coronoid process, and condyle are to the right of your line, it is a right mandible. If the ramus is missing, examine the tooth crypts, which typically increase in size from incisors to molars, to help you orient the anterior portion of the fragment. In standard anatomical position, note that the coarser, external surface of the bone, as well as the mental foramen (fig. 4.9j), are on the side from which the bone comes. Internal features such as the mandibular foramen and lingula (fig. 4.9e, f) are medial, or opposite the side to which it belongs. Alternatively, place the anterior portion toward you with the crypts facing up. The side of the fragment that displays the mandibular fo-

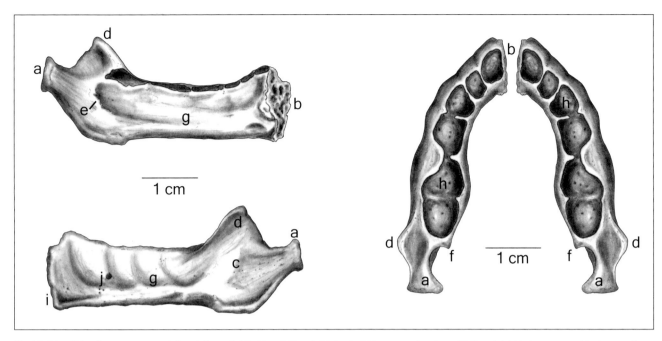

Fig. 4.9 Mandible of a neonate, top left = left medial, bottom left = left lateral, right = superior view of left and right halves: *a*, condyle; *b*, mandibular symphysis; *c*, ascending ramus; *d*, coronoid process; *e*, mandibular foramen; *f*, lingula; *g*, body; *h*, tooth crypts; *i*, mental eminence; *j*, mental foramen.

ramen is the side to which the bone belongs. If only the ramus is present, place the condyle toward you and the coronoid process pointing down. The condyle in a neonate curves toward the side from which the bone comes.

Also, in this position, the side of the ramus that displays the mandibular foramen is the side to which the bone belongs.

The Hyoid

Description at Major Stages

The hyoid (fig. 4.10) is suspended below the mandible by muscles and ligaments, and is the only bone that does not articulate directly with any other bone in the skeleton. The adult hyoid has three major components: the body, and the right and left greater horns or cornua (fig. 4.10a, b). In addition, there are two small components, the lesser horns, that may or not be present. The body is a small ovoid bone that is concave on the posterior surface. The right and left greater horns are long, thin projections of bone that often fuse to the body in adults.

Developing endochondrally, the hyoid may begin to ossify as early as the thirtieth fetal week; however, ossification often does not occur until after birth. The body (fig. 4.10a) is not completely ossified until approximately 2 years of age, while the greater and lesser horns (fig. 4.10b) continue to ossify through puberty. In some cases, the lesser horns and the posterior ends of the greater horns remain cartilaginous. In many cases, however, these components fuse to the body during adulthood. When the greater horns fuse to the body, the hyoid becomes U shaped.

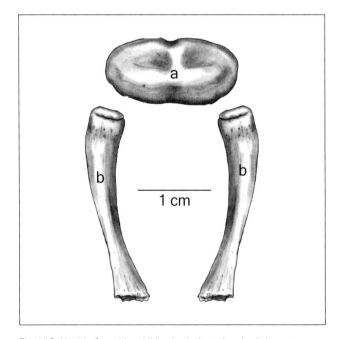

Fig. 4.10 Hyoid of an older child: *a*, body (anterior view); *b*, greater horns or cornua.

Differentiation from Other Bones

Before fusion, the hyoid body (fig. 4.10a) may be mistaken for the unfused anterior arch of the first cervical vertebra (i.e., the atlas). Both are small and have a concave surface in infancy and early childhood. Around age 5 or 6, however, the atlas arch fuses together, preventing confusion. In younger individuals, the way to distinguish these bones is to note that the anterior arch of the atlas has a small tubercle opposite the concave side, which displays a small articular facet for the second cervical vertebra (i.e., the axis). The hyoid body of a single individual is much smaller than the anterior atlas. It might also be possible to mistake the first coccygeal element with its projecting cornua for a hyoid. Note that the coccyx is depressed on its superior surface, from which the cornua project, rather than being concave on the posterior aspect. The hyoid body is far thinner than the coccyx, which is a thicker, more rounded bone.

Unfused greater cornua (fig. 4.10b) are long and thin and could be mistaken for broken processes forming the zygomatic arch. However, they are broad at one end and narrow at the other and have no serrated edges representing sutures. A broken styloid process of the temporal bone might also be mistaken for a greater horn but it shows a break at its thicker end and tapers to a sharp point at its opposite end.

After adolescence, if the greater horns fuse to the body, the complete hyoid bears a slight resemblance to a fetal or infant mandible. The hyoid has a central protuberance resembling the mental eminence of the chin, but it is much smaller and thinner than an infant's mandible and lacks tooth crypts.

Siding Techniques

Siding separate greater horns is difficult in both sub-adult and adult skeletons. The anterior end is wider than the posterior end, so these are easy to distinguish. Trying to differentiate the superolateral and inferomedial aspects, however, is challenging. The superolateral surface is attached to several muscles and ligaments that suspend the bone in the throat. Thus, it will tend to have a slightly rougher surface than the smooth inferomedial aspect. If you can confidently determine which surface is superolateral, place the bone in standard anatomical position with that aspect up and the wider end facing away from you. The bone sweeps up and back, with a concave curve on its superomedial edge and a convex curve on its inferolateral edge. The bone thus bows out (or curves convexly) toward the side from which it comes. In many cases, the greater horns are not developed sufficiently to permit accurate siding.

Chapter 5 The Dentition

■ Every child who survives to adulthood has experienced tooth loss because humans have two sets of teeth. The first set, known as the primary or deciduous dentition, begins to form in utero. These teeth emerge from open crypts but are still under the gums around birth. The second set, known as the secondary or permanent dentition, forms mostly after birth (although certain teeth actually begin formation in utero as well). Permanent teeth emerge as the deciduous teeth are lost. Upon eruption through the gums, only the crown of the tooth (that portion covered with hard enamel and visible above the gum line) is fully formed. Tooth enamel is the hardest substance in the body and helps protect the underlying dentin and pulp cavity (fig. 5.1a–c). The pulp cavity is the inner core of the tooth that contains blood vessels and nerves. Tooth roots continue to develop after eruption and typically are not complete until two years or more after crown completion. Roots are covered with a substance called cementum (fig. 5.1d) that helps secure this part of the tooth in its socket. The juncture of the tooth root and the crown is a constriction known as the neck or, more commonly, the cementoenamel junction (CEJ; fig. 5.1e).

The crown surfaces of each tooth are described by their location in the mouth (fig. 5.2). The main surfaces of the anterior teeth (the incisors and canines) are referred to as labial, lingual, and incisal. The posterior teeth (the premolars and molars) have buccal, lingual, and occlusal surfaces. The lingual surface is the side of the tooth that touches the tongue. The labial and buccal surfaces are opposite the lingual surface. The labial surface touches the lips and the buccal surface touches the cheeks. The incisal or occlusal surface is the biting or chewing area of the tooth. The sides of each tooth are described by their position in the mouth, either toward the midline between the two central incisors (mesial) or away from the midline and toward the back of the mouth (distal). The area between adjacent teeth is interproximal.

Tooth types (incisors, canines, premolars, molars) are typically designated by their initial letters, with permanent teeth distinguished by capital letters (I, C, P, M) and deciduous teeth by small letters (i, c, m). The position of the tooth in the dental arcade is indicated by numbers (e.g., i1, i2). Maxillary and mandibular teeth are often distinguished by superscript and subscript, respectively, of the corresponding tooth number (e.g., i^1 is the deciduous, maxillary, central incisor; I_1 is the permanent, mandibular, central incisor).

The timing of calcification of the crown and root, emergence, and eruption in both sets of dentition has been well studied and, at present, is considered the most accurate approach to determining age at death of subadults. The majority of evidence suggests that environmental factors influence dental development less than skeletal development. Tooth formation and eruption is, therefore, under tighter genetic control than ossification and fusion of skeletal elements. Some of the standards that should be referred to for dental age estimation are Gustafson and Koch (1974), Liversidge et al. (1998), Liversidge and Molleson (2004), Logan and Kronfeld (1933), Schour and Massler (1940), Smith (1991), and Ubelaker (1999).

Teeth are found in only two bones of the skull: the maxilla (upper jaw) and the mandible (lower jaw). In many cases, forming or erupted teeth are still imbedded in the jaws, aiding in their identification. Loose teeth, however, are commonly encountered and must be distinguished from each other for proper identification. This chapter provides simple, straightforward information to help you identify and side isolated human teeth.

Five Steps for Tooth Identification

Differentiating the types of teeth and their position in the jaws (fig. 5.2) is a multistage process. This chapter follows five common steps delineated by various authors (e.g., Anderson 1962; Ubelaker in Bass, 1995; White, 2000); Hillson (1996) is also an excellent reference for identifying and differentiating teeth. The following steps help you answer specific questions that guide you to the proper identification of a loose tooth.

1. To which tooth type does the tooth belong?
2. Is the tooth deciduous or permanent?
3. Is it a maxillary or mandibular tooth?
4. What is the tooth's position in the dentition?
5. Is the tooth from the right or left side?

1. To Which Tooth Type Does the Tooth Belong?

The first step toward identification involves assessing what type of tooth is present. There are four types of teeth: incisors, canines, premolars, and molars (fig. 5.3). Teeth of each type share common characteristics that differentiate them from other tooth types. The basic morphological features of each tooth type are described below. Together, the incisors and canines form the anterior teeth and are used for biting and cutting. The teeth shear past each other, unlike the back teeth (premolars and molars) that come directly together and form grinding surfaces. In incisors and canines, the biting surface of the tooth is referred to as the incisal surface. The grinding surface where the upper and lower premolars and molars contact each other is referred to as the occlusal surface. In each quadrant of the dentition (upper right, upper left, lower right, and lower left), the deciduous dentition consists of two incisors, one canine, and two molars, for a total of twenty teeth. Each quadrant of the permanent dentition is typically comprised of two incisors, one canine, two premolars, and three molars, for a total of thirty-two teeth.

Incisors. The incisors are designed for cutting and stripping and are the most anterior teeth in the mouth. They are shaped like tiny spatulas or flathead screwdriver blades with a sharp cutting edge. When the enamel wears off the incisal surface, the darker dentin below it is exposed as a thin line. The labial surface (toward the lips) is convex, while the lingual surface (toward the tongue) is concave. Also on the lingual surface, just above the CEJ, is a slight bulge known as the tuberculum, from which marginal ridges extend toward the incisal edge (the biting surface). Incisors have a single root.

Canines. Human canines are similar to incisors in having single roots and a crown with one cusp that has marginal ridges. The canine crown tapers to a sharp, central point or cusp rather than having a broad, flat cutting edge, like an incisor. The tuberculum tends to be larger than in incisors, resulting in a thicker appearance at the CEJ in the labial-lingual direction. Extending from the tuberculum is a prominent buttress or ridge that runs up the lingual surface and supports the central cusp. Canine teeth have taller crowns and longer roots than incisors. When worn, the dentin exposure on the incisal edge of a canine is diamond-shaped rather than linear like an incisor.

Premolars. Dentists often refer to premolars as bicuspids or tricuspids because they have two and sometimes three distinct cusps on their crowns. They have more complex roots than incisors and canines that can be single or sometimes double. They are intermediate in morphology between the anterior teeth and the molars. The larger of the two or three cusps is always buccal (toward the cheek) while the smaller cusp(s) is lingual. Premolars are found only in the permanent dentition.

Molars. The molars are designed for grinding. As such, the crowns are bigger than those of other teeth and the roots are more complex, which often helps hold the tooth in its socket. Molar crowns are rectangular in outline and have several distinct cusps (usually four or five). Molars typically have two or three roots.

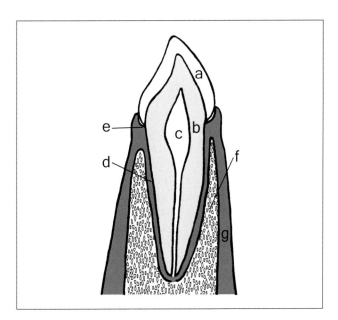

Fig. 5.1 Anatomy of a tooth: *a,* enamel; *b,* dentin; *c,* pulp cavity; *d,* cementum; *e,* CEJ (cementoenamel junction); *f,* bone; *g,* gum.

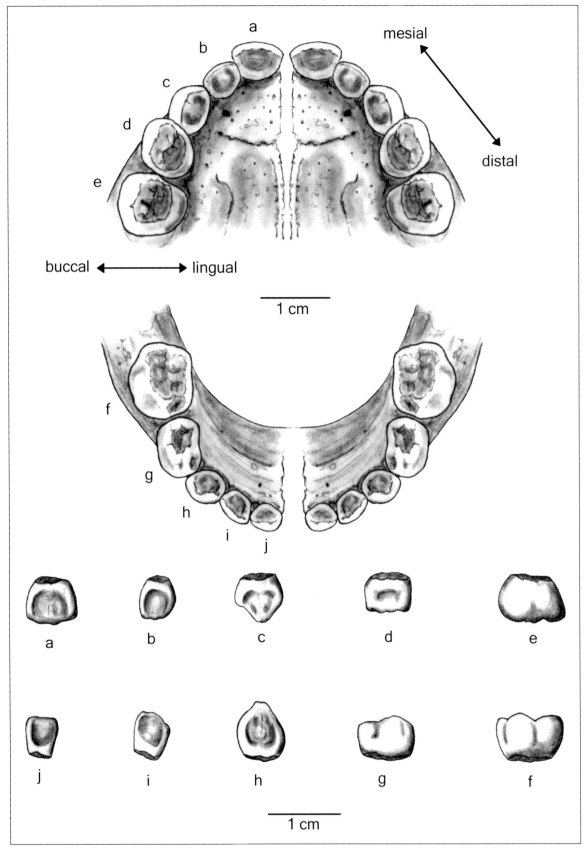

Fig. 5.2 Deciduous dentition of the maxilla (*top*) and mandible (*middle*) in occlusal views with corresponding lingual views (*bottom*) of each tooth; *maxilla: a*, central incisor; *b*, lateral incisor; *c*, canine; *d*, first molar; *e*, second molar; *mandible: f*, second molar; *g*, first molar; *h*, canine; *i*, lateral incisor; *j*, central incisor. All teeth are approximately two times actual size.

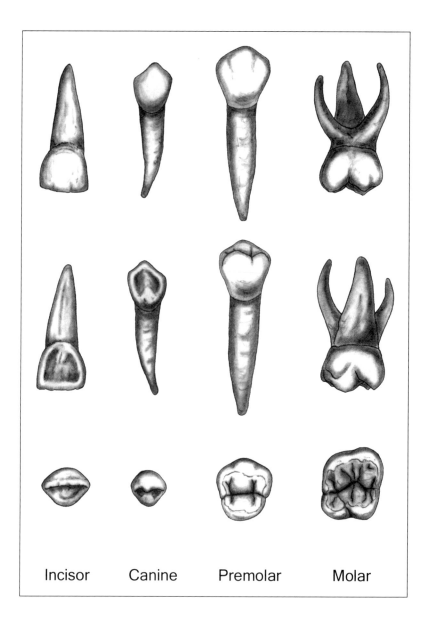

Fig. 5.3 Tooth types: top row = labial/buccal; middle row = lingual; bottom row = occlusal. All teeth are approximately two times actual size.

| Incisor | Canine | Premolar | Molar |

2. Is the Tooth Deciduous or Permanent?

At birth, only the deciduous teeth are well developed. In older infants, the permanent teeth have begun to form, although they do not begin to erupt until about age 6. By age 12, all twenty of the deciduous teeth have normally been shed and all thirty-two permanent teeth have begun development, with most already erupted. Thus, from shortly after birth until about adolescence, a given individual will have both deciduous and permanent teeth present. This combination is often referred to as a mixed dentition (fig. 5.4; see also fig. 10.3). It is, therefore, extremely important to become familiar with the features that distinguish permanent teeth from deciduous teeth (fig. 5.5).

The overall size of the tooth is the first thing to consider. Deciduous teeth are miniature versions of permanent teeth, so they are much smaller in comparison. Even when crowns are not fully formed, the developing permanent teeth are broader than their deciduous counterparts. The roots of permanent teeth are also larger, while deciduous roots are short and slender. Those of deciduous molars are often more divergent than permanent molar roots because they arch over the developing crowns of the premolars.

Next, inspect the crown of the tooth. The crowns of all the deciduous teeth tend to be more bulbous than those of the permanent teeth. The bulbous shape of a deciduous crown is accentuated by its constricted CEJ.

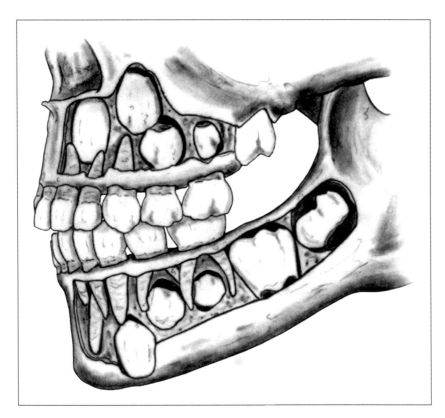

Fig. 5.4 Mixed deciduous and developing permanent dentition of a child approximately 4 years of age.

The enamel of deciduous teeth is thinner than that of permanent tooth crowns. Thus, they often wear quickly and can have a yellow or brown tinge due to the dentin underneath.

3. Is It a Maxillary or Mandibular Tooth?

Incisors. Maxillary incisors are larger and more shovel- or spadelike than mandibular incisors, which are smaller and narrower in shape and appear more rectangular or chisel-shaped (figs. 5.6 and 5.7). The marginal ridges on the lingual surface of the mandibular incisors are either slight or absent, whereas they are very distinct on the maxillary incisors. Finally, the cingulum—a bulge on the crown near the root, often called the tuberculum—is typically broader on the maxillary incisors and narrower on the mandibular. Maxillary incisors have more robust roots than mandibular incisors and are round in cross section. The mandibular roots are somewhat pinched mesiodistally and are, thus, more ovoid in cross section. Note also that maxillary incisors typically show wear facets on the lingual surface, while the mandibular incisors have wear on the labial surface due to the shearing action of these teeth in opposition.

Canines. As with the incisors, the maxillary canine has a broader cingulum, while that of the mandibular tooth is narrower (figs. 5.8 and 5.9). The cusp of the canine tends to be sharper and more pointed in the maxillary than mandibular dentition, which tends to be blunter. The crown is much wider in the maxillary canine, whereas the mandibular canine is thinner and longer, giving it a more rectangular shape. As in incisors, wear facets occur on the lingual surface of maxillary teeth and on the labial surface of mandibular teeth.

Premolars. The easiest way to identify a premolar is to examine the occlusal surface (fig. 5.10). The two cusps of the maxillary premolars are similar in size compared to mandibular premolars, although the buccal cusp is slightly larger and higher. The mandibular premolars can be bi- or tricuspid (two or three cusped); however, the buccal cusp is always larger and higher than the lower and considerably smaller lingual cusp(s). The upper premolars have a crown shape that resembles the number 8 because of the groove that separates the cusps. The occlusal outline of the lower premolar crowns is often round if two cusps are present or almost square when three cusps are present.

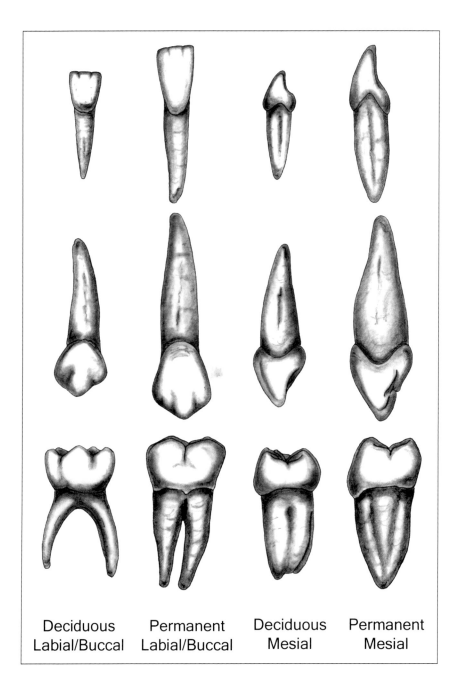

Fig. 5.5 Comparison of the deciduous and permanent teeth: top row = incisor; middle row = canine; bottom row = molar. All teeth are approximately two times actual size.

| Deciduous Labial/Buccal | Permanent Labial/Buccal | Deciduous Mesial | Permanent Mesial |

Both maxillary and mandibular premolars usually have one major root that is much wider buccolingually than incisor or canine roots. Upper premolars sometimes have two roots (see fig. 5.10) and occasionally even three. Three-rooted maxillary premolars have two buccal roots and one lingual like maxillary molars. When there are two roots, one is buccal and the other is lingual. In some cases, these roots are entirely or partially fused together. Lower premolars typically have only one root, although the single rounded root often displays distinct grooves on either side that divide it into buccal and lingual sections and flatten the root mesiodistally.

Molars. A simple way to distinguish maxillary and mandibular molars is to examine the number and position of the roots (figs. 5.11 and 5.12). Maxillary molars typically have three roots (one lingual, one mesiobuccal, and one distobuccal) whereas mandibular molars typically have

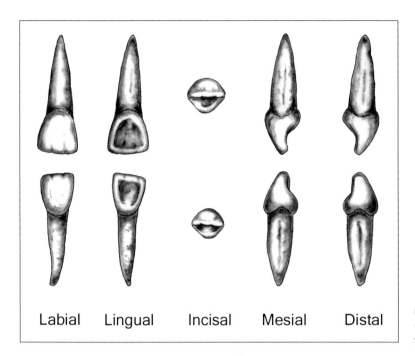

Labial	Lingual	Incisal	Mesial	Distal

Fig. 5.6 Comparison of maxillary (*top*) and mandibular (*bottom*) deciduous incisors. The right lateral incisors are shown (approximately two times actual size).

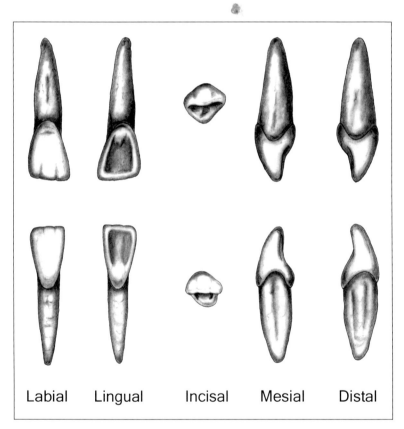

Labial	Lingual	Incisal	Mesial	Distal

Fig. 5.7 Comparison of maxillary (*top*) and mandibular (*bottom*) permanent incisors. The right lateral incisors are shown (approximately two times actual size).

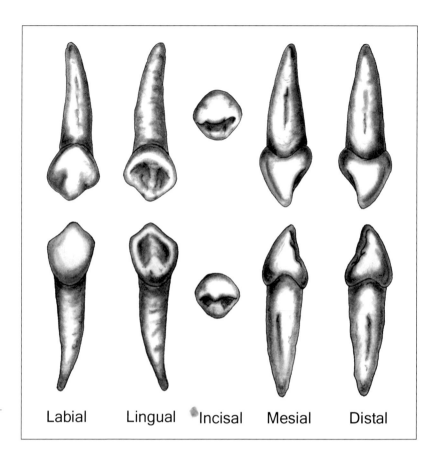

Fig. 5.8 Comparison of maxillary (*top*) and mandibular (*bottom*) deciduous canines from the right side, approximately two times actual size.

| Labial | Lingual | Incisal | Mesial | Distal |

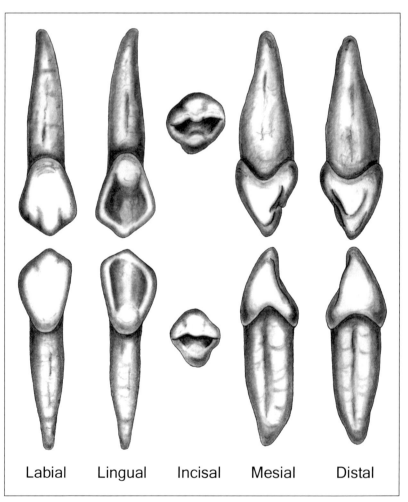

Fig. 5.9 Comparison of maxillary (*top*) and mandibular (*bottom*) permanent canines from the right side, approximately two times actual size.

| Labial | Lingual | Incisal | Mesial | Distal |

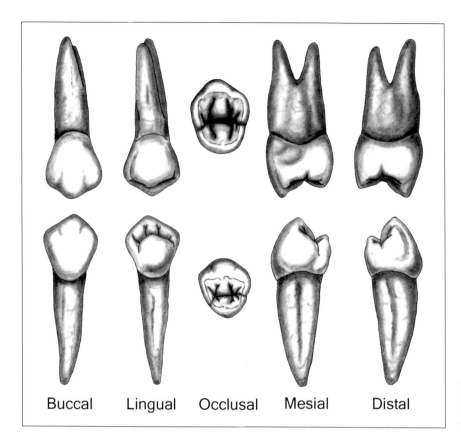

Buccal   Lingual   Occlusal   Mesial   Distal

Fig. 5.10 Comparison of maxillary (*top*) and mandibular (*bottom*) premolars. The right first premolars are shown (approximately two times actual size).

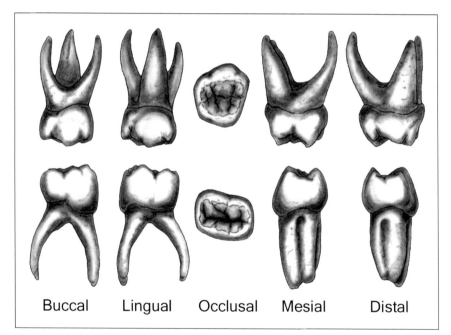

Buccal   Lingual   Occlusal   Mesial   Distal

Fig. 5.11 Comparison of maxillary (*top*) and mandibular (*bottom*) deciduous molars. The right first molars are shown (approximately two times actual size).

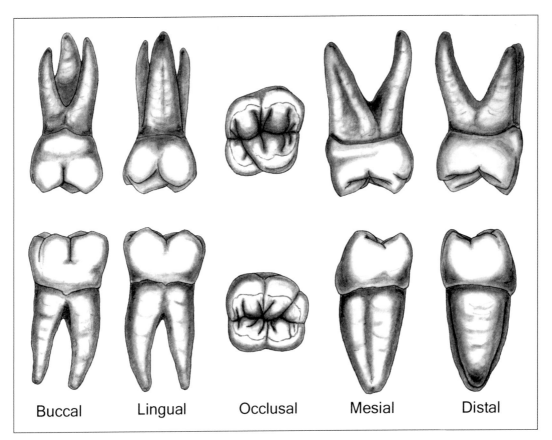

| Buccal | Lingual | Occlusal | Mesial | Distal |

Fig. 5.12 Comparison of maxillary (*top*) and mandibular (*bottom*) permanent molars. The right first molars are shown (approximately two times actual size).

only two (one mesial, one distal). Be aware that these roots may be fused together in the permanent molars but, in many cases, lines of division are visible so you can count them or determine their position.

The number and arrangement of the cusps are also diagnostic of upper versus lower molars. For deciduous first molars, the maxillary and mandibular teeth differ in cusp morphology and the outline of the crown. The maxillary first molar is square and resembles a premolar in cusp configuration, with a groove or gap in the center of the occlusal surface that separates the large buccal cusp and smaller lingual cusp. The mandibular first molar is longer mesiodistally than it is buccolingually, which gives the crown a rectangular shape. The cusp configuration differs from that of any other tooth, because of the close proximity of the buccal and lingual cusp rows. Mesially, there is a small depression separated from a larger distal depression by a constriction, which resembles an hourglass shape. Because the deciduous second molars are miniature versions of permanent molars, the criteria for distinguishing maxillary from mandibular molars in the permanent dentition can be used for these teeth as well.

The maxillary molars of the permanent dentition typically have four cusps (sometimes only three) arranged with two buccal cusps that are roughly similar in size, one large mesiolingual cusp, and a small distolingual cusp. When only three cusps are present it is because the small distolingual cusp is absent. The shape of the crown is, therefore, a square or quadrilateral. The mandibular molars typically have five cusps, or sometimes four, which are arranged more symmetrically than the cusps of the maxillary molars (see fig. 5.12, occlusal views). There are two lingual and two buccal cusps, which are similar in size. The fifth cusp is wedged between the distobuccal and distolingual cusps. The crown of a mandibular molar is longer mesiodistally than a maxillary molar and is, therefore, more rectangular.

4. What Is the Tooth's Position in the Dentition?

Incisors. Is it a central or lateral incisor? Maxillary central incisor crowns are larger and wider than lateral incisors mesiodistally (fig. 5.13). However, the mandibular cen-

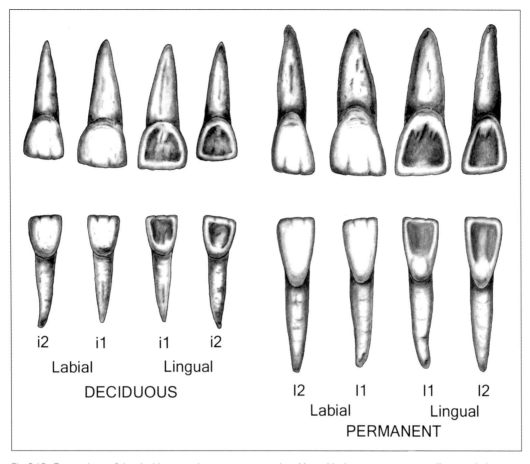

i2   i1   i1   i2
Labial   Lingual
DECIDUOUS

I2   I1   I1   I2
Labial   Lingual
PERMANENT

Fig. 5.13 Comparison of the deciduous and permanent central and lateral incisors: top row = maxillary teeth; bottom row = mandibular teeth. All teeth are from the right side, approximately two times actual size.

tral incisor crown is slightly smaller than a lateral mandibular incisor. Both maxillary and mandibular central incisors are more symmetrical than laterals. Often, the roots of the central incisors are thicker and straighter than the lateral incisor roots, which tend to curve distally. Upper and lower central incisor roots are generally shorter than the corresponding lateral incisor roots. Mandibular and maxillary lateral incisors can be confused, but remember that the mandibular incisor crown and roots are both smaller than their maxillary counterparts.

Premolars. Is it a first or second premolar? The upper first premolars have a larger buccal cusp compared to the lingual cusp, whereas the buccal and lingual cusps of upper second premolars are nearly equal in size (fig. 5.14). The mesial surface tends to be concave in the maxillary first premolars and convex in the second premolars. Finally, maxillary first premolars are more likely to have two discernible roots (buccal and lingual) than the second premolars.

The lower first and second premolars are distinguishable mainly by cusp morphology. A first premolar tends to have a sharp, pointed buccal cusp and a small lingual cusp. The second, on the other hand, has a dull, rounded buccal cusp and often two lingual cusps, with the mesiolingual cusp typically larger than the distolingual cusp. The root of a mandibular first premolar often displays a groove on the mesial aspect, while that of the second premolar lacks a groove.

Molars. A combination of crown and root morphology can be used to discriminate between first and second maxillary and mandibular molars in the deciduous dentition, and among the first, second, and third maxillary and mandibular molars of the permanent dentition.

For deciduous teeth, it is fairly easy to distinguish first and second molars (fig. 5.15). The upper and lower second molars closely resemble permanent molars in their morphology. The first molars, however, differ in their crown configuration. Deciduous first molars are not sym-

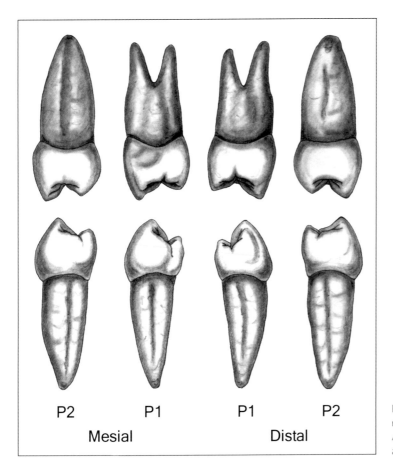

P2   P1   P1   P2

Mesial   Distal

Fig. 5.14 Comparison of the first and second premolars: top row = maxillary teeth, bottom row = mandibular teeth. All teeth are from the right side, approximately two times actual size.

metrical in crown shape and there is a notable difference in cusp morphology, with the upper first more closely resembling a bicuspid premolar (except for the three roots), and the lower first exhibiting a closure of the gap between cusps due to its broad and angled buccal surface.

In the permanent dentition, first molars are the largest of the three, decreasing in size to the third molar, which often has fewer cusps (fig. 5.16). Third molars lack wear facets on the distal surface of the crown, as do the second molars if the thirds have not erupted. The first molars display wear facets on both the mesial and distal aspects, as do the second molars if the thirds have erupted.

For the maxillary molars, the lingual root is largest and is widely separated from the buccal roots in the first molar. In the second molar, the lingual root is largest but is less divergent, and the roots are least divergent or fused to one another in the third molar. The crowns of the upper molars typically display the following cusp pattern: the first has four well-defined cusps; the second has four cusps but the distolingual cusp is reduced or may be absent; and the third is highly variable but often has a dramatically reduced or absent distolingual cusp.

In the mandibular molars, the lower first has two distinct and widely separated roots (mesial and distal) and the mesial root curves toward the distal. The second molars also have two roots but these are occasionally fused. Both roots have a tendency to curve in a distal direction. The two roots of the third molars are often fused and they may also curve distally. The crowns of the lower molars typically display the following cusp pattern: the first has five cusps including the small distal cusp wedged between the distobuccal and distolingual cusps, the second typically has five cusps or possibly four with the distal cusp absent, and the third is the most likely to exhibit only four cusps.

5. Is the Tooth from the Right or Left Side?

Incisors. The key to siding maxillary incisors lies in the morphology of the mesial and distal surfaces of the crown. The mesial surface is straight and has a sharp, almost 90-degree angle (fig. 5.17a) with the incisal edge. In contrast, the juncture of the distal and incisal edges is more

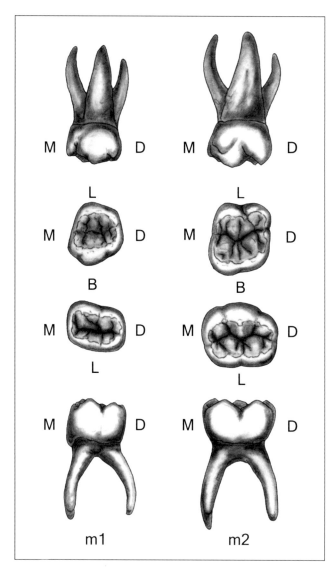

Fig. 5.15 Comparison of the first (m1) and second (m2) deciduous molars. The top two rows show lingual and occlusal views, respectively, of maxillary molars; the bottom two rows show occlusal and lingual views, respectively, of mandibular molars: B, buccal; D, distal; L, lingual; M, mesial. All teeth are from the right side, approximately two times actual size.

if you hold the tooth in anatomical position with the root up and the lingual surface toward you, rotate it slightly from side to side to examine the relative position of the CEJ. The enamel extends higher up the tooth (farther from the incisal edge) on the side to which it belongs. Another siding tip is to note that, in lateral incisors, the apex of the root tends to tilt distally. Thus, when holding the tooth in anatomical position, the apex points to the side from which the tooth comes (fig. 5.17d). Incisor roots also have deeper grooves on the distal side of the root than on the mesial side, also identifying the side the tooth is from in anatomical position.

Determining the side of mandibular incisors is more challenging, but some of the observations that pertain to siding maxillary incisors are also useful for siding lower incisors. Like maxillary incisors, the juncture of the incisal and distal edges in lower incisors is also more rounded than the mesial corner (fig. 5.18a, b). Thus, to side properly, hold the tooth in anatomical position with the root down and the rougher lingual surface toward you. The crown is curved more on the distal aspect and the rounded distoincisal corner (fig. 5.18b). These features indicate the side to which the tooth belongs. Alternatively, orient the labial surface toward you. In this view, the straighter edge of the crown and squarer corner indicate the side from which the tooth comes (fig. 5.18a). This technique is more useful in lateral mandibular incisors but can be ambiguous in the central incisors due to their smaller size and more symmetrical, chiseled shape. Therefore, it is important to examine the root. Look for the grooves on the roots (fig. 5.18c), which are flattened mesiodistally. The distal groove is usually more pronounced than the mesial groove and the root apex often tilts distally like the upper incisors (fig. 5.18d). To use these features in siding a mandibular incisor, hold the tooth in anatomical position. The deeper groove is on the side the tooth is from, and the root apex tilts toward that side as well.

Canines. To side permanent upper and lower canines, examine the incisal edge. The mesial slope from the cusp tip to the corner of the crown is always shorter than the distal (fig. 5.19a, b). To side, place the tooth in standard anatomical position (with the root oriented as it would be in the jaw) with the more rugged, concave lingual surface toward you. The longer, more curved slope is on the side to which the tooth belongs (fig. 5.19b). Beware that in deciduous maxillary canines, the opposite holds true—the mesial slope is always longer than the distal (fig. 5.19A, B). Thus, in orienting as above, remember that for a deciduous upper canine, the longer slope is opposite the side the tooth is from and the shorter slope is on the side from which it comes. In cases where the crown

rounded (fig. 5.17b). Keeping these features in mind, to side a maxillary incisor, orient it in standard anatomical position with the root up and the rugged lingual surface toward you. The rounded corner is on the side from which the tooth comes (fig. 5.17b). Alternatively, you can hold the tooth with the convex, labial surface toward you. In this position, the straighter side of the crown with the squared corner is on the side from which the tooth comes (fig. 5.17a). Another method is to examine the CEJ (fig. 5.17c). On the mesial side, the enamel is lower (closer to the incisal edge) than on the distal side. Thus,

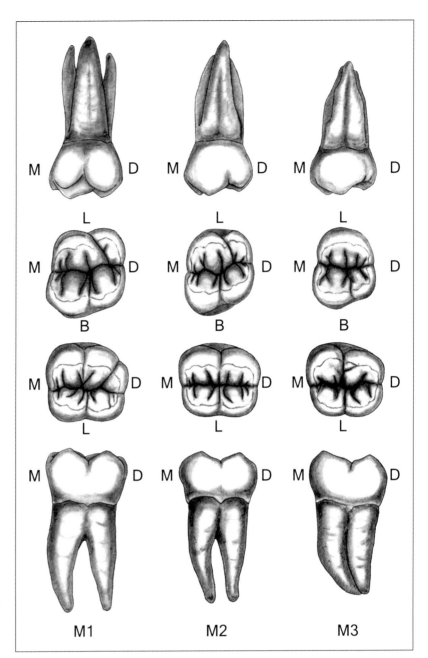

Fig. 5.16 Comparison of the first (M1), second (M2), and third (M3) permanent molars. The top two rows show lingual and occlusal views, respectively, of maxillary molars; the bottom two rows show occlusal and lingual views, respectively, of mandibular molars: B, buccal; D, distal; L, lingual; M, mesial. All teeth are from the right side, approximately two times actual size.

is damaged or very worn, canine roots are helpful in siding the tooth (fig. 5.19c). The distal groove is more pronounced and the apex also angles distally or toward the side the tooth is from when held in anatomical position.

Premolars. It is generally easy to identify the buccal aspect of the tooth in both maxillary and mandibular premolars because it displays the largest cusp (fig. 5.20a, b). This feature is less obvious in maxillary second premolars. For maxillary premolars, the lingual cusp leans toward the mesial side of the tooth (fig. 5.20c). This slant is often easier to observe on a first premolar because of the greater disparity in size of the cusps. Note that any wear present on the occlusal surface of maxillary premolars is heavier toward the lingual side of the crown. In mandibular premolars, the wear tends to be greater on the buccal cusp. Once you have identified the buccal and lingual aspects, note that the roots of all premolars have a tendency

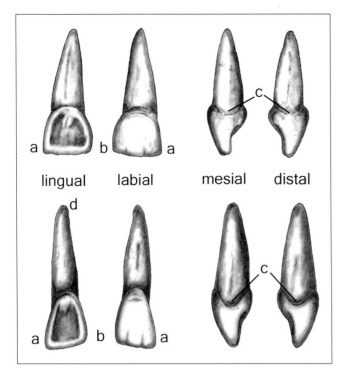

Fig. 5.17 Methods for siding maxillary incisors, top = deciduous central incisor, bottom = permanent lateral incisor: *a*, straight mesioincisal corner; *b*, round distoincisal corner; *c*, CEJ (cementoenamel junction); *d*, root apex. All teeth are from the right side, approximately two times actual size.

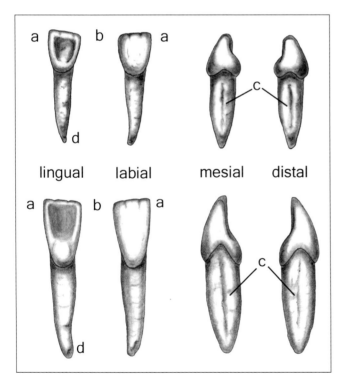

Fig. 5.18 Methods for siding mandibular incisors, top = deciduous lateral incisor, bottom = permanent central incisor: *a*, straight mesioincisal corner; *b*, round distoincisal corner; *c*, root grooves; *d*, root apex. All teeth are from the right side, approximately two times actual size.

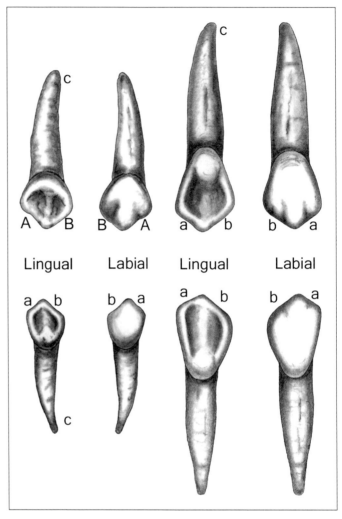

Fig. 5.19 Methods for siding maxillary (*top*) and mandibular (*bottom*) canines, left = deciduous canines, right = permanent canines: *A*, long, mesial incisal edge; *B*, short, distal incisal edge; *a*, short, mesial incisal edge; *b*, long, distal incisal edge; *c*, root apex. All teeth are from the right side, approximately two times actual size.

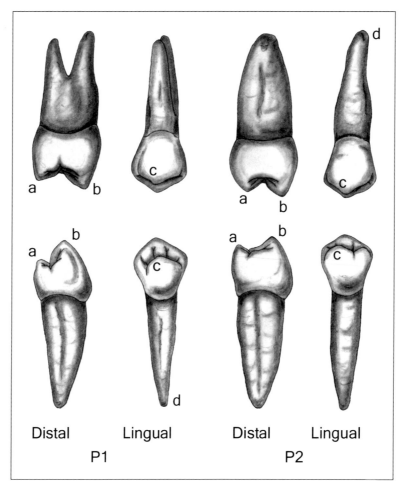

Fig. 5.20 Methods for siding maxillary (*top*) and mandibular (*bottom*) premolars, left = first premolars (P1), right = second premolars (P2): *a*, small lingual cusp; *b*, large buccal cusp; *c*, mesial slant of lingual cusp; *d*, root apex. All teeth are from the right side, approximately two times actual size.

to curve distally (fig. 5.20d). When oriented in standard anatomical position, the root thus curves toward the side to which the tooth belongs.

Molars. For deciduous first molars, whether maxillary or mandibular, a feature that aids in siding is a bulge or ridge located on the mesiobuccal aspect of the tooth (fig. 5.21a). To side a deciduous first molar using this feature, hold the tooth with the roots as they would be held in the jaw (i.e., in anatomical position); the tubercle or bulge indicates the side from which the tooth comes. Tips for siding deciduous second molars coincide with the instructions below for siding permanent molars.

In the maxillary dentition, all molars have one large lingual root and two smaller buccal roots regardless of whether the three roots of the permanent upper molars are fused or not (figs. 5.21b, c and 5.22a, b). In the permanent molars, the thicker of the two buccal roots is usually mesial (fig. 5.22c), while in the deciduous the longer of the two is usually mesial (fig. 5.21b). On the crown, if the fourth cusp is present (i.e., the smallest cusp), it is always located distolingually (figs. 5.21d and 5.22d). Note also that the crown is relatively vertical on its buccal side but bulges outward lingually (figs. 5.21 and 5.22). After identifying the above aspects, orient the tooth with the roots away from you and the distal surface pointing down

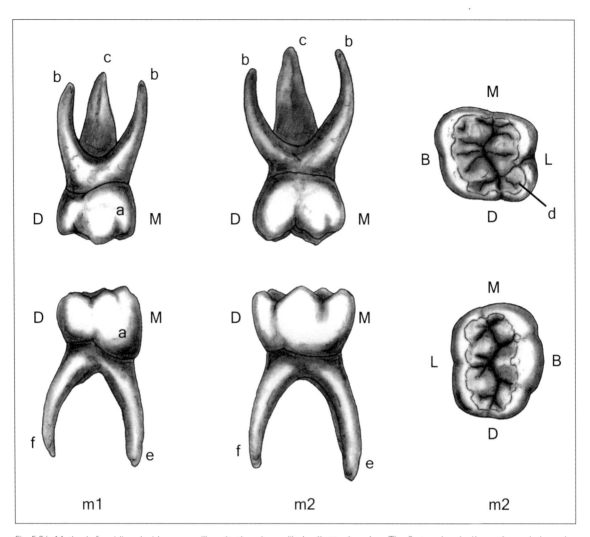

Fig. 5.21 Methods for siding deciduous maxillary (*top*) and mandibular (*bottom*) molars. The first molars (*m1*) are shown in buccal view and the second molars (*m2*), in buccal and occlusal views: B, buccal; D, distal; L, lingual; M, mesial; *a*, mesiobuccal bulge; *b*, buccal root; *c*, lingual root; *d*, distolingual cusp. All teeth are from the right side, approximately two times actual size.

(figs. 5.21 and 5.22). The smallest cusp is toward the side to which the tooth belongs (figs. 5.21d and 5.22d).

For all permanent mandibular molars, the mesial root is thicker in a buccolingual direction and both roots curve distally (fig. 5.23a, b). The mesial root of the deciduous molars tends to be straighter and longer than the distal root (fig. 5.21e, f). Looking at the crown from a mesial, distal, or occlusal perspective, the buccal side bulges while the lingual side is straighter (fig. 5.23). In the occlusal view, the fifth cusp, if present, is distobuccal (fig. 5.23c). The crown outline has a flattened mesial end

and a rounded distal end. These features help you orient the tooth in anatomical position, as it would be in the dental arcade, for proper side identification. When viewed from the distal end of the tooth, note the CEJ slopes down toward the side it is from and the crown bulges outward (is more convex) on the side from which it comes. If you look at the occlusal surface with the distal side toward you, the side with the three cusps indicates the side to which the tooth belongs. If you hold the roots down with the lingual side facing you, the root tips curve distally, or toward the side from which the tooth comes.

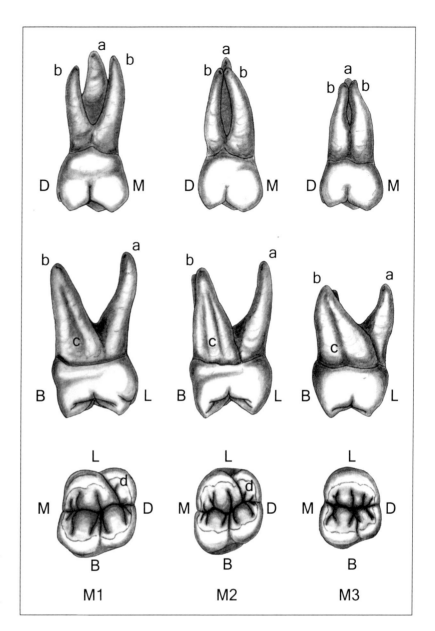

Fig. 5.22 Methods for siding permanent maxillary first (M1), second (M2), and third (M3) molars, top row = buccal, middle row = mesial, bottom row = occlusal: B, buccal; D, distal; L, lingual; M, mesial; *a,* lingual root; *b,* buccal root; *c,* thicker mesiobuccal root; *d,* distolingual cusp. All teeth are from the right side, approximately two times actual size.

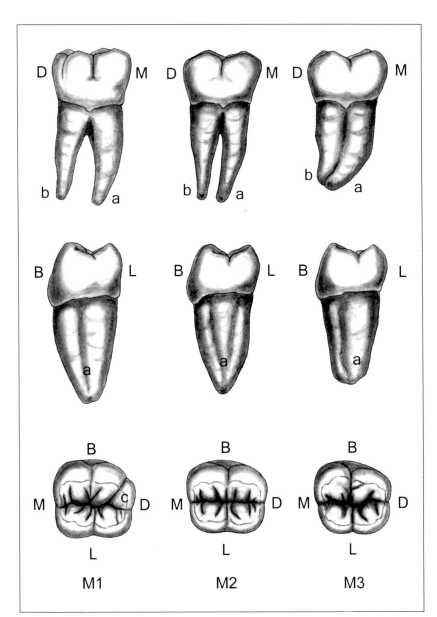

Fig. 5.23 Methods for siding permanent mandibular first (M1), second (M2), and third (M3) molars, top row = buccal, middle row = mesial, bottom row = occlusal: B, buccal; D, distal; L, lingual; M, mesial; *a*, straighter and longer mesial root; *b*, shorter and more curved distal root; *c*, distobuccal cusp. All teeth are from the right side, approximately two times actual size.

PART THREE
The Infracranial Skeleton

The infracranial skeleton refers to the bones situated beneath the skull in an animal with erect posture. The term postcranial, which refers to bones located behind or posterior to the skull, is more accurate for quadrupedal animals, though it is often used interchangeably with infracranial.

The infracranial skeleton is comprised of bones that form the bulk of the axial skeleton, or the trunk, and the appendicular skeleton, or appendages (fig. 1.3). The trunk includes the bones of the vertebral column, ribs, and shoulder and pelvic girdles, while the appendages consist of the bones of the arms and legs. The bones forming the vertebral column and pelvic girdle (vertebrae, sacrum, coccyx, and os coxae) are delineated in chapter 6. Chapter 7 covers the chest cavity and shoulder girdle and includes the ribs, sternum, clavicles, and scapulae. All the long bones of the arms and legs are discussed in chapter 8, while chapter 9 is devoted to the bones of the hands and feet.

Chapter 6 The Vertebral Column and Pelvic Girdle

■ The vertebral column and pelvic girdle, together with the skull and the bones of the chest and shoulder girdle (chap. 7), form the axial skeleton. The vertebral column or spine is comprised of twenty-four true vertebrae, the sacrum, and the coccyx. The twenty-four presacral vertebrae are divided into three groups—cervical, thoracic, and lumbar (fig. 6.1). All bones of the vertebral column develop in a similar manner through endochondral ossification. At birth, all but the first and second cervical vertebrae consist of three elements. The unfused right and left halves of the neural arch form the posterior portion of the adult vertebrae plus the lateral transverse processes and, anteriorly, a small portion of the adult vertebral body. The centrum is the third element, which consists of all but the posterolateral aspects of the adult vertebral body.

The sacrum, while part of the vertebral column, also forms the posterior aspect of the pelvic girdle. The vestigial tailbone—the coccyx—is inferior to the sacrum. The ilium, ischium, and pubis fuse together to form the os coxae or hip bones that complete the pelvis. Together these bones form a stable platform for bipedal locomotion, muscle attachment, and encasement and protection of some of the internal organs.

Cervical Vertebrae

The neck is comprised of seven cervical vertebrae (figs. 6.2–6.4). These are numbered consecutively from superior to inferior so that the uppermost cervical vertebra is designated C1, while the lowest is C7. The first two cervical vertebrae are distinctive at all stages of development. The third through sixth are typical cervical vertebrae, while the seventh can be distinguished in adults. Because its development is identical to that of C3 to C6 and its distinctive features are difficult to discern in infants and young children, C7 is treated here as a typical cervical vertebra.

The Atlas (C1)

Description at Major Stages. The atlas or first cervical vertebra (C1; fig. 6.2) is the most superior of the vertebrae. It articulates superiorly with the occipital condyles and inferiorly with the axis or second cervical vertebra. The atlas develops from three primary centers of ossification: one for each lateral mass (posterior arch segment) and a third for the anterior arch. The atlas begins to ossify in the seventh to tenth week of gestation from two primary endochondral centers. By the fourth fetal month, these elements are the recognizable right and left halves of the posterior neural arch (fig. 6.2a). Each posterior arch initially consists of a large and small projection of bone emanating from an oval portion that has an articular facet on each side. The superior articular facet (fig. 6.2b) is the larger of the two and is cupped to articulate with the occipital condyles. The inferior facets are small ovals (fig. 6.2c). The larger projection of bone sweeping back from the articular area forms the posterior arch. The small anterolateral projection adjacent to the articular facet forms the posterior part of the incomplete transverse foramen (fig. 6.2d). This description applies to the atlas through the first year of life.

The anterior arch (fig. 6.2e) begins to ossify around age 1, and it attains recognizable morphology by age 3 to 4. At this stage, it is generally represented as a thin, straight piece of bone that is slightly concave with a small

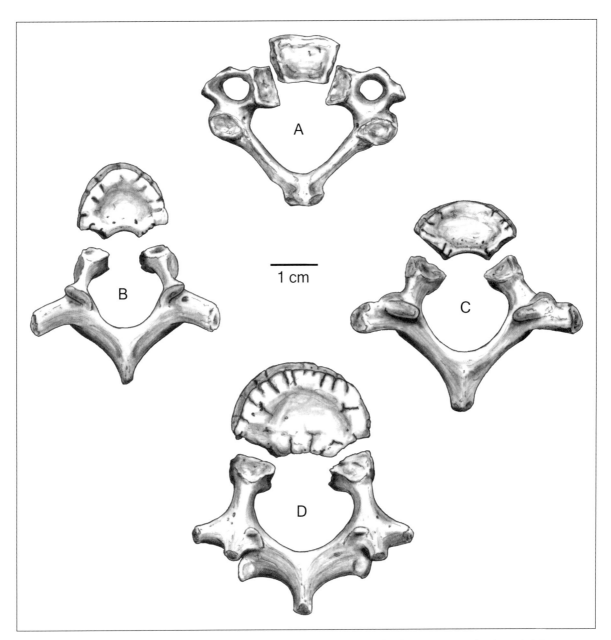

Fig. 6.1 Typical vertebrae from a child, 2 to 4 years old, in superior views, top = anterior, bottom = posterior: A, cervical; B, upper thoracic; C, lower thoracic; D, lumbar.

articular facet on one side, opposite a slight bulge. The bulge represents the anterior tubercle, while the articular facet (fig. 6.2f) on the opposite side is for the odontoid process (dens) of the axis or C2 (fig. 6.3). The transverse foramina are also completed about this time on the posterior arch segment. Between age 4 and 5, the two halves of the posterior arch fuse together, followed by the fusion of the posterior arch to the anterior arch between 5 and 6 years. The atlas may also have two secondary epiphyses that appear and fuse during adolescence on the tips of the transverse processes (fig. 6.2g).

Differentiation from Other Bones. The developing posterior neural arches (fig. 6.2a) of the atlas are identifiable at all stages because of the very large, concave superior articular facets (fig. 6.2b), beneath which are small, flat facets (fig. 6.2c) for the axis. The anterior arch (fig. 6.2e) is also recognizable from its early stages of development because of the anterior tubercle opposite the small articular facet (fig. 6.2f) for the odontoid process of C2. When fused, the atlas is a complete bony ring with cupped facets that articulate with the occipital condyles. Fragments of a mature atlas are easily recognized because its

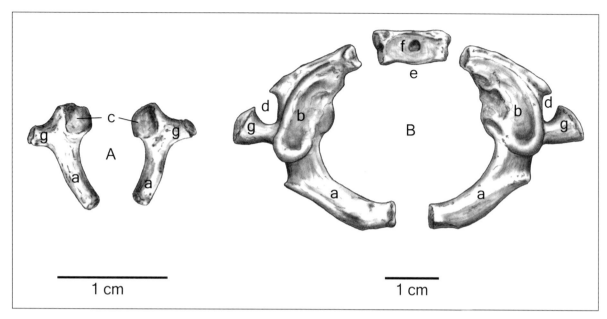

Fig. 6.2 Atlas (C1), A = the posterior neural arches of a perinate (inferior view), B = the unfused posterior neural arches (superior view) and the anterior arch (posterior view) of a child, 3 to 4 years old: *a*, posterior neural arch; *b*, superior articular facet; *c*, inferior articular facet; *d*, transverse foramen; *e*, anterior arch; *f*, articular facet for the odontoid process; *g*, transverse process.

pieces are distinguished by the features noted on unfused components.

Siding Techniques. Up to 5 years of age, the right and left halves that unite to form the posterior arch of the atlas must be sided. To do so, place the larger, concave facet up (fig. 6.2b) and the bigger, posterior projection (fig. 6.2a) toward you so the bone is in standard anatomical position (see fig. 6.2B). The small projection for the transverse process (fig. 6.2g) points to the side from which the bone comes. Thus, if the projection is to the right of the facet, it is the right half of the arch.

The Axis (C2)

Description at Major Stages. The axis or second cervical vertebra (C2; fig. 6.3) articulates superiorly with the atlas (C1) and inferiorly with C3. Its distinct morphology makes it easy to distinguish from all other vertebrae, although its complicated ossification requires differentiating all of its components in infants and young children.

The axis forms from a total of six ossification centers. The centers for each half of the neural arch (fig. 6.3a) are the first to ossify, beginning by the end of the second month in utero. The centrum and paired centers for the body of the odontoid process or dens appear between 4 and 6 fetal months, with the dens centers coalescing soon after their appearance (fig. 6.3b). The tip of the dens appears around 2 years of age.

In a neonate, the axis consists of four components—the two halves of the neural arch, a centrum, and the body of the dens. Each neural arch half has a bulbous anterior articular area that eventually fuses with the centrum. An articular facet is present on the superior aspect (fig. 6.3c), adjacent to the incomplete transverse foramen (fig. 6.3d). The posterior portion of the transverse foramen is formed from a small spicule of bone (fig. 6.3e) on the lateral aspect of the neural arch. The posterior terminus of the lamina is rounded, but it is smaller than the anterior part of the arch. The centrum is squarer than those of other cervical vertebrae. The body of the dens resembles two upside-down commas placed back to back. A groove representing the line of fusion separates the posterior aspect of each half of the body.

Between 3 and 4 years of age, the groove begins to disappear as the dens fuses to the two halves of the neural arch, which also fuse together posteriorly at the same time. The transverse foramina are also completed about this time. Soon thereafter, the centrum fuses to the dens and the neural arch. Thus, as early as 4 years, and maximally by about 6, the axis has only two components—the amalgamated neural arch, dens body, and centrum, plus the small nodule of bone that represents the unfused tip of the dens. A fusion line or groove (fig. 6.3f) persists along the center of the posterior aspect of the dens body until 9 or 10 years of age. The tip fuses to the dens at approximately 12 years of age. The axis also has five secondary ossification centers that appear and fuse during ado-

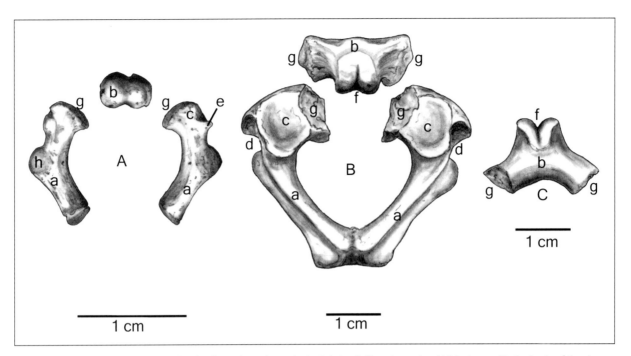

Fig. 6.3 Axis (C2), *A* = the right neural arch of a perinate shown in the inferior (*left*) and superior (*right*) views, with the body of the dens (superior view) at top, *B* = the superior view of the fused neural arch and separate body of the dens from a child, 3 to 4 years old, *C* = posterior view of the body of the dens: *a*, neural arch; *b*, dens or odontoid process; *c*, superior articular facet; *d*, transverse foramen; *e*, posterior portion of the transverse foramen; *f*, line of fusion on dens body; *g*, articulation between neural arch and centrum/body of the dens; *h*, inferior articular facet.

lescence. These epiphyses are for the transverse processes, the tips of the bifid spinous process, and the inferior surface of the centrum (annular ring).

Differentiation from Other Bones. The axis has recognizable features for each component early in its development. The neural arches (fig. 6.3a) and centrum are thicker than those of other cervical vertebrae. It displays a curved shape without distinct projections. A large, roughened area (fig. 6.3g) is present on one end that represents the articulation for the centrum and the dens (fig. 6.3b). The ends of the neural arch halves are larger and blockier than those of other cervical arch components, and the transverse foramen (fig. 6.3d) is defined by a very thin spicule of bone (fig. 6.3e) emanating from the lateral aspect of the posterior arch (or lamina). The centrum of a neonate is square compared to the more wedge-shaped centra of C3 through C7. The separate body of the dens is a small, curvy element, and its forked tip is unlike any other vertebral element. Once united with the neural arches and centrum, the C2 of a child closely resembles the adult bone. The superior projection of the dens remains indented at its apex until the small nodule at its tip fuses around age 12.

Siding Techniques. Because the two halves of the dens are fused before birth, they appear as separate halves for only a short period in fetal development. It is far more important to identify them as components of the axis than to attempt siding them. Like the other cervical vertebrae, the unfused halves of the neural arch must be sided in individuals younger than 3 to 4 years of age, when they unite posteriorly. Place the bulbous articular end (fig. 6.3g) away from you. Note that the posterior aspect of the arch angles down when properly positioned and the inferomedial surface is concave. In this view (which corresponds to standard anatomical position), the arch curves out toward the side it is from and the small lateral projection for the transverse process (fig. 6.3e) is also on the side from which the bone comes.

Typical Cervical Vertebrae (C3–C7)

Description at Major Stages. The typical cervical vertebrae, C3 through C7 (fig. 6.4), form in the same general pattern as C1 and C2, but with slight differences in appearance and fusion time. Each is formed from right and left neural arches and a centrum (fig. 6.4a, b). These elements first appear in C7 during early fetal life, and centra progressively appear superiorly, reaching C3 by the fourth fetal month. At birth, the three-part cervical vertebra is distinguished by the developing transverse foramina (fig. 6.4c) on each neural arch half and by its small,

the superior and inferior surfaces of the centrum, and one on each end of the bifid spinous process (fig. 6.4d). The spinous process of C7 is not bifurcated like those of other cervical vertebrae. Thus, it has only one epiphysis for the spinous process. This is the only epiphysis that is likely to be found separately as a small cap that is difficult to distinguish from those of the thoracic vertebrae below it.

Differentiation from Other Bones. All cervical vertebrae have common features that help distinguish them as a group from other vertebrae. These are the only vertebrae that have foramina (fig. 6.4c) for passage of the vertebral artery on either side of the neural arch. The presence of a transverse foramen is, therefore, diagnostic of a cervical vertebra. While incomplete in infants and very young children, the transverse foramina are still identifiable because the posterior aspect of the transverse process is formed early in development and creates a semicircular indentation in the anterolateral aspects of the paired neural arches. In addition, the posterior portions of each neural arch (the laminae) are long and thin.

On C3 through C7, a small superior articular facet (fig. 6.4e) is evident and forms an upward angle at the corner of the neural arch. The opposite inferior articular facet (fig. 6.4f) is generally more rounded than the superior facet and does not angle as sharply. The projecting spurs (fig. 6.4g) that form the posterior portion of the transverse process become thicker inferiorly so that all are more robust than that of C2. The united neural arch in all but C7 typically has a bifid spinous process.

The unfused cervical centra are small and flat in comparison to thoracic and lumbar elements (fig. 6.1). They become progressively larger from C3 to C7. While the centrum of C2 is shaped more like a square, those of typical cervical vertebrae are shaped like a slice of bread —wider and billowed at the top (anterior aspect) with slightly angled sides and a narrower bottom (posterior aspect).

Siding Techniques. Unfused neural arch halves must be sided in children younger than 3 or 4 years of age. To side, it is useful to orient the bone in standard anatomical position. Place the transverse foramen (fig. 6.4c) away from you with the superior articular facet up (fig. 6.4e). This facet protrudes from the bone, angling up and away from you. On the inferior surface, the facet (fig. 6.4f) angles down and away from you. The inferior margin of the lamina angles downward slightly, while the superior border is slightly concave. In anatomical position, the portion of the arch on which the articular facet lies is toward the side from which the bone comes (see fig. 6.4A, right). Thus, if you follow a line from the posterior aspect of the arch to the articular facet, the line points to the correct side.

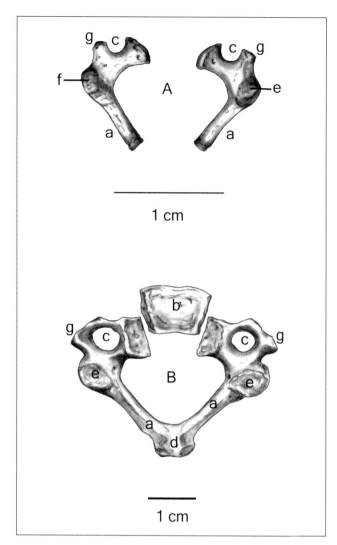

1 cm

1 cm

Fig. 6.4 Typical cervical vertebra, A = the right neural arch of a perinate shown in the inferior (*left*) and superior (*right*) views, B = the superior view of the fused neural arch and separate centrum from a child, 2 to 4 years old: *a*, neural arch; *b*, centrum; *c*, transverse foramen; *d*, spinous process; *e*, superior articular facet; *f*, inferior articular facet; *g*, transverse process.

relatively flat centrum. Centra are shaped much like a slice of bread with a somewhat scalloped anterior border (similar to the top crust of a bread slice). The anterior aspect is broad and convex, while the posterior aspect is narrower. The superior surface of a centrum slopes down toward the anterior edge, while the inferior aspect is flat.

The halves of the neural arch fuse around 2 years of age and subsequently fuse to the centrum between ages 3 and 4. The transverse foramina are completed at the same time. Typically, C3 through C6 have six secondary epiphyses that appear and fuse during adolescence. These epiphyses occur on the tips of each transverse process, on

Thoracic Vertebrae

The twelve thoracic vertebrae are inferior to the cervical vertebrae and superior to the lumbar vertebrae. In addition to articulating with the vertebrae above and below, each articulates with a pair of ribs to form the thoracic cavity. The thoracic vertebrae are numbered consecutively from superior to inferior so that the first element is labeled T1 and the last is designated T12.

Description at Major Stages

Like the typical cervical vertebrae, each thoracic vertebra develops from three primary centers of ossification, two for the neural arch halves and one for the centrum (fig. 6.5a, b). These all appear by the tenth week of gestation and are recognizable soon thereafter. At birth, each thoracic vertebra continues to be represented by the same three components.

The neural arches of the lower thoracic vertebrae are the first to fuse, progressing superiorly during the first and second years of life. Generally, between about 1 and 3 years of age, most thoracic vertebrae consist of two elements—a complete neural arch and an unfused centrum. Fusion of the neural arch to the centrum in the lower thoracic vertebrae begins around 3 to 4 years of age, and progresses superiorly, completing fusion by 5 to 6 years of age. The thoracic vertebrae also have five secondary epiphyses that appear during early adolescence and fuse by early adulthood. They are found on the superior and inferior surfaces of the centrum, on the tips of the transverse processes, and on the end of the spinous process.

Differentiation from Other Bones

It is most difficult to distinguish the components of fetal or neonatal thoracic vertebrae from those of lumbar vertebrae. The neural arch halves lack the transverse foramina that identify the cervical vertebrae and can be separated from lumbar neural arches by their prominent transverse processes (fig. 6.5c) and more angular, thinner laminae. The facet pattern of thoracic vertebrae also distinguishes them. With the exception of T12, both the superior (fig. 6.5d) and inferior articular facets (fig. 6.5e) are small, flat surfaces oriented vertically. They increase in

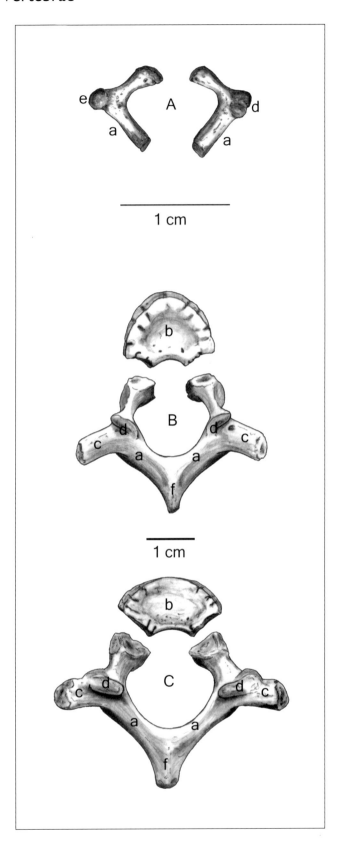

1 cm

1 cm

Fig. 6.5 Typical thoracic vertebrae, A = the right neural arch of a perinate shown in the inferior (*left*) and superior (*right*) views, B = the superior view of the fused neural arch and separate centrum of an upper thoracic from a child, 2 to 4 years old, C = the superior view of the fused neural arch and centrum of a lower thoracic from a child, 2 to 4 years old: *a,* neural arch; *b,* centrum; *c,* transverse process; *d,* superior articular facet; *e,* inferior articular facet; *f,* spinous process.

size from T1 through T12, so that T11 and T12 are more similar to lumbar neural arches.

A neural arch half from T1 can often be differentiated because it resembles the cervical arches closely in size and shape yet lacks the transverse foramen. The neural arch halves of T11 and T12 are more difficult to separate from the lumbar arches because of greater similarity in size and shape. The transverse process is still more prominent and the laminae are thinner and angled more sharply than their lumbar counterparts. In T12, the less robust transverse process and the lumbarlike, convexly curved inferior articular facet, even at very young ages, permit it to be separated from other thoracic arches. The flat, vertically oriented superior articular facet separates it from the lumbar facet pattern (see below).

Thoracic centra are generally thicker and more rounded than those of the cervical segment (fig. 6.1). They are smaller than the lumbar centra, but increase in size from T1 to T12. While the centrum of T1 is difficult to distinguish from a cervical centrum because of similarity in shape, the superior surface is even rather than sloping down toward the anterior aspect. The centra of the lower thoracic vertebrae are broader (transversely across the center) and are rounded anteriorly.

For unfused neural arches and centra, the increasing size from T1 through T12 is the only way to identify specific thoracic elements, and it is very difficult to place them in proper sequence even when preservation is good. Generally, only T1 and T12 are likely to be differentiated with confidence. In older children for whom the centrum and neural arch are fused, the presence of an obvious costal facet (for the head of the corresponding rib) on the body (near the neurocentral juncture) is the easiest way to separate a thoracic vertebra from lumbar or cervical vertebrae. Costal facets also develop on the transverse processes of all but T11 and T12. As in adults, T1 and T12 of older children are distinguishable by their transitional features.

The epiphyses of thoracic vertebrae include small caps for the ends of the spinous (fig. 6.5f) and transverse processes. These caps are smaller than long bone epiphyses such as the medial epicondyle of the humerus or the lesser trochanter of the femur. They are more convex than epiphyses for the bones of the hands and feet. The annular rings are semicircular flakes that are readily distinguishable from epiphyses for the vertebral border of the scapula or those on the bones of the hip. In all cases, they are thin, flat, and more curved due to the small diameter of the vertebral bodies.

Siding Techniques

If the thoracic neural arches are unfused, they can be sided by placing the arch with the small projection for the superior articular facet (fig. 6.5d) facing up, and the large projection of the lamina toward you (see fig. 6.5A, right). The inferior border of the arch just anterior to the transverse process and facets is always concave and should be oriented away from you, along with the rounded surface for the centrum. In this view (which corresponds to standard anatomical position), the small, lateral projection for the transverse process is on the side from which the bone comes.

Lumbar Vertebrae

The five elements of the lumbar spine form the lower back. They are situated between the thoracic vertebrae above and the sacrum below them. As with other vertebrae, each articulates with the element above and below it via superior and inferior articular facets. The elements are numbered superiorly to inferiorly from L1 to L5.

Description at Major Stages

Like the thoracic and typical cervical vertebrae, the lumbar vertebrae initially consist of two neural arch halves and the centrum (fig. 6.6a, b). In general the centra ossify first, followed by the neural arches. The centra begin to ossify superiorly, reaching L5 by the end of the third fetal month. Neural arches follow the same ossification pattern, reaching L5 by the end of the fourth fetal month.

At birth, the lumbar vertebrae are characterized by the three main components. The neural arches of the upper lumbar vertebrae begin to fuse together posteriorly by about age 1, although fusion in L5 may not occur until the fifth year. Between ages 2 and 3, the centrum and neural arches begin to fuse, culminating with L5 by age 4. The lumbar vertebrae also have seven secondary epiphyses that appear and fuse during adolescence. Two of these epiphyses occur on the mamillary processes, two on the transverse processes, annular rings for the superior and inferior surfaces of the centrum, and one for the tip of the spinous process.

Differentiation from Other Bones

The elements of the lumbar vertebrae are the largest, most robust parts of the presacral vertebral column at all ages. In a neonate, the neural arches are thicker superiorly to inferiorly than thoracic or cervical arches and lack the defining features of those segments, such as transverse

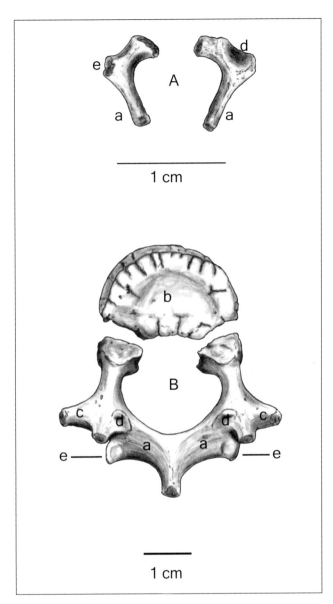

Fig. 6.6 Typical lumbar vertebra, A = the right neural arch of a perinate shown in the inferior (*left*) and superior (*right*) views, B = the superior view of the fused neural arch and separate centrum of a lumbar from a child, 2 to 4 years old: *a*, neural arch; *b*, centrum; *c*, transverse process; *d*, superior articular facet; *e*, inferior articular facet.

foramina of the cervical vertebrae and large transverse processes of the thoracic spine. In lumbar vertebrae, the transverse processes (fig. 6.6c) are rudimentary and are not readily apparent in infants and young children. In older children it is evident that the lumbar neural arch lacks costal facets. The defining curvature of the superior (fig. 6.6d) and inferior articular facets (fig. 6.6e) is evident by late childhood. The superior articular facets are concave, while the inferior facets are oriented somewhat laterally on the anterior aspect of the laminae and are slightly convex.

The centra of lumbar vertebrae are larger than those above them (fig. 6.1). They are thicker superiorly to inferiorly and broader transversely than they are anteroposteriorly, giving them an oblong shape. As in adults, L5 is distinguished by its wedge shape. The anterior aspect of the centrum is thicker than the posterior aspect, so it slants from front to back.

For epiphyses, the shapes are similar to those described for the thoracic vertebrae. The mamillary process epiphyses are very small, curved caps that are less regular in appearance than epiphyses for the transverse and spinous processes.

Siding Techniques

The neural arches of the lumbar vertebrae are more difficult to side because of the attenuated transverse processes (fig. 6.6c). However, they still bear small projections at the lateral aspects of the laminae where the superior articular facets (fig. 6.6d) are located. To distinguish the right and left side requires identification of the superior and inferior borders. The superior border is straighter than the inferior border, which is concave. Place the inferior border on a table with the rounded surface for the centrum facing away from you and the posterior end of the lamina toward you (so that the bone is in standard anatomical position). The small projection with the superior articular facet is on the side from which the bone comes.

Differentiating Vertebrae from Other Bones

During the fetal and infant stages of development, the vertebral elements have very similar shapes and are hard to distinguish from one another, but they are unlike other bones in the skeleton. In general, vertebral arches consist of two bony projections that join together in an L or T shape. During the fetal stage, a neural arch exhibits a boomerang shape depending on the degree of angle and helps differentiate it from rib fragments.

An unfused anterior arch of the atlas could be mistaken for the unfused body of a hyoid bone but is easily distinguished by the small facet on the center of the posterior surface for articulation with the dens. The centra may be confused with the sternebrae. Although the vertebral centra have the same general shape, the sternebrae are very flat and have a thin, smooth cortex. The vertebral centra, in contrast, show vascular channels on the superior and inferior surfaces that give them an uneven appearance. Vertebral centra are generally thicker and rounded. The greatest confusion lies with cervical centra, which are the smallest and flattest in the vertebral column.

In late childhood and adolescence, the composite vertebra closely resembles the adult morphology. Thus, in older children (those with fully fused centra and neural arches), a vertebra is distinctive and should not be confused with other bones of the body. Rules used in adults for differentiating cervical, thoracic, and lumbar vertebrae and specific elements within each category can, therefore, be applied.

The Sacrum

The sacrum (figs. 6.7–6.9) is located at the base of the vertebral column. It articulates superiorly with the fifth lumbar vertebra, laterally with the ilium and inferiorly with the coccyx. The sacrum is typically composed of five elements numbered S1 to S5 from superior to inferior. These elements are separate in children and fuse together in adults to form a single wedge-shaped bone that is broad at the top and tapers to a narrow apex inferiorly.

Description at Major Stages
The ossification of the sacrum is complex. While each of the sacral elements has the three typical primary centers of all vertebrae, representing the neural arches and centrum (figs. 6.7a, b and 6.8a), the first three sacral elements have additional ossification centers (fig. 6.7c) that form the lateral wings or alae and the articular surface for the hip bones. The sacrum generally ossifies from twenty-one primary centers plus at least fourteen secondary centers or epiphyses.

The first to third sacral elements typically form from five ossification centers. Two wedge-shaped anterolateral centers on each side (fig. 6.7c and 6.8b) form the front portion of the alae or wings. The posterior part of each ala is formed from the neural arch (fig. 6.7a and 6.8a). Ossification data on the sacral elements is variable, with some investigators (e.g., Fazekas and Kósa, 1978) indicating much later times of appearance than others. In general, the centra begin to ossify around the third fetal month, while the neural arches appear at 4 to 6 fetal months. The centers for the alae appear between 6 and 8 fetal months.

The remaining sacral elements, S4 and S5, consist of the three standard ossification centers for the centrum and neural arches. The centra of S4 and S5 begin to ossify in the fourth and fifth fetal months, respectively. The neural arches, like those of S1 through S3, appear between 6 and 8 fetal months.

In late-term fetuses and infants, the sacrum thus normally consists of twenty-one separate elements. At birth, some of these centers are not clearly defined and they do not usually develop recognizable morphology until about 1 year of age. In infants, the centra differ in shape from S1 to S5, with S1 the largest and S5 the smallest. The superior surfaces are broader than the inferior surfaces in all sacral centra (see fig. 6.9). The neural arches also decrease in size from S1 to S5, as do the alar or costal centers from S1 to S3. The neural arches of S1 are recognizable early in development because of their larger size and prominent superior articular facets. The alar elements (figs. 6.7 and 6.8) are blocky, wedge-shaped or somewhat pyramidal bones with smooth, concave anterior surfaces and billowy articular surfaces for the neural arch.

Between ages 2 and 5, the neural arches and elements of the alae fuse together in S1 to S3 and fuse soon after to the centrum. The neural arches of S4 and S5 fuse to the centrum between 2 and 6 years of age. By age 6 or 7, therefore, the sacrum consists of five unfused segments (fig. 6.9). Because the neural arches fuse to the alar elements and centra initially, rather than first uniting posteriorly as in the presacral vertebrae, the spinous processes are delayed in development. The laminae continue to grow toward each other, fusing at the spinous process between age 7 and 15. The five sacral segments of an older child or adolescent are readily identifiable at this stage because of their transverse breadth and sweeping alar surfaces in the upper elements and their narrow anteroposterior dimension in lower elements.

Around puberty, several secondary centers or epiphyses appear. The number of epiphyses varies by individual; however, they are consistently found on the superior and inferior aspects of the body (annular rings), two lateral plates for the auricular surface where the sacrum articulates with the ilium, and two narrow strips for the lateral margins below the level of the auricular surface. At least fourteen epiphyses, therefore, develop. Frequently, small epiphyses appear for the tips of the spinous and transverse processes, as in other vertebrae. In the unified sacrum, these are fused to form the median crest and the lateral crests on the posterior aspect of the bone. Around age 12, the sacral elements begin to unite laterally, starting with S5 and S4 and progressing superiorly. Fusion of the annular rings coincides with this sequence. The epiphyses for the auricular surfaces and inferior lateral margins generally appear by age 15 or 16 and fuse in the late teens. By age 20, the sacral segments are all united laterally but space may still remain between the bodies of upper elements until the late 20s.

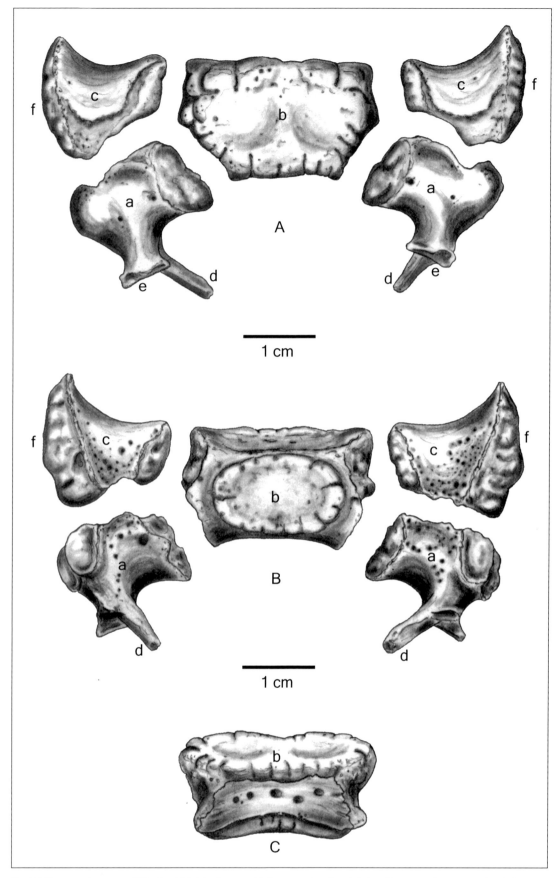

Fig. 6.7 First sacral segment (S1) of a child, 1 to 2 years old, A = superior, B = inferior, C = posterior: *a*, neural arch; *b*, centrum; *c*, ala; *d*, lamina; *e*, superior articular facet; *f*, articular surface for the auricular surface.

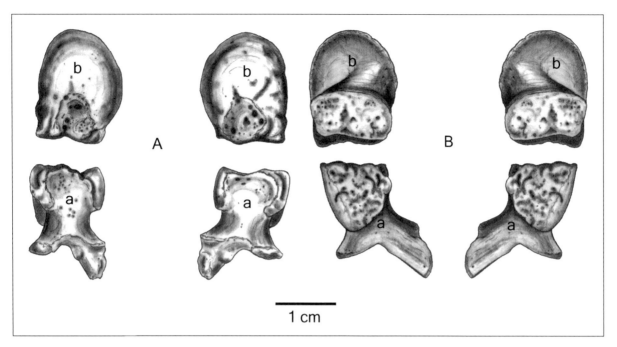

Fig. 6.8 First sacral segment (S1) of a child, 1 to 2 years old, A = lateral, B = medial: *a*, neural arch; *b*, anterolateral center for the ala.

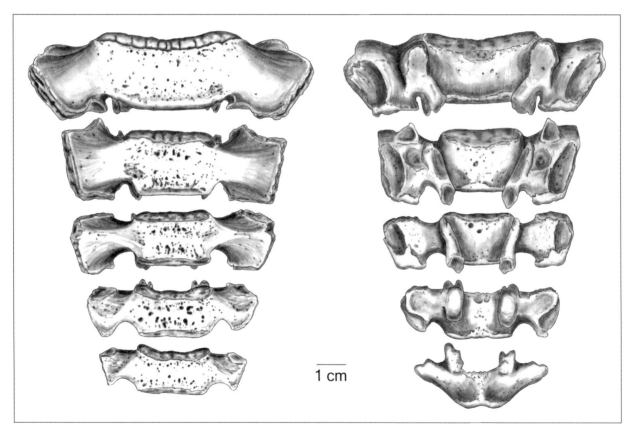

Fig. 6.9 Unfused sacral segments of an adolescent, left = anterior, right = posterior.

Differentiation from Other Bones

Before fusion, the separate elements of the sacrum can be confused with other aspects of the developing skeleton, particularly the presacral vertebrae. A separate neural arch can be differentiated from other vertebrae by a much larger and thicker articular projection that meets the centrum. An S1 neural arch (figs. 6.7a and 6.8a) is distinguished by its very large superior articular facet and blocky anterior portion with billowy surfaces on the anterior and medial aspects for articulation with the centrum and the ala. For children of 3 years or more, the neural arches of the vertebrae are already fused together posteriorly, while those of the sacrum are open.

Sacral centra may also be confused with those of the other developing vertebrae. The S1 centrum (fig. 6.7b), in particular, resembles that of L5 in size but it is not wedged like the L5 centrum, which is taller anteriorly than posteriorly. The S1 centrum is more rectangular and the short end has a cut corner, making it hexagonal. Centra of the lower sacral segments could be confused with those of the cervical vertebrae due to their smaller size. Sacral centra, unlike all other vertebral centra, have straight to slightly concave anterior margins, whereas those of presacral vertebrae are convex. Sacral centra are broader transversely than in the anteroposterior direction, unlike the cervical centra. They also display larger superior surfaces than inferior surfaces. Like the other vertebral centra, sacral centra have crenulated borders for the passage of blood vessels, which distinguishes them from the smooth sternebrae.

The anterior portion of the ala (figs. 6.7c and 6.8b) may resemble a carpal bone of the wrist or a tarsal of the ankle (e.g., the lunate or talus), but during fetal and infant development it is much too large to be confused with a carpal. A tarsal (e.g., the calcaneus and talus), however, may be similar in size. The developing carpals and tarsals in infants are more rounded than the alar elements of a sacrum.

Siding Techniques

To side a separate right or left sacral neural arch, place it on a table with the posterior lamina (fig. 6.7d) facing toward you, the anterior metaphyseal surfaces away from you, and the superior articular facet (fig. 6.7e) up, as shown in figure 6.7A. The superior articular facet is displaced to one side of the lamina, indicating the side from which the bone comes. The large anterior aspect also points toward the side to which the arch belongs. Thus, if the axis of the arch angles to the right in this position, it is from the right side.

To side the separate alae, hold the large articular surface for the auricular surface (figs. 6.7f and 6.8A, b) toward you with the saddle surface facing up, as in figure 6.8A (left). A large bump is present on the surface facing you, just above a large porous, vascular area. The bump in relation to the vascular area is toward the side from which the bone comes. Thus, a bump to the left of the vascular area indicates it is a left ala.

The Coccyx

The coccyx is inferior to the sacrum. The coccygeal elements comprise what is colloquially referred to as the tailbone. This vestigial tail anchors pelvic muscles and ligaments. The number of coccygeal vertebrae is variable, as is the development.

Description at Major Stages

The mature coccyx is usually composed of four vertebral segments that may fuse or remain as separate elements. It is generally accepted that each coccygeal element arises from one ossification center that forms a body, although the first element may have separate centers for the cornua or superior horns that articulate with the sacrum. The first coccygeal center appears by the end of fetal development or in infancy. The remaining two or three elements usually begin developing superiorly to

inferiorly between age 3 and puberty. Early in development, the coccygeal bodies are nondescript ovoids. They attain their final adult morphology by puberty.

Differentiation from Other Bones

The coccygeal vertebrae are usually not identifiable until after the advent of puberty. In older children, the first coccygeal element is easily distinguished from other coccygeal vertebrae due to the small projecting cornua at its superior border. It might be confused with a hyoid bone, although the body of the hyoid is much thinner, while the coccyx is thicker and more rounded. The nondescript, rounded bodies of the lower coccygeal elements are distinguished from other bones at this stage because all others have developed distinctive features.

The Os Coxa

The os coxa or hip bone (figs. 6.10 and 6.11) is sometimes referred to by the misnomer "innominate," meaning "no name." Its plural form is os coxae. Each mature bone articulates anteriorly with its counterpart at the pubic symphysis, inferiorly and laterally with the femora at the acetabulum (hip socket), and posteriorly with the sacrum at the auricular surface or sacroiliac joint. The os coxa develops from the fusion of three different bones: the ilium, the ischium, and the pubis (figs. 6.10a–c and 6.11a–c). At birth, these three separate elements are present and recognizable. The first of the elements to fuse together are the ischium and the pubis, which unite inferiorly to form the ischiopubic ramus between 4 and 8 years of age. The ilium subsequently fuses with the combined ischiopubic portion at the acetabulum between 11 and 14 years in females and 14 to 17 years in males to form the os coxa.

Beginning around age 9 or 10, secondary centers of ossification appear in the acetabulum. In adolescents, these separate bones can often be identified in isolation. These centers develop in the Y-shaped cartilage separating the pubis, ischium, and ilium and form part of the articular surface and most of the acetabular rim. The first center to appear is for the os acetabuli at the anterior aspect of the acetabulum, between the pubis and ilium. It is somewhat triangular in shape. The posterior epiphysis is usually larger and arises around age 10 or 11 between the ilium and ischium to form a triangular wedge along the rim of the acetabulum. A third center develops between 12 and 14 years at the superior rim of the acetabulum, just inferior to the anterior inferior iliac spine. This center often develops an extension toward the latter feature and is irregular in shape compared to the other acetabular bones. A variable number of small ossicles also tend to

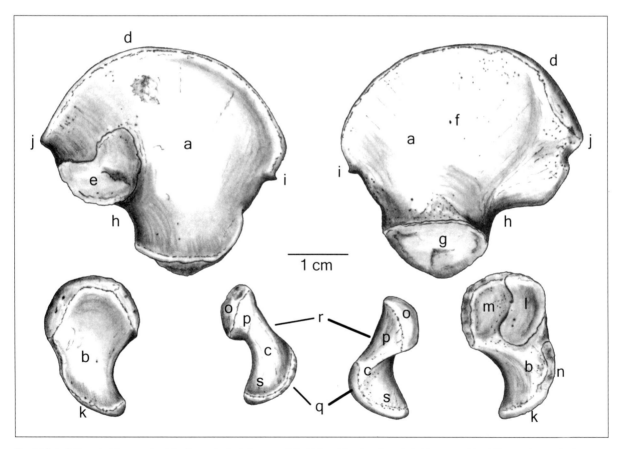

Fig. 6.10 Left ilium, ischium, and pubis of a perinate, left = medial, right = lateral: *a*, ilium; *b*, ischium; *c*, pubis; *d*, iliac crest; *e*, auricular surface; *f*, nutrient foramen; *g*, acetabular surface of ilium; *h*, greater sciatic notch; *i*, anterior superior iliac spine; *j*, posterior superior iliac spine; *k*, inferior ramus of ischium; *l*, lunate surface; *m*, acetabular fossa; *n*, ischial tuberosity; *o*, acetabular surface of pubis; *p*, superior ramus of pubis; *q*, pubic symphysis; *r*, obturator crest; *s*, inferior ramus of pubis.

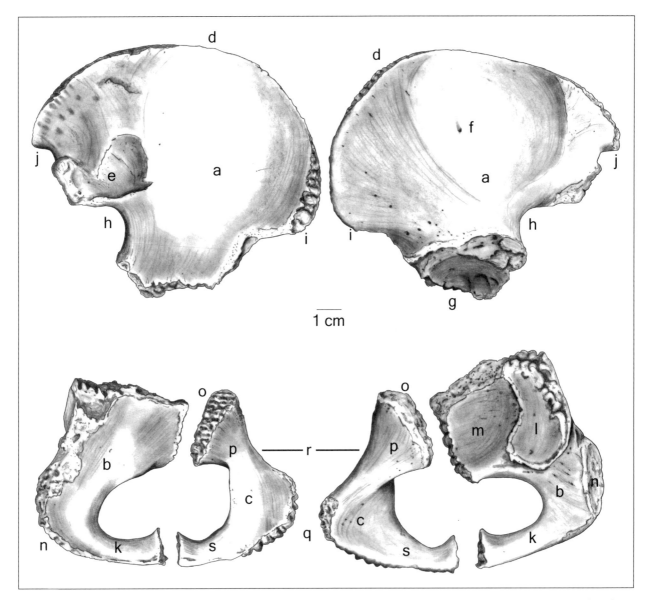

Fig. 6.11 Left ilium, ischium, and pubis of a child, left = medial, right = lateral: *a*, ilium; *b*, ischium; *c*, pubis; *d*, iliac crest; *e*, auricular surface; *f*, nutrient foramen; *g*, acetabular surface of ilium; *h*, greater sciatic notch; *i*, anterior superior iliac spine; *j*, posterior superior iliac spine; *k*, inferior ramus of ischium; *l*, lunate surface; *m*, acetabular fossa; *n*, ischial tuberosity; *o*, acetabular surface of pubis; *p*, superior ramus of pubis; *q*, pubic symphysis; *r*, obturator crest; *s*, inferior ramus of pubis.

appear within the Y-shaped cartilage. Fusion of the acetabular elements begins earlier in females than males. For females, fusion occurs between 11 and 15 years. In males, it takes place between age 15 and 17. Scheuer and Black (2000:357–63) provide an excellent discussion of the complex development and fusion of the acetabulum and should be consulted for further detail. The major acetabular bones, when separate, are identifiable as blocky bones with a curved rim on one aspect and a smooth, concave articular surface opposite a rougher, convex external aspect.

Additional epiphyses that appear for each of the three primary bones of the os coxa are described below. The growth and fusion of all elements of the os coxa are not complete until adulthood. To understand the development of the os coxa, it is important to consider each of these bones separately.

The Ilium

The ilium (figs. 6.10a and 6.11a) is the largest and most superior portion of the os coxa. It is considered a flat bone because of its broad blade. The ilium articulates posteromedially with the sacrum. It unites inferiorly at the acetabulum or hip socket, with the pubis anteriorly, and the ischium posteriorly to form the adult bone.

Description at Major Stages

The ilium begins to ossify before the other components of the os coxa, at 2 to 3 fetal months. By 4 to 5 fetal months, it is recognizable. The ilium is easily identified in third trimester fetuses, infants, and children by its broad blade with distinctive features. The superior border of the blade has a long metaphyseal surface called the iliac crest (figs. 6.10d and 6.11d), which changes in thickness throughout its length and is slightly S shaped. On the medial and posterior aspect of the blade is an articular surface shaped like an ear, hence it is called the auricular surface (figs. 6.10e and 6.11e). This surface articulates with the opposing auricular surface of the sacral ala to form the sacroiliac joint. The lateral side of the blade has a large nutrient foramen (figs. 6.10f and 6.11f) in the middle of the blade. The inferior aspect of the bone is thick and rounded and contributes to the acetabulum. The acetabular surface (figs. 6.10g and 6.11g) is somewhat crenulated around the edges where it eventually fuses with the pubis, ischium, and secondary acetabular bones. Inferior to the auricular surface and extending to the acetabular area is the broad concavity of the greater sciatic notch (figs. 6.10h and 6.11h). This feature is present very early in development.

Even in young children, the adult morphology of the ilium is well developed. The bone thickens anteriorly above the acetabular surface to form a buttress known as the iliac pillar. The width of the superior border thickens noticeably toward its anterior margin as well. This buttress is present but slight at birth. It becomes much more pronounced after a child begins to walk because of its relationship to biomechanical stressors associated with weight bearing. The most anterior extension of the superior border terminates at the projection of the anterior superior iliac spine (figs. 6.10i and 6.11i), while the posterior aspect ends at the posterior superior iliac spine (figs. 6.10j and 6.11j). The posterior inferior iliac spine is just below, on the lateral side opposite the auricular surface. The bump for the anterior inferior iliac spine is not well developed in infants and very young children but is discernible in older children as a bulge between the auricular aspect and the anterior superior iliac spine.

Two epiphyses generally develop for the ilium. A small cap for the anterior inferior iliac spine begins to ossify around ages 10 to 13, but this center is sometimes linked to the acetabular epiphysis and is not always found separately. This epiphysis fuses completely between ages 18 and 20. The second epiphysis is the iliac crest, which begins ossifying from two separate centers around age 12 or 13 in females and 14 to 15 in males. These separate centers grow toward the midpoint of the crest and unite to form a single iliac crest epiphysis that subsequently begins to fuse to the blade of the ilium between 17 and 20 years and is complete by age 23. When separate, the long, thin epiphysis for the iliac crest will follow the S-shaped curvature of the ilium. The anterior portion is wider than the posterior portion, and is especially thick toward its posterior end where it forms the iliac tubercle atop the iliac pillar. The opposite, anterior end of this portion often has a hooklike extension that covers the anterior superior iliac spine. The posterior portion of the crest epiphysis is more uniform in width, but is a little narrower where it joins the anterior part and slightly wider posteriorly. The epiphysis is very thin superoinferiorly and quite porous.

Differentiation from Other Bones

Being a flat, bladelike bone, the ilium, or fragments thereof, may be confused with the scapula or flat bones of the skull at all ages. In fetal and infant remains, the ilium is most often confused with the scapula. The ilium is thicker and has more rounded contours than a scapula and lacks the scapular spine. Look for the distinctive auricular surface (figs. 6.10e and 6.11e), the rounded acetabular area (figs. 6.10g and 6.11g), the iliac crest (figs. 6.10d and 6.11d), or even the nutrient foramen (figs. 6.10f and 6.11f) to ensure correct identification as the ilium. Fragments of the ilium at any age can also be distinguished from those of the scapula because of the presence of thin cortices encasing an inner layer of spongy (trabecular) bone. Thus, iliac fragments more closely resemble cranial fragments than scapular fragments. The borders of the ilium, however, are rounded and not serrated as for cranial sutures, and the surface lacks distinguishing cranial features such as meningeal impressions or grooves of various sulci.

Iliac crest epiphyses or fragments are often mistaken for ribs because they are thin and curved. The iliac crest epiphysis is easy to distinguish from a rib by noting its bubbly, porous surface. In contrast, a rib presents smooth surfaces.

Siding Techniques

Before fusion, the ilium is easily sided at all stages of development. To side this bone, hold the acetabular surface (figs. 6.10g and 6.11g) toward you and the iliac crest (figs. 6.10d and 6.11d) away from you, with the auricular surface up (figs. 6.10e and 6.11e). The auricular surface is on the side from which the bone comes (see figs. 6.10 and 6.11, left). You can also position the bone with the iliac crest up, the acetabular surface down, and the auricular surface facing you. Again, the auricular surface and the greater sciatic notch (figs. 6.10h and 6.11h) are on the side to which the bone belongs. Another method is to orient the ilium in standard anatomical position with the acetabular area down, the iliac crest up, and the auricular surface back and toward the sagittal plane (midline of your body). The smooth, lateral surface of the bone with its large nutrient foramen (figs. 6.10f and 6.11f) is on the side from which the bone comes.

Siding epiphyses of the ilium is difficult. The indistinct caps of the anterior inferior iliac spines cannot be sided with any accuracy unless both os coxae are present to per-mit fitting onto the bones. This procedure also ensures accurate siding of iliac crest epiphyses. These can be sided in isolation, however, by noting the thickness and curvature of the crest. When oriented properly, the anterior half of the crest is concave on its medial edge, curving toward the widest area for the iliac tubercle. Posterior to the tubercle, the crest narrows considerably and past the midpoint the medial edge curves convexly toward the wider, somewhat rounded posterior end. When viewing the superior aspect of a crest epiphysis, place the anterior end away from you and the posterior end toward you. The bulge of the iliac tubercle is toward the side to which the epiphysis belongs. Note that this technique also works for an isolated anterior portion of the crest epiphysis. If the posterior portion is isolated, place the narrowest end away from you and the wider end toward you. The concavity is on the side from which the epiphysis comes.

The Ischium

The ischium (figs. 6.10b and 6.11b) is located laterally and inferiorly to both the ilium and the pubis and forms the posteroinferior aspect of the os coxa. It contributes substantially to the formation of the acetabulum and its superior border forms the lateral and inferior margins of the obturator foramen.

Description at Major Stages

The ischium forms endochondrally from one primary ossification center, beginning between 3 and 5 fetal months. It is recognizable early in its development and generally maintains the same shape until the inferior ramus (figs. 6.10k and 6.11k) fuses with that of the pubis between 4 and 8 years of age.

In isolation, the ischium is shaped like a small hook or comma. The wider part is superior and the narrow curved part is inferior. A crescent-shaped articular surface is located on the lateral aspect of the superior portion of the ischium. This feature forms the inferior part of the lunate surface (figs. 6.10l and 6.11l) for articulation with the head of the femur. Anterior to the articular surface is an indentation for the acetabular fossa (figs. 6.10m and 6.11m). This fossa, which deepens as the bone develops, is only a slight depression in infants. Above this, the acetabular portion of the ischium has two contiguous epiphyseal surfaces. The larger posterosuperior surface is for the ilium, while the smaller anterior surface is for the pubis. The anteroinferior part of the ischium is the ramus, which eventually fuses to the pubis to form the ischiopubic ramus. The posterior aspect of the ramus bears a thick and roughened oval known as the ischial tuberosity (figs. 6.10n and 6.11n). One secondary ossification center arises between ages 13 and 16 for the epiphysis of the ischial tuberosity. This epiphysis is a curved cap with irregular edges that resembles a large cornflake that covers the area of the tuberosity as well as the inferior aspect of the ramus. It begins to fuse between ages 16 and 18 and is fully fused by 21 to 23 years. Occasionally, a small epiphysis forms for the ischial spine, a projection located just above the ischial tuberosity.

Differentiation from Other Bones

The ischium is quite distinct throughout development. Its hook or comma shape, along with distinguishing features such as the lunate surface (figs. 6.10l and 6.11l) and the ischial tuberosity (figs. 6.10n and 6.11n), makes it unlikely to be confused with another bone. In older infants and in children, the unfused pubis has a hook shape with a curved, roughened component (the pubic symphysis) that is similar to the ischium (at the ischial tuberosity), but the ischium is larger and more robust at all stages. In commingled remains, however, the ischium and pubis of different individuals could be confused. The square acetabular end and large articular crescent for the lunate surface on the lateral aspect of the ischium distinguish it from the pubis.

When fused with the pubis, the united bones form a ring to create the obturator foramen. The ischial portion is still distinctive because it forms the majority of the acetabulum and, at this stage, the indentation for the acetabular fossa becomes marked adjacent to the articular lunate surface. The thickened ischial tuberosity is unmistakable. The epiphysis for the ischial tuberosity is generally not difficult to distinguish from other epiphyses due to its fairly large size and substantial curvature.

Siding Techniques

To side an isolated ischium, hold the ischial tuberosity (figs. 6.10n and 6.11n) toward you with the thicker portion of the acetabular surface (figs. 6.10l, m and 6.11l, m) up and the thin ramus down (figs. 6.10k and 6.11k). The smooth side is medial, while the lateral side of the bone has the articular surface for the femoral head (lunate surface) and indentation for the acetabular fossa. These features are on the side from which the bone comes. If you only have the acetabular surface (if the ramus is broken) hold the thicker metaphyseal edge (for the ilium) toward you and the lunate surface facing up. The articular surface is toward the side to which the bone belongs.

The Pubis

The pubis (figs. 6.10c and 6.11c) is the most anterior of the three bones of the os coxa. It articulates medially with the opposite pubis, inferiorly with the ischium, and superiorly at the acetabulum with the ilium and ischium. The contribution to the acetabulum (figs. 6.10o and 6.11o) is less than that of the ischium. The borders of the pubis also form part of the obturator foramen.

Description at Major Stages

The pubis forms endochondrally, typically from one primary ossification center. It is the last of the pelvic elements to begin ossifying, at 4 to 6 fetal months. During fetal and infant growth, the pubis is very small in comparison to the ilium and ischium. It has a characteristic hook shape after birth, but it remains much smaller and less robust than the ischium.

In the developing pubis, the actebabular surface is thicker and rounder than the longer, flatter body. In late-term fetuses and neonates, the pubis consists of only the acetabular aspect, the superior ramus (figs. 6.10p and 6.11p), and the pubic symphysis (figs. 6.10q and 6.11q). The latter is a narrow, roughened surface on the most medial aspect for articulation with the opposite pubis. At this stage, the shape of the bone has been characterized as a dumbbell. Because it is slightly indented on the superior ramus and the anterolateral (outer) aspect has a short ridge, it appears twisted on that side. The opposite or posteromedial (internal) aspect is smooth.

In older infants and in children, the acetabular end has a smooth lateral articular surface. This articular aspect forms the anteroinferior portion of the lunate surface for articulation with the femoral head. A small, indented vascular surface is situated at the center of the acetabular end for ligament attachments to the femoral head. The superior and medial surfaces of the acetabular end are crenulated metaphyseal areas. The superior metaphyseal surface is for the ilium, while the medial surface is for the ischium. Although not readily observable at birth, a sharp ridge known as the obturator crest (figs. 6.10r and 6.11r) on the superior aspect of the superior ramus, extending between the acetabular end and the pubic symphysis, is present in older infants and children. The inferior aspect of the superior ramus is somewhat concave where it forms part of the obturator foramen. As the bone grows from infancy to childhood, the inferior pubic ramus (figs. 6.10s and 6.11s) ossifies below the pubic symphysis. This development gives the bone a hook-shaped appearance as it extends inferiorly and posteriorly toward the inferior ramus of the ischium. The narrow, flat inferior ramus of the pubis completes fusion with its ischial counterpart by 8 years of age. At this stage, the two bones form a ring encircling the obturator foramen and meeting superiorly at the acetabulum. At this juncture, the metaphyseal surfaces are separated by a cartilaginous strip that later ossifies to form the fused acetabulum (see above).

The pubic symphysis presents the typical appearance of an epiphyseal surface with its ridges and furrows that characterize it throughout childhood and early adulthood. The changes associated with aging of the pubic symphysis are due to secondary ossification that begins around age 20.

Differentiation from Other Bones

The pubis of a fetus or neonate is much smaller than the other pelvic bones and is distinguished by its rounded end and slightly twisted appearance. It might be confused with an unfused vertebral neural arch but the pubis is much thicker, more rounded, and it lacks distinctive vertebral features such as transverse foramina or processes.

In older infants and children, an unfused pubis can be mistaken for an ischium. The pubis has a hook shape with a curved, roughened component (the pubic symphysis) that is similar to the area of the ischial tuberosity. However, the pubis of a single individual is smaller and thinner than the ischium at all stages. In commingled remains, the pubis can be distinguished from an ischium by noting the obturator crest (figs. 6.10r and 6.11r) extending between the pubic symphysis (figs. 6.10q and 6.11q) and the rounded, crenulated acetabular end (figs. 6.10o and 6.11o). In contrast, the acetabular end of the ischium is a much flatter square with a large articular crescent for the lunate surface.

Siding Techniques

The pubis of a fetus or neonate may seem much harder to side than those of older individuals because its features are less developed, but siding is simple when you orient the pubis in approximately standard anatomical position. To do so, hold the pubis with the rounded acetabular end (figs. 6.10o and 6.11o) toward you, the pubic symphysis (figs. 6.10q and 6.11q) away from you, and the concave inferior aspect of the ramus down (figs. 6.10s and 6.11s). The smooth side is internal, while the irregular, slightly twisted side is external and indicates the side from which the bone comes. This method works well at all ages.

To side an unfused pubis in older infants and children, several other methods can be employed. When held as above, the obturator crest (figs. 6.10r and 6.11r) angles toward the side to which the bone belongs. Likewise, if you orient the pubic symphysis toward you and the acetabular end away from you with the obturator crest up, it also angles toward the side from which the bone comes. These methods are useful when only the superior ramus (figs. 6.10p and 6.11p) is preserved. Alternatively, hold the symphyseal surface toward you with the inferior ramus (thin projection) pointing down. The side of the symphysis that is convex (dorsal) is the side to which the bone belongs. This technique works well when only the symphyseal area is present. If you only have the acetabular portion, hold the acetabular surface toward you, with the broader metaphyseal surface of the ilium pointing up. The smoother, flatter articular surface is on the side from which the bone comes.

Chapter 7   The Chest and Shoulder Girdle

■ The chest or thorax is composed of the rib cage and the sternum (breastbone). These bones protect vital organs and serve as areas for muscle attachment. The shoulder girdle, which gives anchor and stability to the arm, consists of the scapula (shoulder blade) and the clavicle (collarbone).

The Ribs

There are typically twelve pairs of ribs (fig. 7.1), numbered 1 through 12 from superior to inferior, for a total of twenty-four. All ribs are crescent-shaped blades with a flattened end and a rounded end. The rounded ends or heads (fig. 7.1a) articulate with the thoracic vertebrae posteriorly, while the flat, anterior ends are the sternal ends (fig. 7.1b). The ribs appear early in development with endochondral ossification beginning between 8 and 9 fetal weeks in ribs 5 through 7. By 11 to 12 fetal weeks, all ribs have usually begun to ossify. At birth, the ribs are readily recognizable and resemble adult ribs in all but their size and vertical angulation. In fetal and neonatal remains, the ribs are relatively horizontal from end to end. Throughout childhood, they gradually angle downward so that adult ribs, rather than being straight across, are much higher at the vertebral end than the sternal end in standard anatomical position.

Around puberty, most of the ribs develop three very small epiphyses at the vertebral end of the shaft. One of these epiphyses is for the articular surface of the rounded head, while the others form the articular and nonarticular portions of the tubercle, a prominent bulge near the head that articulates with the transverse process of the associated thoracic vertebra. Because the eleventh and twelfth ribs lack tubercles, they develop only one epiphysis for the head. The epiphyses fuse to the shaft of the rib between 17 and 25 years. Due to their small size, they are often overlooked in archaeological contexts.

Ribs 1 through 7 are known as true ribs because they articulate with the sternum via cartilage. Ribs 8 through 10 are called false ribs because they articulate indirectly with the sternum via cartilage that attaches to that of the true ribs above them. The last two ribs (11 and 12) are designated floating ribs because they have no cartilaginous connection to the other ribs or to the sternum and hang free.

General features of the ribs include the shaft or body (fig. 7.1c). The external surface of a rib shaft is rougher and slightly convex compared to the very smooth internal or visceral surface. The superior edge of the shaft is blunt and convex, while the inferior edge is sharp and concave. The internal aspect of the inferior border of all but the twelfth rib is marked by the costal groove (fig. 7.1d) for blood vessels and nerve fibers, which is most prominent toward the posterolateral aspect of the shaft and disappears anteriorly (toward the sternal end). The sternal end is generally roughened and cupped for cartilage or tapers to a point in the floating ribs. The posterior or vertebral end of a rib is characterized by the knobby head and a constricted neck (fig. 7.1e) that separates the head from the tubercle (fig. 7.1f). Just anterolateral to the tubercle is the angle (fig. 7.1g), where the shaft takes a sharp curve. The angle is marked on the external surface by a diagonal line that serves for attachment of muscles of the back and on the internal surface by the deep but narrow costal groove. The curvature of the ribs decreases from the first to the twelfth rib. The necks are much longer and more slender in upper ribs than in lower ribs due to the greater curvature at the angle.

Ribs increase in length from the first through seventh ribs, then decrease in length through the twelfth rib. Features of the first, second, eleventh, and twelfth ribs permit them to be distinguished easily from the other, typical ribs, even in late fetal and neonatal remains. These ribs are treated separately from ribs 3 through 10 for purposes of identification and siding. In adults, the tenth rib can also be differentiated but it is grouped here with typical ribs because the distinguishing features are difficult to discern in infants and children.

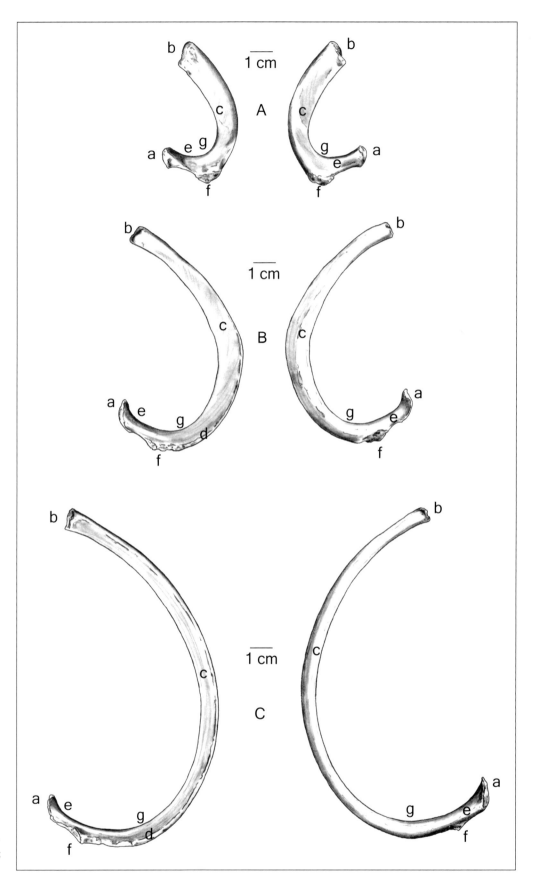

Fig. 7.1 Left ribs of a child, left = inferior, right = superior: A, first rib; B, second rib; C, typical rib; a, head; b, sternal end; c, shaft; d, costal groove; e, neck; f, tubercle; g, angle.

First Rib

Description at Major Stages. The first rib (fig. 7.1A) is the broadest, flattest, and most curved of all ribs and it is also one of the shortest. It is compressed superior to inferior so it lies flat on a table, whereas ribs 3 through 12 are thinner in an anterior-posterior orientation so their shafts are raised off a table when complete. The sternal or anterior end of the first rib is wider or more flared than the opposite vertebral end with its small, rounded head. The neck of a first rib is long, with a prominent tubercle set off at a right angle to it. Even in infants, the inferior (internal or visceral) surface of a first rib is convex and smoother than the superior (external) surface. A shallow depression for a short costal groove is located at the medial border of the neck. The superior surface of the first rib is slightly concave. As it develops in childhood, it becomes increasingly marked by depressions for the subclavian grooves on either side of a small ridge called the scalene tubercle.

Siding Techniques. To side the first rib, orient the bone in standard anatomical position (see fig. 7.1A, right) with the neck and tubercle (fig.7.1A, e, f) facing you. When oriented properly with the inferior surface on a table, the head (fig. 7.1A, a) inclines downward slightly (i.e., it does not point up in the air). If you have mistakenly placed the superior surface down, the head and neck will be raised off the table and you need to flip the bone over. When placed in anatomical position, the tubercle is lateral, or toward the side from which the bone comes.

Second Rib

Description at Major Stages. The second rib (fig. 7.1B) is longer and less curved than the first. It looks more like a lower rib except that it is more strongly curved and lies almost flat on a table because the smooth, internal (visceral) surface is directed inferiorly. The superior or external surface is roughened, with a prominent bump or tuberosity near the midshaft becoming evident in childhood. The inferior or internal surface has a short costal groove at the angle.

Siding Techniques. The same technique described for the first rib also works for the second rib. Thus, even if you are having trouble distinguishing the superior (external) and inferior (internal) aspects, the head (fig. 7.1B, a) will be raised off the table if you have oriented the rib incorrectly. Also note that the tubercle (fig.7.1B, f) is oriented downward when properly positioned, as in ribs 3 through 10.

Ribs 3 through 10

Description at Major Stages. The third rib still has a long neck and more pronounced curvature than the ribs below it (fig. 7.1C). Its superoinferior orientation is transitional between the more inferiorly oriented internal surface of the second rib and the more vertically inclined internal aspect of the fourth rib. The curvature of the ribs decreases as you progress down the rib cage. The tubercle in these ribs is oriented inferiorly and the costal groove becomes deeper and longer from ribs 3 through 7, and decreases in prominence from ribs 8 through 11. In adults, the tenth rib can be distinguished from ribs 3 through 9 because it is shorter and straighter and has a rounder head with only a single articular facet. A double, saddle-shaped facet characterizes the heads of ribs 2 through 9 because they articulate with two adjacent vertebral bodies. Unlike ribs 11 and 12, however, rib 10 has a tubercle. Because the difference in the articular aspect of the head is difficult to identify in ribs of children who lack head epiphyses, the tenth rib is categorized here as a typical rib.

Siding Techniques. To side ribs 3 through 10, hold the head (fig. 7.1C, a) toward you (flattened sternal end away from you) with the tubercle pointing down (fig. 7.1C, f). Note that the blunt superior surface is up, and the sharp margin with the costal groove (fig. 7.1C, d) is down and faces inward. The rib curves out toward the side that it is from; the external surface, which lacks the costal groove, is also on the side from which it comes. For vertebral fragments of ribs, these features are recognizable and permit siding. For sternal ends only, siding depends upon identification of the rounded superior margin and sharper inferior edge, even on fragments that lack a portion of the costal groove. Observe that the superior edge of the rib is straight, while the inferior edge is not as regular and is slightly indented. By orienting the superior and inferior borders properly, with the sternal end pointing away from you, the coarser and somewhat convex external aspect is on the side to which the rib belongs. For midshaft fragments, note that the costal groove is deeper and broader posteriorly, and shallower anteriorly. Using this feature, orient the deeper, wider part of the groove toward you and facing down. With the costal groove facing you, the widest end is on the side from which the bone comes. If you hold it so the broken end with the widest part of the groove is toward you, the external surface opposite the groove is on the side to which the fragment belongs.

Ribs 11 and 12

Description at Major Stages. Ribs 11 and 12 differ from other ribs in their morphology. They are two of the smallest ribs and lack the curvature of the ribs above them. They do not articulate with the sternum, nor do they have a cartilaginous connection to the other ribs, so the sternal ends taper to a point and lack the cupped or billowy articular surface seen on all the other ribs. In addition, because these ribs do not articulate with a transverse process on the eleventh and twelfth thoracic vertebrae, no neck or tubercle is present. Like the first and tenth ribs, the head of an eleventh or twelfth rib is rounded with only a single facet for articulation with one vertebral body. The eleventh rib is longer than the twelfth rib. It often has a groove on the external aspect of the neck in older individuals. Rib 12 can be easily distinguished in adults by its lack of an angle and costal groove. The presence or absence of these features in the eleventh and twelfth ribs is difficult to discern in neonates but becomes more obvious throughout childhood. Rib 12 is often attenuated and its internal surface inclines superiorly.

Siding Techniques. To side the eleventh rib, follow the procedures outlined for ribs 3 through 10. In cases where the costal groove is difficult to observe, remember that the superior border of the rib is straight, while the inferior border is uneven. Orient this uneven border down. Hold the head toward you and the nonarticular sternal end away from you. The smoother surface is the internal aspect and the coarser, convex external surface is on the side from which the rib comes. The rib curves out slightly toward the side to which it belongs. To side the twelfth rib, hold the vertebral end toward you with the nonarticular sternal end away from you. Like the other ribs, the superior border is straight, while the inferior border is uneven and contributes to the change in width of the rib near the midpoint. When held with the head straight on, the shaft angles downward when properly positioned. If the rib shaft slants upward, you have misidentified the superior and inferior aspects and must flip the bone over. With the bone oriented with the superior side up, the twelfth rib also curves slightly toward the side from which it comes.

Differentiating Ribs from Other Bones

Because of their narrow, bladelike shape and distinctive ends, whole ribs do not resemble any other bone in the body. They are identifiable very early in development because of their characteristic shape. When fragmentary, small pieces of ribs are generally thin and flat. The cortex or dense outer covering of a rib is very thin, whereas the internal part of the bone is light and airy with thin spicules of bone (trabeculae) giving it a webbed appearance. There is no marrow cavity such as that seen in long and short bones of the limbs or the clavicle. A rib fragment could be mistaken for a piece of the scapula or ilium, but these bones are larger and the scapula is much thinner. The superior and inferior edges of a rib fragment identify its narrow shaft, while scapula and ilium fragments do not show two parallel borders. A rib shaft fragment might also be mistaken for a piece of cranial vault bone. Vault bones will generally have identifying internal features such as meningeal grooves, a sulcus, a foramen, or a serrated sutural border. Look for the presence of the parallel margins and costal groove (fig. 7.1d) to distinguish a rib shaft fragment.

The epiphyses of the ribs are very small. Those for the articular aspect of the tubercle and the head are round to oval in shape. The head epiphysis is more of a disk, while that of the tubercle is thicker and more like a small cap. These epiphyses could be mistaken for those found in the metacarpals, metatarsals, and phalanges of the hands and feet or for the vertebral epiphyses on the spinous and transverse processes. Careful excavation and labeling in the field are important in distinguishing these epiphyses.

The Sternum

Description at Major Stages

The sternum (fig. 7.2) is located in the anterior portion of the rib cage in the midline of the chest. It articulates with both clavicles, and directly and indirectly via cartilage to ribs 1 through 10. The adult sternum is comprised of three main parts—the manubrium, sternal body, and xiphoid process. The manubrium (fig. 7.2a) is the thickest, most superior part of the sternum, while the xiphoid process is variable in appearance and forms the inferior terminus of the sternum. The entire sternum is preformed in cartilage. Although the number of ossification centers is variable, the sternum generally develops from six primary centers. One ossification center forms the manubrium; another is for the xiphoid process; and the remaining four comprise the sternal body. Prior to fusion into the composite sternal body, these four segments are known as sternebrae (fig. 7.2b). The sternebrae frequently ossify from paired centers that fuse together during their development. Thus, it is not uncommon to find more than four elements for a sternal body in a given subadult skeleton.

Ossification of the sternum commences with a center in the manubrium that appears at about 5 fetal months. The first sternebra appears shortly thereafter. By 8 fetal months, the second and third sternebrae begin to mineralize. At birth, therefore, the sternum generally consists of at least four indistinct nodules of bone. The fourth sternebra does not start to ossify until the first year after birth, while the xiphoid process can commence ossification as early as 3 to 6 years of age but frequently remains cartilaginous well into adulthood.

By the late third trimester and during infancy, each portion of the sternum that is present appears as a thin, circular disk of bone. The manubrium is the largest seg-

longer circular. The manubrium resembles a hexagon and the sternebrae are more rectangular. By approximately 8 years, the clavicular and jugular notches (fig. 7.2c, d) on the superior aspect of the manubrium resemble their adult form. At this time, the sternal bodies are generally square, thin bones. The third and fourth sternebrae typically fuse together between 4 and 10 years and these fuse to the second sternebra in adolescence (generally between age 11 and 16). Finally, the first sternebra fuses to form a complete sternal body between ages 15 and 20.

Differentiation from Other Bones

For fetal and infant remains, the sternal segments, including the manubrium, are often misclassified as vertebral centra, particularly those of the cervical vertebrae. Vertebral centra tend to be thicker and more consistent in shape, whereas the sternal elements are thinner, irregular disks of bone. The anterior and posterior surfaces of the sternal elements are thin and smooth, while the vertebral centra appear to have thin layers of dense, furrowed bone above and below a porous interior. The internal porosity reflects the complex development and vascularity of the vertebrae, and is absent in a sternal element. While cervical centra are flatter than thoracic and lumbar centra and more easily confused with sternebrae, they also display more crenulated surfaces than a sternal element.

Before the basilar part fuses to the lateral portions of the occipital bone, it may be misidentified as the manubrium. However, the characteristic adult shape of the manubrium is not present until well after the basilar part is no longer a separate element. In the case of commingled juvenile remains, remember that the basilar part displays portions of the occipital condyles as well as a smooth, U-shaped curve for the foramen magnum situated between the condylar facets.

In older children and adolescents, the manubrium has attained its adult morphology and the sternal body demonstrates scalloped edges at the costal facets where the sternebrae are fused together. When fully fused, the long, flat sternal body is unlikely to be misidentified.

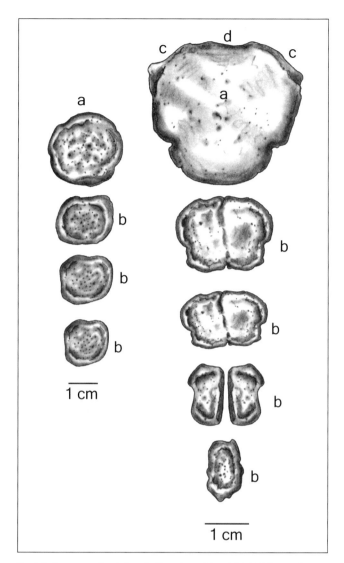

Fig. 7.2 Sternum of an infant (*left*) and an older child (*right*), anterior view: *a*, manubrium; *b*, sternebra; *c*, clavicular notch; *d*, jugular notch.

ment, and size decreases inferiorly. The manubrium becomes recognizable in late infancy as a flat bone with relatively straight sides and an inferior ovoid articular area. By around 3 years of age, each sternal portion is no

The Clavicle

Description at Major Stages

Although the clavicle (fig. 7.3) is unique in its morphology and development, it is classified as a short bone because of its tubular shape. The clavicle acts as a strut or support for the shoulder joint and anchors many muscles. It articulates medially with the manubrium of the sternum, laterally with the scapula, and inferiorly with the first rib. The clavicle begins to ossify before any other bone of the body, commencing in the fifth week in utero. The ossification of the clavicle is complicated, and it appears to be the only infracranial bone to employ intramembranous ossification. It develops both intramembranously and endochondrally from two primary ossification centers that form the shaft. Additionally, there is one secondary center that forms the medial or sternal epiphysis (fig. 7.3C). This epiphysis may begin to ossify around puberty but frequently does not appear until the late teens. While the clavicle is the first bone to ossify, its medial epiphysis is the last to fuse, generally in the mid-20s. A lateral epiphysis may also develop around age 19 to 20 but,

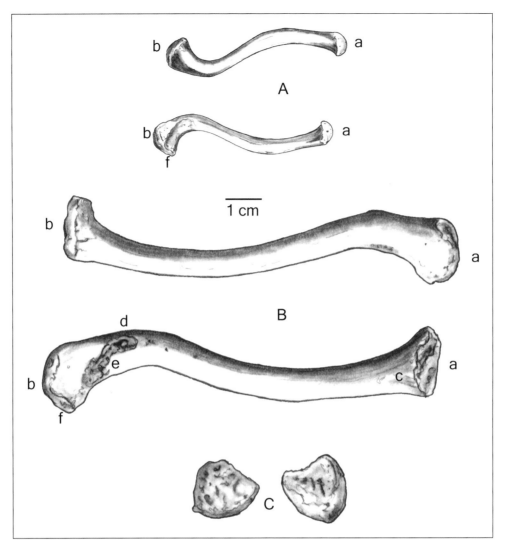

Fig. 7.3 Left clavicle of a perinate (A) and an adolescent (B), top = superior, bottom = inferior; and a left medial epiphysis of an adolescent (C), left = metaphyseal view, right = medial view of articular surface: *a*, medial/
sternal end; *b*, lateral/acromial end; *c*, costal tuberosity; *d*, conoid tubercle; *e*, oblique/trapezoid line; *f*, facet for
acromion process of scapula. Actual size.

when actually separate, it fuses very quickly, so it is rarely
found in archaeological contexts.

By the eleventh fetal week, the shaft reflects its distinctive S-shaped adult morphology, distinguishing it from
all other bones. The medial or sternal end (fig. 7.3a) of
the bone is round in cross section. The epiphyseal surface
of the medial metaphysis is a vertically oriented ovoid.
It flares inferiorly (downward) noticeably at all ages. The
lateral or acromial end (fig. 7.3b) is flat in cross section,
giving it an oblong appearance on the metaphyseal surface. The inferior aspect of the clavicle is marked on the
medial end by a roughened indentation known as the costal tuberosity (fig. 7.3c), a nutrient foramen in the midshaft region, and the conoid tubercle (fig. 7.3d) and the
oblique trapezoid line (fig. 7.3e) on the lateral end. In fetal and neonatal clavicles, the nutrient foramen is the most

obvious of these features, but it can sometimes occur on
the posterior aspect of the midshaft area. The superior
surface is very round and smooth.

The medial epiphysis initially appears as a small, oval
piece of bone that is smaller than the medial end of the
shaft. It is often a cap that is separate, but can also be a thin
flake that forms on the metaphyseal surface of the shaft.

Differentiation from Other Bones

Unless fragmentary, the clavicle is distinct enough to
prevent confusion with other bones from early fetal development onward. Small clavicular shaft fragments may be
confused with long bone shaft fragments; however, the
small circumference aids identification. In fragmentary
condition, the lateral or acromial end (fig. 7.3b) of the
clavicle is most often confused with the acromion process

of the scapula. In children, the most obvious difference is the epiphyseal nature of the scapular acromion process. An acromial end of the clavicle will exhibit a break rather than a billowy metaphyseal surface. The clavicle also displays the conoid tubercle (fig. 7.3d) on its inferior aspect, while the acromion process is smooth. The articular facet on the clavicle is lateral (fig. 7.3f), whereas it is antero-medial on an acromion process of the scapula. A further distinction is the cross section. The lateral end of a clavicle, while flat, becomes round as it extends medially, while the acromion process continues medially to the pronounced ridge of the scapular spine. A clavicle fragment may also be mistaken for a piece of a rib. The clavicle is more robust, rounder, and has a thicker cortex with a narrow medullary cavity in its shaft.

The medial epiphysis (fig. 7.3C) for the clavicle is frequently not very distinct, but it is unlikely to be confused with other epiphyses because of its late development and persistence long after other similarly shaped epiphyses have fused. It can appear as an irregular flake in the center of the surface of the metaphysis or as a separate, thin cap with a smooth, slightly convex, articular surface.

Siding Techniques

For a neonatal clavicle (fig. 7.3A), determining which side the bone is from is most easily accomplished by identifying the medial, lateral, inferior, and superior aspects of the bone. Doing so allows you to place the bone in standard anatomical position with the rougher inferior surface and majority of the medial metaphyseal end down and the rounded superior surface up. Place the conoid tubercle (fig. 7.3d) down and toward you (because it is inferior and posterior on the shaft). You can inspect the curvature of the shaft near the rounded medial end. If ori-ented correctly, the bone bows out anteriorly (away from you) at the medial end (fig. 7.3a), then curves posteriorly toward the lateral end. In anatomical position, the flat acromial end (fig. 7.3b) is, thus, on the side to which the bone belongs. Alternatively, place the clavicle with the smooth, superior surface on a table and the rounded, medial end pointing away from you (the inferior surface is identified by the presence of the nutrient foramen). The medial end curves toward the side from which the bone comes.

To side fragments consisting of only the medial or lateral portions of the clavicle, it is generally easiest to orient the bone in standard anatomical position by observing the curvature. For a medial end, remember that the costal tuberosity (fig. 7.3c) is inferior, the medial metaphysis flares downward, and the bone curves out anteriorly. The rounded end is medial, or opposite the side the bone is from, while the broken end is on the side from which the bone comes. For a lateral portion, place the rugged surface with the conoid tubercle and trapezoid line (fig. 7.3d, e) down and the smooth surface up. The posterior part curves out toward you and the flat, acromial end indicates the side to which the bone belongs. Alternatively, if you only have the lateral or acromial end, hold the flat end up and the roughened inferior surface toward you. The end of the bone curves toward the side from which it comes.

The medial epiphysis (fig. 7.3C) is very difficult to side due to its nondescript nature. Unless both medial ends are present to permit fitting them to each clavicle, there are no reliable siding techniques for separate medial epiphyses. The lateral epiphysis, when present, is usually not separate.

The Scapula

The scapula (figs. 7.4 and 7.5) is classified as a flat bone because of its broad blade, which serves as an anchor for several muscles. It articulates laterally with the humerus and superiorly and anteriorly with the clavicle. The anterior aspect of the blade is a shallow concavity known as the subscapular fossa (fig. 7.4a) for the subscapularis muscle, which separates the bone from the back of the rib cage. The blade is situated between ribs 2 and 7.

Description at Major Stages

The body of the scapula begins to ossify endochon-drally around 7 to 8 fetal weeks. By 12 to 14 fetal weeks, it has recognizable morphology. At this stage and at birth, the scapula has a thin, bladelike surface that is flat on both sides. The dorsal or posterior side has a large projecting ridge of bone called the scapular spine (fig. 7.4b) at the superior part of the blade. This spine extends laterally into the acromion process (figs. 7.4c and 7.5a), which has an epiphyseal surface on its end. Below the spine is the infraspinous fossa (fig. 7.4d), while the supraspinous fossa (fig. 7.4e) is above the spine. In adults, these are pronounced hollows immediately adjacent to the spine. In fetuses and infants, however, they are much shallower.

The blade of the fetal/neonatal scapula has a somewhat triangular or sail shape with two long borders and one short margin. The longest border is a broad, convex curve. This margin is the vertebral or medial border (fig. 7.4f) and is further distinguished by a thin epiphyseal surface along its edge. The straighter edge opposite the vertebral border is the axillary or lateral border (figs. 7.4g and 7.5b). It is a relatively straight margin that is concavely curved from the inferior angle (the point

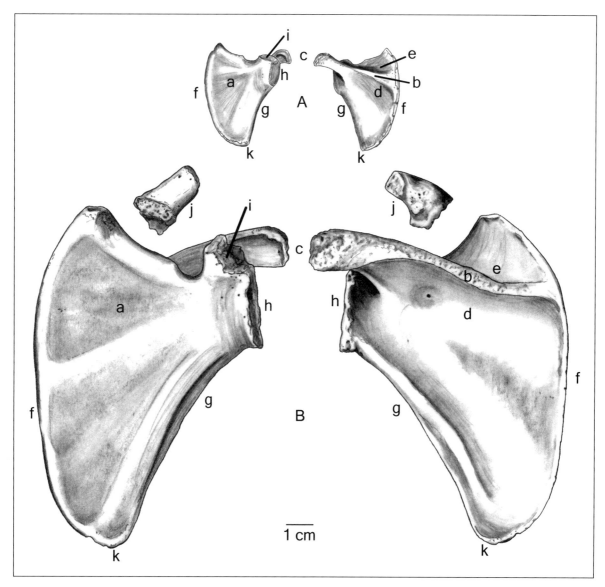

Fig. 7.4 Left scapula of a perinate (A) and a young child (B), left = anterior; right = posterior: *a*, subscapular fossa; *b*, scapular spine; *c*, acromion process; *d*, infraspinous fossa; *e*, supraspinous fossa; *f*, medial/vertebral border; *g*, lateral/axillary border; *h*, glenoid cavity; *i*, epiphyseal surface for the coracoid; *j*, coracoid epiphysis; *k*, inferior angle.

where it meets the curved vertebral border) to the epiphyseal surface of the glenoid cavity or fossa (figs. 7.4h and 7.5c). The shortest border is superior and somewhat irregular. It flares upward to meet the vertebral border at the superior angle and ends laterally at the glenoid cavity, where the bone articulates with the head of the humerus. The glenoid cavity has an epiphyseal surface on its lateral aspect (fig. 7.5d) and a contiguous surface on its superior aspect (fig. 7.4i) for the epiphysis of the coracoid process (fig. 7.4j). Thus, in a fetus or neonate, the scapula resembles the adult form but it is less angular. The fingerlike coracoid process has not yet formed, while the acromion process is attenuated because the projecting spine lacks its epiphysis.

The scapula has approximately seven secondary ossification centers, but not all of these appear as separate, recognizable epiphyses. One of the largest and most easily identified epiphyses is for the coracoid process (fig. 7.4j), which begins to ossify in the first year of life. Because the other epiphyses commence ossification in late childhood and adolescence, the coracoid process is the only scapular epiphysis present in older infants and young children. At this stage, the coracoid process looks like a tiny, crooked little finger. It is broader and thicker inferomedially, where it has a roughened metaphyseal surface that eventually fuses to the superior aspect of the glenoid area. The more superolateral end is a small, blunt projection.

In addition to the body of the coracoid process, scapu-

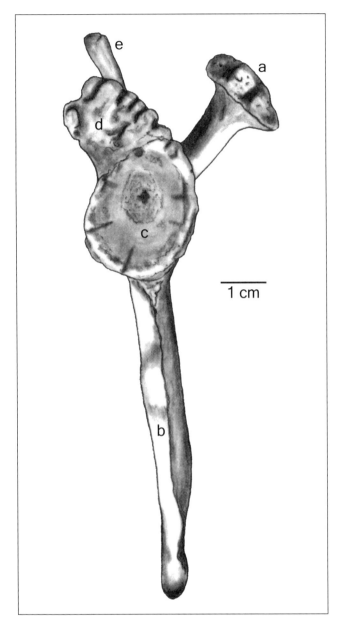

Fig. 7.5 Left scapula of a young child, medial view: *a*, acromion process; *b*, lateral/axillary border; *c*, glenoid cavity; *d*, epiphyseal surface for the coracoid; *e*, superior border.

pect or angle of the coracoid process and the thin, flaky epiphysis for the articular surface of the glenoid cavity develops. The latter is evident during fusion as an irregular deposit of very smooth bone on the rough epiphyseal surface. An epiphysis at the lateral end of the coracoid (the apex) may also form and join with the angle epiphysis as it fuses in the late teens.

Distinct epiphyses develop between 13 and 16 years of age for the acromion process (figs. 7.4c and 7.5a) and at age 15 to 17 for the inferior angle (fig. 7.4k) and vertebral border (fig. 7.4f). The acromial epiphysis is a U-shaped piece of bone with the opening of the U showing a rough metaphyseal surface and the bottom of the U displaying a smooth surface. The lateral half of the articular facet for the clavicle is located on the shorter arm of the U. It generally fuses to the spine between age 18 and 20 but can remain separate throughout life as the os acromiale. The epiphysis for the inferior angle varies in size from a small cap to a broader crescent. It is a narrow ridge of bone with a billowy metaphyseal surface and a smoother nonarticular aspect that forms the apex of the scapula. The rim of the vertebral border also forms at the same time and is generally comprised of multiple, thin strips of bone that fuse to the blade of the scapula. These epiphyses are generally completely fused between 20 and 23 years of age.

Differentiation from Other Bones

When complete, the scapula of a fetus or infant is most likely to be confused with the lateral parts of an unfused occipital bone because of their similar shape and double projections at one end. The scapula is much larger, with a thinner blade that curves more gradually than the border of a lateral part. The glenoid cavity (figs. 7.4h and 7.5c) at the lateral end and the large spine on the posterior aspect (fig. 7.4b) differentiate the scapula from the lateral part of the occipital. The lateral part shows a large portion of the occipital condyle on one of the bony projections or limbs. Another feature distinguishing the lateral occipital is the smooth and curved edge that represents the border of the foramen magnum.

Fragments of the scapula blade may be confused with other thin, flat developing bones of the skull or pelvic area. The spine of the scapula (fig. 7.4b) is generally the best preserved area because it is thicker than other parts of the bone. When present, the spine should eliminate confusion with other bones. In cases where only a fragment of the blade is present, look at the borders (fig. 7.4f, g). The scapula is longer and more angular than the broad ilium, particularly if the inferior angle (fig. 7.4k) is apparent. While the top of the ilium also curves much like the vertebral border of the scapula, even in infants it is twice as thick as this border of the scapula. An ilium also displays the ear-shaped articular surface for the sacrum. The bor-

lar epiphyses develop for the subcoracoid, the angle of the coracoid, the glenoid cavity, acromion process, inferior angle, and vertebral border. The subcoracoid is the earliest of these to appear (around age 8 to 10) and fuses first with the coracoid process between 14 and 15 years and then with the superior aspect of the glenoid cavity by age 16 to 17. This ossification center does not typically appear as a separate, identifiable epiphysis. Instead, it is usually observed at the top of the glenoid cavity as the composite coracoid fuses to the body of the bone. Around age 14 to 15, a small cap appears at the superomedial as-

ders of cranial vault bones are serrated sutures, and the internal features of these bones (e.g., meningeal grooves, presence of a sulcus, etc.) distinguish them from a scapula.

An unfused coracoid process (fig. 7.4j) can be mistaken for the transverse process of a thoracic vertebra but it lacks an articular facet and has significant curvature. The epiphyses for the inferior angle and vertebral border are most likely to be confused with the epiphysis of the iliac crest. The latter is broader and curves in an S shape, whereas the thinner epiphyses of the scapular margins are much straighter. The acromial epiphysis is generally recognizable with its U shape and presence of a portion of the articular facet for the clavicle.

Siding Techniques

To side a complete scapula at any age, orient it with the spine (fig. 7.4b) facing you and toward the top of the bone, which corresponds to standard anatomical position (see fig. 7.4, right). The concave anterior surface, well-developed in children and adults, is away from you. The spine projects laterally toward the side the bone is from and the glenoid cavity (fig. 7.4h) is also on that side. Alternatively, place the scapular spine up and the glenoid cavity toward you, as shown in figure 7.5. The spine with its acromial surface (fig. 7.5a) is opposite the side the bone is from, while the glenoid cavity (fig. 7.5c) and the articulation of the coracoid process (fig. 7.5d) are on the side

from which the bone comes. Also, in the same orientation, the short superior border (fig. 7.5e) of the bone indicates the side to which it belongs.

To side the coracoid epiphysis (fig. 7.4j), hold the metaphyseal surface toward you with the concave surface facing up (the blunt end should point upward). The side that the tip of the coracoid process points toward is the side from which the bone comes. Another method is to hold the metaphyseal surface down with the projection up and toward you. The process curves toward the side to which the epiphysis belongs. For an unfused acromion process, point the metaphyseal surface away from you and the smoother surface down. The facet for the clavicle indicates the side from which the bone comes. Note also that this facet is on the shorter arm of the U formed by the epiphysis. Epiphyses for the inferior angle are very hard to side without reference to the scapular blades. The difficulty is in determining which aspect is anterior and which is posterior. The anterior surface is very slightly concave, while the posterior is slightly convex; however, the unfused epiphysis is often relatively flat. If you can identify the front and back of the bone confidently, place the posterior surface on the table with the tip of the epiphysis toward you. The epiphysis extends up and away from you on the side it is from because the medial border of the epiphysis is longer.

Chapter 8   The Bones of the Arms and Legs

■ This chapter contains all the bones of the arms and legs, including the humerus, ulna, radius, femur, tibia, fibula, and patella. With the exception of the patella, all these bones are considered long bones because of their length and tubular shape. The patella, which does not appear until childhood, is technically a sesamoid because it is located within a tendon.

The Bones of the Arm

The major bones of the arm consist of the humerus, radius, and ulna. All three of these bones are long, tubular bones with proximal and distal ends, as well as epiphyses that appear and fuse to the shaft of the bone at specific times. Separate epiphyses are described with each major bone. An interesting developmental pattern is that the bones of the arm are only longer than the corresponding bones of the leg during the first trimester in utero, likely reflecting our common ancestry with apes. In all subsequent stages of development, human leg bones are longer than the analogous arm bones.

The Humerus

Description at Major Stages. The humerus (figs. 8.1–8.3) is the major bone of the upper arm. It articulates proximally with the scapula, and distally with the radius and ulna. The growing humerus consists of a shaft (figs. 8.1a and 8.2a) and proximal and distal epiphyses. During the first trimester, the humerus begins as a cartilage model and starts to ossify during the seventh week in utero (fig. 8.1A). There are at least two proximal epiphyses, for the head (figs. 8.1b and 8.2b) and greater tubercle (figs. 8.2c and 8.3c) and, possibly, a third for the lesser tubercle, although its existence has been questioned (Scheuer and Black, 2000:281). The proximal epiphysis for the head typically begins to ossify between birth and 6 months of age, and between 3 months and 3 years for the greater tubercle. These centers are generally considered to fuse together between 5 and 7 years, forming a single, united epiphysis (fig. 8.3A). The distal epiphysis initially consists of four secondary ossification centers. These are the capitulum (figs. 8.1c, 8.2d, and 8.3B),

trochlea (figs. 8.2e and 8.3D), and medial (figs. 8.1d, 8.2f, and 8.3C) and lateral (fig. 8.2g) epicondyles. The capitulum begins to ossify between 6 months and 2 years of age, whereas the trochlea does not form until 8 years of age and quickly fuses to the capitulum. The medial epicondyle begins to form after the fourth year of life, while the lateral epicondyle forms after the tenth.

The humeral diaphysis displays distinct morphological characteristics from the time of ossification. It is fairly round throughout the midshaft, although both ends form other characteristic shapes. Bilateral flaring at the distal end creates an inverted V shape. The metaphyseal surface of the distal end of the shaft is approximately four times as wide medially to laterally as it is anteroposteriorly, resulting in a flattened appearance. A large indentation is present on one side of the distal end. This depression is the olecranon fossa (fig. 8.1e), which identifies the posterior aspect of the humerus. At the proximal end, the diaphysis appears straighter on the lateral side and curved on the medial side, with the latter flaring outward where the epiphysis for the head eventually fuses. The proximal metaphyseal surface is ovoid, but a portion is pinched inward. This pinched area represents the intertubercular sulcus (figs. 8.1f and 8.2h) and identifies the anterolateral aspect of the bone. A nutrient foramen is present in the middle of the shaft and its entrance is directed distally. This foramen identifies the anteromedial aspect of the bone.

The proximal epiphysis for the head (figs. 8.1–8.3) initially appears as an oval piece of bone. At first, the epiphysis is thin and porous, with a bubbly appearance. The posterior aspect is rounded, whereas the anterior has a hooked projection at its lateral edge. The area opposite

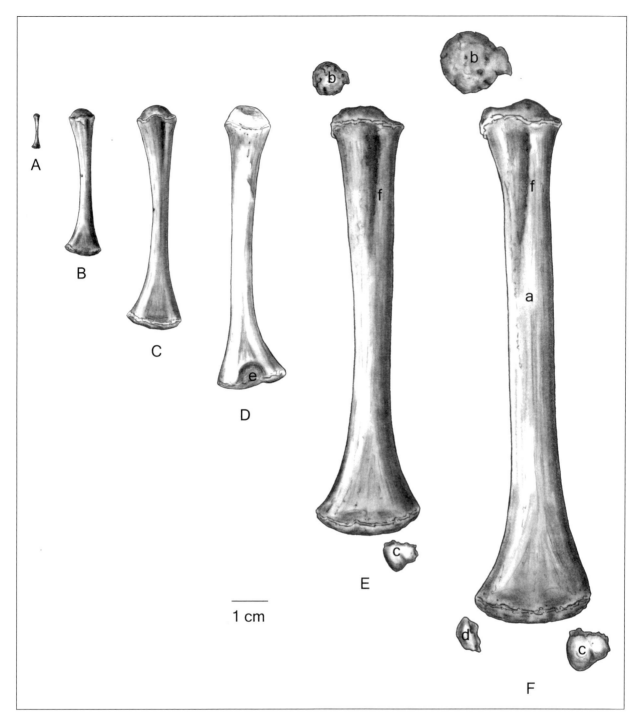

Fig. 8.1 Left humerus shown in actual size at approximate ages, A = first trimester, B = second trimester, C = third trimester, D = perinate, E = 1.5 years, F = 5 years: a, diaphysis; b, head; c, capitulum; d, medial epicondyle; e, olecranon fossa; f, intertubercular sulcus. All shafts are shown in an anterior view except D, which is posterior. Epiphyses are in proximal and distal views to show the articular surfaces.

the roughened metaphyseal surface is somewhat bulbous and represents the humeral head. This bulbous portion is raised more in the medial direction than the lateral. The greater tubercle first appears as a nodule and begins to fuse to the lateral projection between 2 and 6 years of age. Once the greater tubercle (figs. 8.2c and 8.3c) has fused to the head, the combined epiphysis displays a smooth, rounded articular surface. The nonarticular tubercle is somewhat crenulated and forms the lateral aspect of the epiphysis. It is situated between the intertubercular sulcus and the posterior notch that marks the line of fusion between the formerly separate centers of ossification.

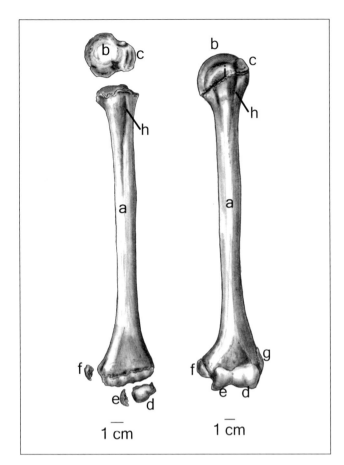

Fig. 8.2 Left humerus, anterior view, at approximate ages, left = 9 years, right = 15 years: *a*, diaphysis; *b*, head; *c*, greater tubercle; *d*, capitulum; *e*, trochlea; *f*, medial epicondyle; *g*, lateral epicondyle; *h*, intertubercular sulcus; *i*, lesser tubercle. Epiphyses (except *f*) are in proximal and distal views to show the articular surfaces.

Based on radiographic studies, this combined epiphysis typically fuses to the humeral diaphysis between 13 and 17 years in females and between age 16 and 20 in males. Scheuer and Black (2000:281), however, note that direct observation of bone generally places fusion approximately two years later than fusion data from radiographic studies.

The capitulum (figs. 8.1c, 8.2d, and 8.3B) is rounded, tapering medially and dropping off sharply at the lateral edge. The anterior aspect is smooth and rounded, while the posterolateral edge is irregular and more pointed. The trochlear epiphysis (figs. 8.2e and 8.3D) is rather indistinct and exists as a separate entity only in late childhood. Like the epiphyses for the medial and lateral epicondyles, the separate epiphysis for the trochlea is difficult to recognize. These epiphyses can appear as thin crescents or nodules when they begin to ossify. The capitulum, trochlea, and lateral epicondyle (fig. 8.2g) generally completely fuse to one another between 10 and 14 years of age. These subsequently fuse to the distal diaphysis between 11 and 15 years in females and between 12 and 17 years in males. The medial epicondyle (figs. 8.1d, 8.2f, and 8.3C) is the last distal epiphysis to fuse to the diaphysis, generally between ages 13 and 15 in females and between 14 and 16 in males. It is only in adolescence, after the union of the capitulum, trochlea, and lateral epicondyle, that the small, caplike epiphysis of the medial epicondyle is generally recognizable.

Differentiation from Other Bones. Bones of similar size and thickness that may be confused with the humerus at each stage of development are the tibia and the femur. The

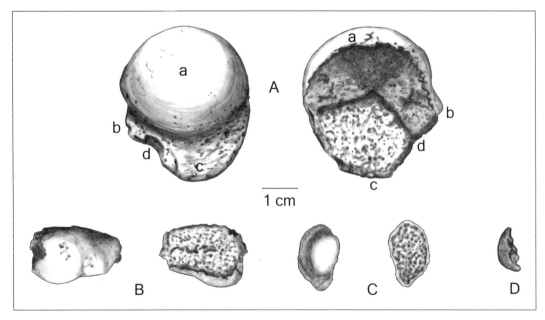

Fig. 8.3 Left humeral epiphyses for the head (*A*), capitulum (*B*), medial epicondyle (*C*), and trochlea (*D*), left = articular/external view, right = metaphyseal view: *a*, head; *b*, lesser tubercle; *c*, greater tubercle; *d*, intertubercular groove.

humerus and tibia are similar in length and diameter until approximately 1 year of age when the tibia becomes the longer bone. After the first fetal trimester, the femur is longer than the humerus at each developmental stage; this difference can help identify both bones when each is present in a burial.

For fetal and neonatal remains, the humerus is distinguishable from the femur and tibia by the deep depression of the olecranon fossa (fig. 8.1e), situated on the distal, posterior aspect of the bone. The proximal end of the humerus is rounded, whereas this portion of the femur is larger and more rectangular in shape. Moreover, the billowy femoral epiphyseal surface for the lesser trochanter differentiates it from the humerus. The midshaft of the humerus is round like the femur, but it is smaller in diameter and lacks the posterior ridge (linea aspera) that marks the femur. As the linea aspera develops, the femur begins to resemble a teardrop in cross section, whereas the humeral midshaft is more rounded throughout childhood. In contrast, the tibia is triangular in cross section due to the anterior crest. In the humerus, the nutrient foramen is situated on the anteromedial aspect of the diaphysis; in the femur and tibia, the nutrient foramen is located on the posterior surface. Note also that the nutrient foramen for the humerus enters the bone in the distal direction, toward the elbow. In the tibia, the nutrient foramen also enters the bone distally, but in the femur, it proceeds proximally.

In infancy and later stages, the intertubercular groove (figs. 8.1f and 8.2h), proximally, and the olecranon fossa (fig. 8.1e), distally, continue to be key features that separate the humerus from the femur and tibia. In early childhood, the further development of the humeral head and distal epiphyses are features that aid in identification of the bone (figs. 8.1–8.3).

The humeral head is easily distinguished from the femoral head in older children by its smooth surface, which lacks the indentation found on the femoral head, and by the protuberances at the lateral aspect from the fusion of the greater and lesser tubercles. In early stages of ossification, however, the epiphyses for the femoral and humeral heads are very similar in appearance. The humeral head from a single skeleton is much smaller and not as rounded as the femoral head epiphysis. It is readily identified by a hooked projection at its anterolateral border (fig. 8.1b). A separate distal epiphysis for the capitulum is recognizable as a small, rounded knob. A combined distal epiphysis has two rounded eminences. The separate medial epicondyle is a small cap that is notable because it lacks an articular surface.

Siding Techniques. For a perinatal humerus (fig. 8.1D), determining which side the bone is from is most easily accomplished by identifying the olecranon fossa (fig. 8.1e)

at the distal end of the shaft on the posterior surface. In standard anatomical position, the distal end points down with the olecranon fossa facing you and the intertubercular groove (fig. 8.1f) facing up and away from you. In this position, note that the proximal end of the bone projects medially, or opposite the side to which the bone belongs, while the indentation of the intertubercular groove is displaced laterally, or toward the side to which the bone belongs. At the distal end, the bone curves more medially, while the lateral side is relatively straight and marks the side from which the bone comes.

Additional methods of siding the bone rely on holding the humerus out of anatomical position. One option is to hold the bone with the anterior surface facing you. Locate the nutrient foramen and note that it indicates the medial aspect of the bone so, in this position, it is on the same side to which the bone belongs. The humeral head and the distal end also flare more toward the side to which the bone belongs in this view. Alternatively, if you hold the bone with the posterior surface facing you and the distal aspect pointing down, determine which of the medial and lateral borders of the olecranon fossa is longer proximally to distally (in the long axis of the shaft). The longer border is on the side from which the bone comes. These features continue to aid in siding the humerus throughout childhood.

To side the proximal epiphysis, place the metaphyseal surface on a table with the large, round head (fig. 8.3A, a) away from you and the biggest nonarticular area toward you (see fig. 8.3A, left). The smaller nonarticular tubercle, known as the lesser tubercle (fig. 8.3A, b), is on the side to which the bone belongs. The lesser tubercle is separated from the greater tubercle (fig. 8.3A, c) by the intertubercular groove (fig. 8.3A, d), a shallow depression. This groove is anterior, so when positioned facing away from you, it will be toward the side from which the bone comes. For younger individuals where the lesser tubercle is not yet fused, place the metaphyseal surface on a table with the head away from you and the tubercle (nonarticular portion) facing you. There is a large notch present (where the lesser tubercle will eventually fuse) that is on the side to which the bone belongs. To side an unfused head only, note that the posterior aspect is rounded, whereas the anterior has a hooked projection at its lateral edge (fig. 8.1E, b and 8.1F, b). With the anterior aspect facing away from you, the hook is thus on the side from which the bone comes.

For the unfused distal capitulum (fig. 8.3B), the anterior aspect is smooth and rounded, while the posterior, lateral edge is irregular and more pointed. Place the metaphyseal surface on a table with the sharper edge away from you. The widest part of the epiphysis is on the side to which the bone belongs. Alternatively, place the metaphyseal surface on a table with the bulbous portion toward you. The nonarticular area faces you and the serrated edge is on the side from which the bone comes.

The Radius

Description at Major Stages. The radius (figs. 8.4–8.6) is one of the two bones in the lower arm. In standard anatomical position, the radius lies on the lateral side. It articulates proximally with the ulna and humerus and distally with the ulna, scaphoid, and lunate. The growing radius consists of a shaft (figs. 8.4a and 8.5a) and a proximal and distal epiphysis. During the first trimester, the radius begins as a cartilage model and starts to ossify during the seventh week in utero (fig. 8.4A). The proximal epiphysis (figs. 8.4b and 8.5b) begins to ossify around 5 years of age. The distal epiphysis (figs. 8.4c and 8.5c) typically begins to ossify between the first and third years.

The radial diaphysis is discernible from the time of ossification as a tubular bone with small diameter and distinctive ends. The distal end of the bone flares bilaterally. The opposite or proximal metaphyseal end is round. A large bump is present just below the proximal metaphysis. This bump, known as the radial tuberosity (figs. 8.4d and 8.5d), is present from the third month in utero and is a distinguishing feature of the radius throughout life. The nutrient foramen is located on the anterior surface in the middle of the diaphysis and enters the bone in a proximal direction (toward the elbow).

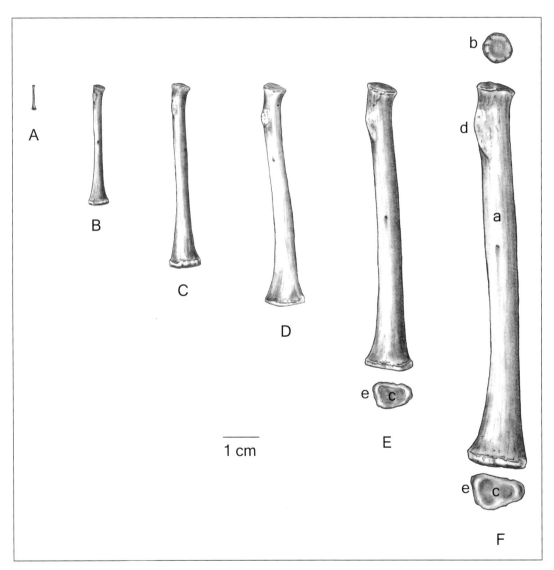

Fig. 8.4 Left radius, anterior view, shown in actual size at approximate ages, A = first trimester, B = second trimester, C = third trimester, D = perinate, E = 1.5 years, F = 5 years: a, diaphysis; b, head; c, distal epiphysis; d, radial tuberosity; e, ulnar notch.

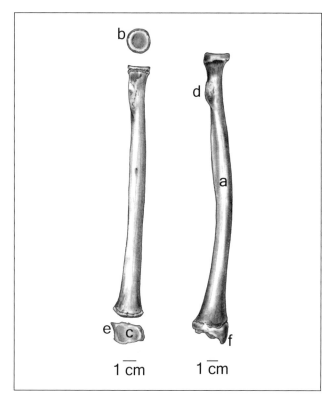

Fig. 8.5 Left radius, anterior view, at approximate ages, left = 9 years, right = 15 years: *a*, diaphysis; *b*, head; *c*, distal epiphysis; *d*, radial tuberosity; *e*, ulnar notch; *f*, styloid process.

The proximal epiphysis for the head of the radius initially appears as a circular disk of bone that displays a roughened surface on the metaphyseal side and a smooth articular surface on the other side (fig. 8.4F, b). The articular surface becomes slightly concave by around 10 years of age (fig. 8.6A). The proximal epiphysis typically fuses to the shaft between 11 and 15 years in females and between 14 and 17 in males. Again, it appears to be later in direct observation of dry bone versus radiographs.

The distal epiphysis begins to ossify as early as infancy and no later than the third year of life (fig. 8.4c). It soon becomes recognizable as a thin, wedge-shaped bone. A smooth articular surface, often marked by nutrient foramina, is present on the distal aspect. The metaphyseal surface is rough. During growth, the epiphysis thickens and, by age 10, it is rectangular with a diagonal cut at one corner (fig. 8.6B). This diagonal corner identifies the posterolateral border. Opposite this border, on the medial side of the epiphysis, a distinct notch (figs. 8.4e, 8.5e, and 8.6a) provides the articulation for the ulna. The dorsal tubercle is also evident as a bump on the posterior aspect of the epiphysis. Two concavities on the articular surface, for the scaphoid and lunate, are evident by this time. By adolescence, a large bony protuberance known as the styloid process (fig. 8.5f) is present and identifies the lateral aspect of the epiphysis. The distal epiphysis fuses to the shaft between 14 and 17 years in females and between ages 16 and 20 in males.

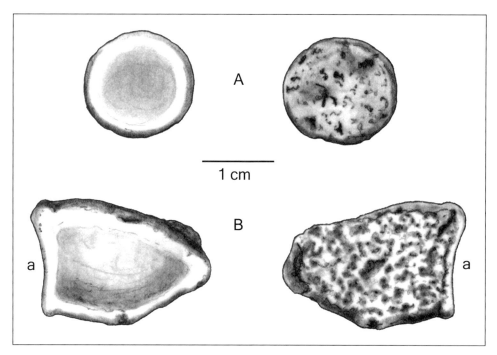

Fig. 8.6 Left radial epiphyses for the head (A) and distal end (B), left = articular view, right = metaphyseal view: *a*, ulnar notch. Orientation: anterior is at the top.

Differentiation from Other Bones. The radius is the shortest of the long bones after the first fetal trimester. Bones that may be confused with the radius at each stage of development are the ulna and fibula. However, the proximal end of the radius is easily separated from the ulna and fibula because of the presence of the radial tuberosity (figs. 8.4d and 8.5d). For fetal and neonatal remains, the rounded proximal end and flared distal end of the radius (fig. 8.4A–D) help distinguish it from both the fibula and the ulna. In more mature juveniles, the radius is typically more triangular in cross section at the midshaft, whereas it is circular proximally and rectangular distally. In neonates, the radial shaft is approximately the same diameter as the ulna. A broken distal ulna can be easily mistaken for a proximal radius. The distal ulna, however, is broader medially to laterally, giving it a more oval shape than the round radial head. Proximal and distal fibula shaft fragments must be distinguished from the radial and ulnar heads. A proximal radius fragment exhibits the radial tuberosity and angled neck between this bulge and the head. The distal radius is much broader than the distal ulna and both ends of the fibula.

The radial epiphyses ossify much earlier than those of the ulna. The epiphysis for the radial head is distinctive. It is much more developed and exhibits an indentation on the articular surface by the time the distal ulnar epiphysis has ossified to the point where it might be confused. The distal radial epiphysis is small and wedge-shaped, with two slight depressions on the articular surface that distinguish it from other long bone epiphyses.

Siding Techniques. For the radius of neonates and older children, determining which side the bone is from is best done by identifying the radial tuberosity (figs. 8.4d and 8.5d), which signifies the proximal end. The nutrient foramen identifies the anterior aspect. If the nutrient foramen is absent, as it sometimes is, the anterior aspect of the distal end is fairly flat to slightly concave and smooth, whereas the posterior aspect is convex and slightly irregular because of the dorsal tubercle ridge.

Holding the bone in standard anatomical position with the anterior aspect up and the flared distal end pointing away from you, the proximal end shows a bulge on the medial aspect for the radial tuberosity and the distal end curves medially to meet the ulnar head. These features, therefore, are opposite the side to which the bone belongs when held in this manner.

Taking the bone out of anatomical position provides some simple ways of siding the shaft. By holding the radius with the anterior surface facing you and the proximal end up, the radial tuberosity is on the side from which the bone comes (see figs. 8.4 and 8.5). Alternatively, if the proximal end is missing, hold the bone with the anterior surface facing you and the distal end away from you. The

ulnar notch (figs. 8.4e and 8.5e) is on the side to which the bone belongs. If the distal end is missing, the radial tuberosity is more visible if the anterior surface is facing you and identifies the side from which the bone comes (as above). These features continue to aid in siding the radius throughout childhood.

The proximal epiphysis (fig. 8.6A) is very difficult to side before it fuses to the shaft. The only means of siding is to attempt fitting a well-developed epiphysis to the radial shaft. Unless both shafts are present, however, this method may not be accurate. The distal epiphysis (fig. 8.6B) can be sided by placing the articular surface on a table with the thick end away from you. The epiphysis is rectangular in shape with one corner missing. This missing corner (or more curved edge) is on the side to which the bone belongs.

The Ulna

Description at Major Stages. The ulna (figs. 8.7–8.9) is the medial bone in the lower arm in standard anatomical position. It articulates proximally with the humerus and radius and, distally, connects directly only with the radius. The growing ulna consists of a shaft (figs. 8.7a and 8.8a) and a proximal and distal epiphysis. During the first trimester, the ulna begins as a cartilage model and starts to ossify during the seventh week in utero (fig. 8.7A). The proximal epiphysis (figs. 8.8b and 8.9A) begins to ossify around 8 years of age in females and around 10 years in males. The distal epiphysis (figs. 8.7b, 8.8c, and 8.9B) typically begins to ossify between ages 5 and 7 years.

The ulnar diaphysis is quite distinct from the time of ossification and is easily identifiable when undamaged. The bulbous olecranon process (figs. 8.7c and 8.8d) marks the proximal end. While this feature is somewhat less pronounced in infants than older children, the bulging proximal end is readily observable early in development. The shallow depression or concavity below this knob is the trochlear notch (figs. 8.7d and 8.8e), which identifies the anterior aspect of the ulna. The opposite (distal) end is straight and narrow and the metaphyseal surface is round. The nutrient foramen is located in the proximal half of the bone, typically on the anterior surface, and enters in a proximal direction.

The proximal epiphysis (figs. 8.8b and 8.9A) begins to ossify much later than that of the radius and is separate for only a few years. It appears as a somewhat elongated cap with a crenulated metaphyseal surface and a smooth articular surface. It has a small projection or hook extending downward on the anterolateral aspect. The proximal epiphysis typically fuses between 12 and 15 years in females and between 13 and 17 in males.

The distal epiphysis (fig. 8.7F, b) first appears as a small, thin, circular disk with a roughened metaphyseal surface

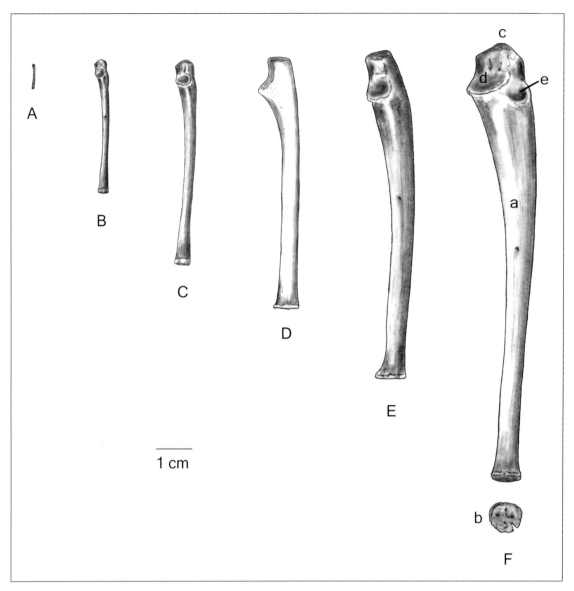

Fig. 8.7 Left ulna shown in actual size at approximate ages, A = first trimester, B = second trimester, C = third trimester, D = perinate, E = 1.5 years, F = 5 years: a, diaphysis; b, distal epiphysis/head; c, olecranon process; d, trochlear notch; e, radial notch. All are shown in an anterior view except D, which is lateral.

and a bubbly articular surface with scalloped edges. During growth, the epiphysis thickens and the articular surface becomes smoother (fig. 8.9B). By early adolescence, a bony process, known as the styloid process (figs. 8.8f and 8.9a), is present and identifies the posterior aspect of the epiphysis. The distal epiphysis fuses between 15 and 17 years in females and between 17 and 20 in males.

Differentiation from Other Bones. Bones of similar size and thickness that may be confused with the ulna at each stage of development are the radius and fibula. However, the bulbous proximal end of the ulna is easily distin-guishable from the more tubular ends of the radius and fibula. For fetal and neonatal remains, the ulna and fibula are similar in length, but the fibula is uniformly thin and straight throughout the entire diaphysis. The ulna, on the other hand, is curved and thicker in the proximal half (fig. 8.7A–D). After birth, the fibula begins to increase in length at a faster rate than the ulna. Separating the distal ulna (head) from the proximal and distal ends of a fibula is challenging in neonates. The proximal end of the fibula is very small in diameter and more rounded, with a tubular shaft and straight sides. When viewed from the distal end, the ulna is broader and more ovoid in shape

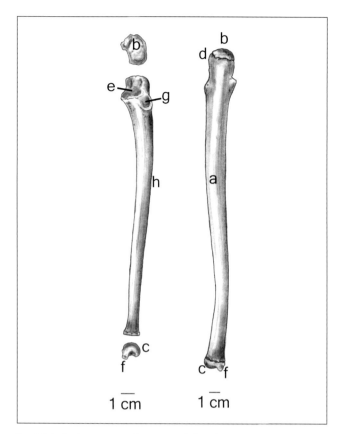

Fig. 8.8 Left ulna, at approximate ages, left = 9 years, anterior; right = 15 years, posterior: *a*, diaphysis; *b*, proximal epiphysis/olecranon; *c*, distal epiphysis/head; *d*, olecranon process; *e*, trochlear notch; *f*, styloid process; *g*, radial notch; *h*, interosseous crest.

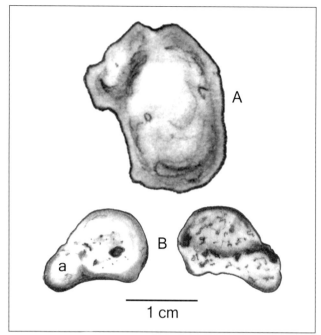

Fig. 8.9 Left ulnar epiphyses for the proximal olecranon (A) shown in superior view and distal head (B), left = articular view, right = metaphyseal view: *a*, styloid process.

and the posterior edge is flat rather than curved like the fibula.

The radius is always shorter than the ulna; it does not display a distinct process with an articular notch like the ulna, and its distal end displays bilateral flaring. In more mature juveniles, the ulna is typically more triangular in cross section proximally and circular distally.

The age of appearance is useful in identifying ulnar epiphyses, because they begin to ossify much later than those of the radius. The proximal olecranon epiphysis (fig. 8.9A) is shaped like a cap. While it could be confused with the femoral greater trochanter epiphysis, it is much smaller and has an articular surface that the greater trochanter lacks. The distal ulnar epiphysis (fig. 8.9B) could be confused with that of the radial head since both are relatively flat circles of bone. When compared to the radial head epiphyses from the same skeleton, the distal ulnar epiphysis is smaller and more irregular because it begins to ossify much later. In later stages of ossification, the development of the styloid process (figs. 8.8f and 8.9a) and the convexity of the head distinguish the distal ulna

from the radial epiphysis, which has a smooth, concave articular surface.

Siding Techniques. For a neonatal ulna, determining which side the bone is from is accomplished by first identifying the trochlear notch (figs. 8.7d and 8.8e), which signifies the proximal end and the anterior aspect. Orient the bone in standard anatomical position with the proximal end up and trochlear notch away from you. Note that the articular surface extends laterally, or on the side to which the bone belongs. In infants, the depression for the proximal articulation of the radial head, known as the radial notch (figs. 8.7e and 8.8g), can be difficult to discern, but it is readily observable in older children and is on the side the bone is from when it is held in anatomical position. Note also that the sharp ridge of the interosseous crest (fig. 8.8h) is on the side from which the bone comes.

Taking the bone out of anatomical position and holding it with the anterior surface facing you and the proximal end up (see fig. 8.7F), note that the proximal end curves toward the side to which the bone belongs. For infants only, if the proximal end is missing, the nutrient foramen occurs on the anterior surface and enters the diaphysis proximally (toward the elbow). Holding the bone the same way, the distal metaphysis is curved on the side the bone is from, while the opposite side is straight up and down.

To side the proximal epiphysis, place the rough metaphyseal surface on a table with the rounded portion facing you (see fig. 8.9A). The hook or small projection is on the side from which the bone comes.

To side the distal epiphysis (fig. 8.9B), place the rough metaphyseal surface on a table with the round portion of the epiphysis away from you. The projection or styloid process (fig. 8.9a) is on the side to which the bone belongs. Alternatively, you can view the epiphysis with the metaphyseal surface down, the rounded portion toward you, and the styloid process away from you and pointing up. In this view, a notch or indentation is located adjacent to the styloid process and indicates the side from which the bone comes.

The Bones of the Leg

The bones in the legs are the femur, tibia, fibula, and patella. Like the bones of the arm, the leg is comprised of three long, tubular bones with proximal and distal ends, and epiphyses that appear and fuse to the shaft of the bone at specific times. Separate epiphyses are described with each major bone. The patella or kneecap is classified as an irregular bone and does not begin to ossify until early childhood.

The Femur

Description at Major Stages. The femur (figs. 8.10–8.12), the largest bone in the human skeleton, is found in the upper leg. It articulates proximally with the pelvis and distally with the tibia and the patella. The femur develops from five ossification centers. The primary center forms the shaft (figs. 8.10a and 8.11a), with four secondary centers. Three are for the proximal epiphyses that become the head (figs. 8.10b, 8.11b, and 8.12A) and the greater and lesser trochanters (figs. 8.10c, d, 8.11c, d, and 8.12B, C), and one is for the distal epiphysis (figs. 8.10e, 8.11e, and 8.12D). The femoral shaft begins to mineralize between the seventh and eighth weeks in utero (fig. 8.10A). From its inception, the femur is tubular. The distal end is slightly flared, while the proximal end already shows the development of what will become the femoral neck (figs. 8.10f and 8.11f). As the femur progresses through the fetal growth stages, the general shape of the shaft or primary center remains similar, with its distal end flared and the neck extending medially at the proximal end. From the second trimester on, several distinct anatomical landmarks begin to take shape on the shaft, including the epiphyseal surface of the lesser trochanter (fig. 8.10g), the linea aspera (fig. 8.10h), and the nutrient foramen.

The distal epiphysis typically appears between 36 and 40 fetal weeks and usually begins to ossify before birth. In most cases, the distal epiphysis is the only femoral epiphysis to appear before birth, although occasionally the proximal epiphysis for the head is also present. During fetal development, the distal epiphysis has a distinctive shape, with two rounded protuberances on the articular surface that eventually form the medial and lateral condyles (figs. 8.10i, j, 8.11g, h, and 8.12a, b). The metaphyseal surface of this epiphysis, like all others, has a roughened texture where it joins the growth plate. Between 3 and 5 years of age, the distal epiphysis achieves its characteristic adult shape, making it much easier to differentiate from other epiphyses. While it is the first long bone epiphysis to form, it is one of the last to fuse to the shaft. Fusion generally occurs earlier in females than males with an approximate age range of 14 to 18 years and 16 to 20 years, respectively.

The appearance of the proximal epiphysis that forms the femoral head (figs. 8.10b and 8.11b) is variable, but usually occurs after birth and within the first year of life. During early development, the epiphysis is nondescript and may resemble others in the body (e.g., the epiphysis for the head of the humerus). It is generally flattened on the metaphyseal surface and rounded on the articular surface. One feature that helps identify this epiphysis is the beginning of the cavity that forms the fovea capitis (figs. 8.11i and 8.12c). By early childhood, the epiphysis attains its characteristic shape, with its rounded articular surface and depressed fovea capitis. The metaphyseal surface is flattened but somewhat indented. At this stage, the head resembles a toadstool cap in shape. The epiphysis typically reaches its distinctive shape between 10 and 12 years of age. The proximal end of the femoral shaft also reflects the adult shape, as the neck is well developed and the metaphysis has a convex surface, while the adjacent metaphyseal side of the epiphysis has a concave surface. Fusion of this epiphysis usually begins between 12 and 16 years in females and between 14 and 19 years in males.

The epiphysis that forms the greater trochanter (figs. 8.10c, 8.11c, and 8.12B) usually appears between the ages of 1 and 5 years. Between 6 and 9 years, this epiphysis achieves a notable crescent shape due to the presence of the trochanteric fossa (fig. 8.12d). Fusion to the shaft generally occurs later in males than females, with an approximate age range of 16 to 18 years and 14 to 16 years, respectively. The epiphysis that forms the lesser trochanter (figs. 8.10d, 8.11d, and 8.12C) appears between 7 and 12 years and fuses around 16 to 17 years.

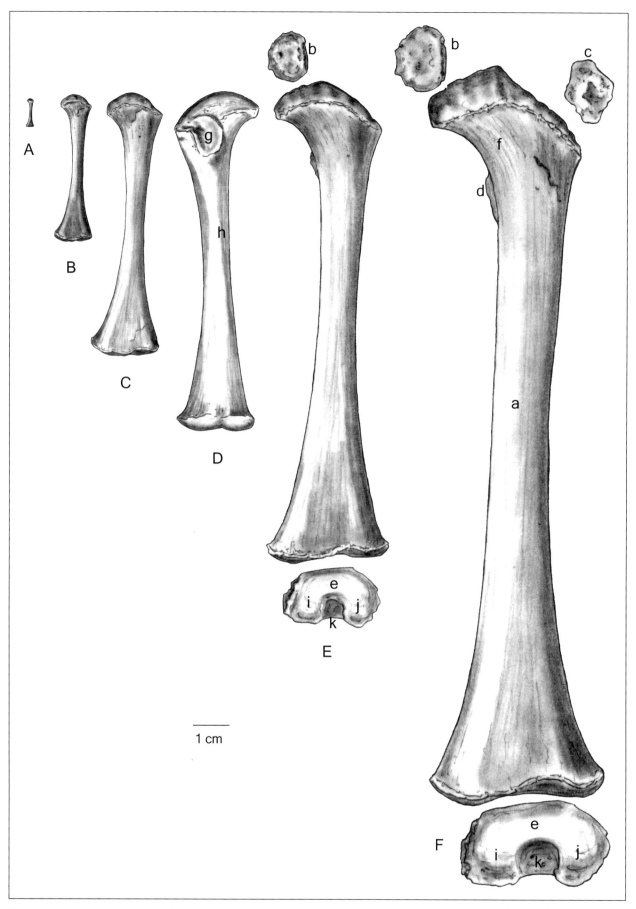

Fig. 8.10 Left femur shown in actual size at approximate ages, A = first trimester, B = second trimester, C = third trimester, D = perinate, E = 1.5 years, F = 5 years: *a*, diaphysis; *b*, head; *c*, greater trochanter; *d*, lesser trochanter; *e*, distal epiphysis; *f*, neck; *g*, epiphyseal surface for lesser trochanter; *h*, linea aspera; *i*, medial condyle; *j*, lateral condyle; *k*, intercondylar fossa. All are shown in an anterior view except D, which is posterior.

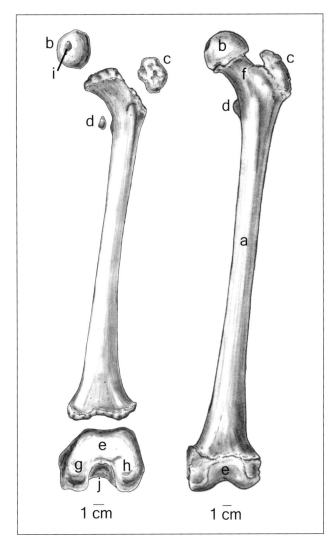

Fig. 8.11 Left femur, anterior view, at approximate ages, left = 9 years, right = 15 years: *a,* diaphysis; *b,* head; *c,* greater trochanter; *d,* lesser trochanter; *e,* distal epiphysis; *f,* neck; *g,* medial condyle; *h,* lateral condyle; *i,* fovea capitis; *j,* intercondylar fossa.

Differentiation from Other Bones. The femur is the longest bone in the human skeleton except during the first fetal trimester. Bones of similar size and thickness that may be confused with the femur at each stage of development are the humerus and the tibia. When all these bones are present (from the second trimester onward), the femur is the longest. If preservation is poor, or where multiple individuals are commingled, length alone cannot be used to distinguish the femur from a humerus or tibia.

For fetal and neonatal remains, the epiphyseal surface for the lesser trochanter (fig. 8.10g) is the most distinctive feature. Located on the posterior metaphysis at the proximal end of the bone, the presence of this roughened, ovoid surface identifies the bone as a femur. The medial curvature of the proximal humerus is similar, but the width of its metaphysis is much smaller and its posterior aspect is smooth and rounded. The proximal tibia is also flared medially, but is angulated anteriorly due to its protruding tuberosity. At midshaft, the femur is rounded anteriorly and shows a nutrient foramen posteriorly. The ridge of the linea aspera (fig. 8.10h) is variably developed but is evident along the lateral margin of the posterior shaft from the surface for the lesser trochanter to the flared distal end of the bone where it becomes the lateral supracondylar line. In contrast, the midshaft region of the humerus is smaller and rounder. The nutrient foramen and interosseous crest on the posterior tibia are easily mistaken for the features on the posterior femur. Note, however, that the tibial shaft is much more angular than that of the femur due to its well-developed anterior crest. The distal femur lacks the deep indentation that marks the posterior aspect of the distal humerus and is more flared and much wider than either the distal humerus or tibia.

In infancy and later stages, these characteristics continue to be useful in differentiating the femur from the humerus and tibia. In early childhood, the further development of the femoral neck (figs. 8.10f and 8.11f) and epiphyseal surface for the greater trochanter are key features that aid in identification of the bone. The proximal tibia, though flared, is straight up and down, while the humerus curves only slightly medially. Only the femur shows the elongated medial extension at the proximal extremity of the shaft.

Femoral epiphyses can generally be easily distinguished from those of other bones. An exception is in the early stages of ossification of the femoral head, when it lacks the development of the fovea capitis and more closely resembles the humeral head. The femoral head, however, is larger and more rounded than the humeral head from the same individual, and the latter has a notable hooked projection. The crescent shape of the greater trochanter is distinctive in its early development. By late childhood, the trochanteric fossa is evident and the epiphysis resembles its adult shape by puberty. Its lack of articular surfaces aids in its identification at all stages. When recovered, the small epiphysis for the lesser trochanter is an ovoid cap, unlike most other long bone epiphyses. The medial epicondyle of the humerus is similar in appearance, but it is much smaller than the lesser trochanter epiphysis.

The distal epiphysis of the femur is one of the most easily identified epiphyses at most stages of development because it begins to ossify before birth, at which point it is an indistinct oval marked by numerous foramina. At this stage, it can be confused with the proximal tibial epiphysis, which appears just before or immediately after birth and is, therefore, similar in size and shape. To separate these epiphyses confidently requires careful recovery and labeling in the field. During infancy and early childhood, the distal femoral epiphysis begins to develop recogniz-

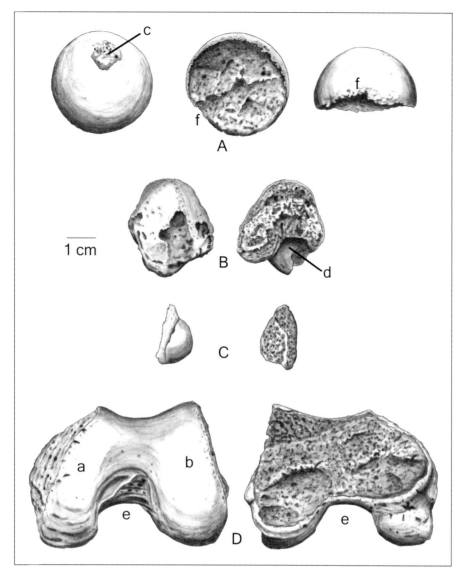

Fig. 8.12 Left femoral epiphyses for the head (*A*), greater trochanter (*B*), lesser trochanter (*C*), and distal end (*D*): *a*, medial condyle; *b*, lateral condyle; *c*, fovea capitis; *d*, trochanteric fossa; *e*, intercondylar fossa; *f*, notch.

able articular condyles that are separated by the indentation of the intercondylar fossa (figs. 8.10k, 8.11j, and 8.12e), thereby distinguishing it from the flatter proximal tibial epiphysis.

Siding Techniques. For a neonatal femur, determining which side the bone is from is most easily accomplished by locating the surface for the lesser trochanter (fig. 8.10g) on the posterior aspect and holding the bone in standard anatomical position (see fig. 8.10D). The proximal end curves medially, opposite the side to which the bone belongs. Thus, if you view the anterior aspect of the bone with the lesser trochanter surface up and away from you, the neck (figs. 8.10f and 8.11f) and head curve toward the side from which the bone comes (see fig. 8.10E). This siding technique works for all ages.

In early childhood, another method is to orient the bone in anatomical position and note that the surface for the greater trochanter is toward the side to which the bone belongs. Distally, even in neonates, the bone flares more medially and is somewhat straighter laterally. The ridge of the linea aspera extends distally into the lateral supracondylar line, sweeping toward the side from which the bone comes. These features continue to aid in siding the femur throughout childhood.

Femoral epiphyses generally cannot be sided until early childhood and, even then, siding is quite difficult. For these reasons, careful excavation and bagging of epiphyses with each bone in the field is imperative. In late childhood and adolescence, femoral epiphyses are more easily identified and sided as they develop their adult morphology. Nonetheless, bagging the epiphyses by side while in the field will save time and possible misidentification in the lab.

To side the head, note that the fovea capitis (figs. 8.11i and 8.12c) is medial, but displaced posteriorly. Place the articular surface on a table with the fovea capitis facing directly away from you. A slight notch (fig. 8.12f) is present on the border of the metaphyseal surface that is facing you. This notch is toward the side to which the bone belongs.

The greater trochanter (fig. 8.12B) is irregular in shape, with a flat and rough metaphyseal side and bulbous body, and a deep notch for the trochanteric fossa (fig. 8.12d) on one side. To side a separate greater trochanter, hold the bone with the pointed end up and the fossa toward you. The body of the epiphysis is on the side from which the bone comes. Another method is to hold the epiphysis with the pointed end up and the bulbous projection toward you. In this view, the notch is opposite the side it is from while the superior projection is on the side to which the epiphysis belongs. Alternatively, place the metaphyseal surface on a table with the notch for the trochanteric fossa facing away from you. The larger side of the epiphysis represents the side to which the bone belongs. In older children, the greater trochanter is more developed and the trochanteric fossa is not visible from the nonmetaphyseal surface. In this case, hold the metaphyseal surface toward you and the fossa pointing down (see fig. 8.12B, right). In this view, the metaphyseal surface looks similar to the outline of a horse's head, with a long nose projecting to one side. The metaphyseal surface or nose of the horse is thicker and extends more toward you on the side from which the epiphysis comes.

To side the distal epiphysis (fig. 8.12D), orient it with the metaphyseal surface on the table, the articular surface up, and the depression or notch separating the condyles, the intercondylar fossa (fig. 8.12e), away from you. The edge of the intercondylar fossa is curved more on the medial side and is much straighter on the lateral side, or the side to which the epiphysis belongs. Note also that the articular surface extends toward you on the side from which the bone comes. Another way to side the bone is to place the metaphyseal surface up, the articular surface on the table, and face the intercondylar fossa toward you (see fig. 8.12D, right). On the edge farthest from you, the margin slopes upward and farther away from you on the side to which the epiphysis belongs.

The Tibia

Description at Major Stages. The tibia (figs. 8.13–8.15) is the larger of the lower leg bones. In standard anatomical position the tibia lies on the medial side. It articulates proximally with the femur and the fibula, and distally with the fibula and the talus. The growing tibia consists of a shaft (figs. 8.13a and 8.14a) and proximal and distal epiphyses (figs. 8.13b, c, 8.14b, c, and 8.15). During the first trimester, the tibia begins as a cartilage model and starts to ossify during the eighth week in utero (fig. 8.13A). Toward the end of the third trimester the proximal epiphysis also begins to ossify. The identification of this epiphysis can be used to identify a full-term infant in archaeological and forensic contexts. The distal epiphysis does not typically begin to ossify until the second year of life.

The tibial shaft displays distinct morphological characteristics from the time of ossification. A unilateral flare is present on one end of the bone. This flare distinguishes the proximal end from the distal end, which is narrower and straighter. The metaphyseal surface of the distal end of the shaft is somewhat rhomboid shaped, while the proximal metaphyseal surface displays a rounded edge opposite a more pointed edge. A very large nutrient foramen is present and denotes the posterior aspect of the proximal third of the shaft. The anterior surface displays a pronounced ridge (the anterior crest) that corresponds to the shin.

During early development, the proximal epiphysis appears as a porous, oval nodule. By 3 to 4 years of age, the articular surfaces begin to become distinct and the epiphysis as a whole appears somewhat kidney shaped. The intercondylar eminence (figs. 8.13d, 8.14d, and 8.15a) becomes observable around this time as a bulge or slight bumps between the developing articular condyles. These features gradually become more distinct as growth continues and the articular surfaces become smoother throughout childhood. During early adolescence, the proximal epiphysis is identified by the presence of a large tuberosity that extends perpendicular to the condylar surface. This perpendicular projection is known as the tibial tuberosity (fig. 8.14e) and identifies the anterior and lateral aspect of the bone. Directly behind the tuberosity, on the posterior aspect of the epiphysis, is a smooth, oval articular facet. This facet represents the articulation for the proximal end of the fibula. The distal portion of the tibial tuberosity does not unite with the proximal epiphysis until 12 to 14 years of age. The proximal epiphysis fuses typically between 13 and 17 years in females and between 15 and 19 in males.

The metaphyseal surface of the distal epiphysis (fig. 8.15B), like all others, has a roughened texture where it joins the growth plate, but it also displays a small ridge that identifies the medial aspect of the bone. The articular surface appears smooth and concave. Overall, this epiphysis is somewhat square or rhomboid shaped like the distal end of the shaft. As growth occurs, the shape of the epiphysis changes as one corner of the square begins to

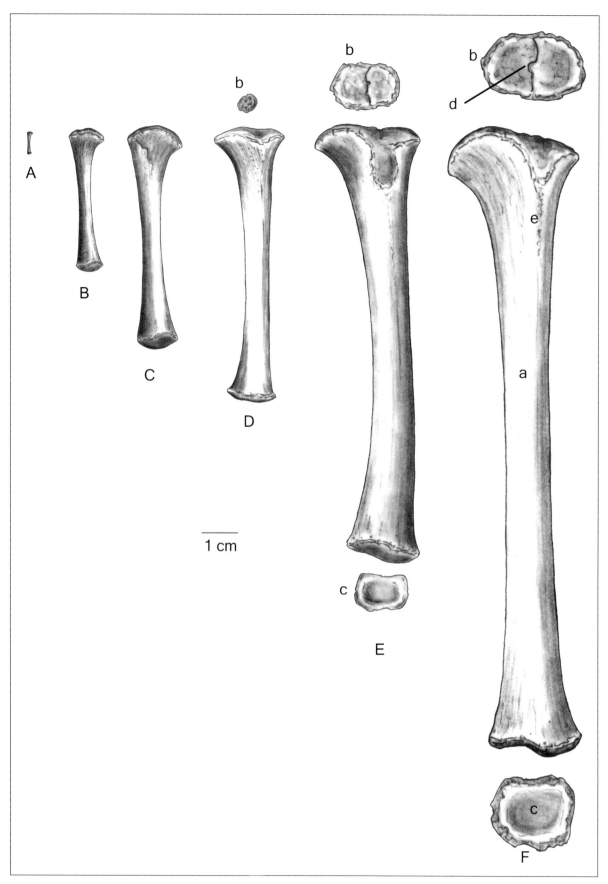

Fig. 8.13 Left tibia shown in actual size at approximate ages, *A* = first trimester, *B* = second trimester, *C* = third trimester, *D* = perinate, *E* = 1.5 years, *F* = 5 years: *a*, diaphysis; *b*, proximal epiphysis; *c*, distal epiphysis; *d*, intercondylar eminence; *e*, anterior crest. *A–C* shown in a posterior view; *D–F*, in anterior.

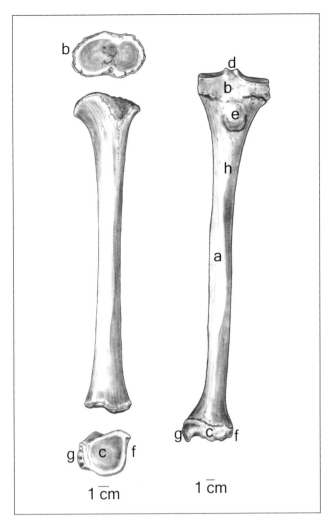

Fig. 8.14 Left tibia, anterior view at approximate ages, left = 9 years, right = 15 years: *a*, diaphysis; *b*, proximal epiphysis; *c*, distal epiphysis; *d*, intercondylar eminence; *e*, tibial tuberosity; *f*, fibular notch; *g*, medial malleolus; *h*, anterior crest.

project outward at an angle of approximately 45 degrees. This projection represents what eventually becomes the fibular notch (figs. 8.14f and 8.15b) and identifies the anterior and lateral aspect of the bone. On the opposite (i.e., medial) side of the projection, an outgrowth of bone begins to appear by 3 or 4 years of age that represents the developing medial malleolus (figs. 8.14g and 8.15c). By adolescence, the fibular notch and medial malleolus are distinct and useful in identifying the lateral and medial aspects, respectively. The distal epiphysis fuses to the diaphysis between 14 and 16 years in females and between 15 and 18 in males.

Differentiation from Other Bones. Bones of similar size and thickness that may be confused with the tibia at each stage of development are the humerus and the femur. The tibia and humerus are similar in length and diameter until approximately 1 year of age. At this stage, the tibia becomes

the longer bone. The nutrient foramen on the tibia is typically very large relative to those on the other long bones. The tibia lacks the large indentation, the olecranon fossa, that characterizes the distal end of the humerus. A distinction from other long bones is the sharp ridge present on the anterior surface of the tibia. This anterior crest (figs. 8.13e and 8.14h) gives the tibia a cross section that is typically triangular at one end and square at the other. In contrast, the humerus is round at one end and flattened at the other. The femur is always longer than the tibia at each developmental stage, and this helps distinguish the bones when both are present. The proximal ends of the tibia and femur flare medially and can be easily confused unless other features, such as the billowy surface for the lesser trochanter, are considered. It helps to remember that the distal end of the tibia is square (or rhomboid shaped), whereas it is flattened and flared both medially and laterally in the femur. The cross section of a femur shaft is more rounded than that of the tibia; as the linea aspera develops, it becomes teardrop shaped rather than triangular like the tibia. In infancy and later stages, these characteristics continue to be useful in differentiating the tibia from the humerus and femur. In early childhood, the further development of the femoral neck and surface for the greater trochanter are key features that distinguish it from the tibia. The proximal tibia, though flared like a proximal humerus, has a bulge on the anterior surface and lacks the indentation that represents the intertubercular groove of the proximal humerus.

Differentiating the tibial epiphyses from other long bone epiphyses is most difficult early in development when the proximal epiphysis is generally the same size and shape as that of the distal femoral epiphysis (fig. 8.13D, b). By early childhood, however, it can be separated by its oval shape and its flatness. The smooth articular surfaces and small bumps marking the intercondylar eminence develop throughout childhood and become the primary features for recognition (fig. 8.15A). The distal epiphysis (fig. 8.15B) is initially round to oval but is flatter than the epiphyses for the femur and humerus. In shape, it more closely resembles the epiphysis of the distal radius, but the latter is much smaller.

Siding Techniques. Determining the side for a perinatal tibia is most easily accomplished by identifying the nutrient foramen on the proximal third of the posterior surface. Hold the tibia either with the posterior surface facing you and the nutrient foramen toward the top, or with the anterior crest (figs. 8.13e and 8.14h) up and the distal end pointing away from you. The proximal end flares on one side, while the other side is straighter and marks the side from which the bone comes. The same holds true for the distal end of the shaft. Also, the nutrient foramen typically dominates one half of the posterior surface over the other and is on the side to which the bone belongs.

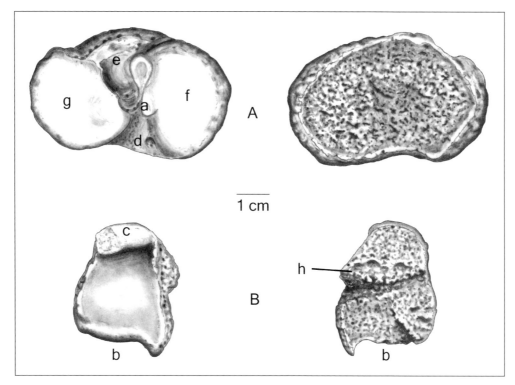

Fig. 8.15 Left tibial epiphyses for the proximal (A) and distal (B) ends: *a*, intercondylar eminence; *b*, fibular notch; *c*, medial malleolus; *d*, posterior intercondylar fossa; *e*, anterior intercondylar fossa; *f*, medial condyle; *g*, lateral condyle; *h*, bump for siding.

The anterior surface can be used to side the bone and is useful especially when only the tibial shaft is present. If you can determine the proximal and distal aspects of the shaft, hold the proximal end up with the anterior surface facing you. The anterior border curves distally toward the side to which the bone belongs. These features continue to aid in siding the tibia throughout childhood.

Tibial epiphyses generally cannot be sided until early childhood and, even then, siding is quite difficult. In late childhood and adolescence, tibial epiphyses are more easily identified and sided as they attain their adult morphology. To side the proximal epiphysis, first orient it in standard anatomical position by placing the metaphyseal surface on a table and the straighter side with the smaller indentation or fossa (fig. 8.15d) toward you (see fig. 8.15A, left). The rounded side with the larger fossa (fig. 8.15e) is, therefore, away from you. The larger fossa angles anteriorly and laterally, or toward the side from which the bone comes. As in adults, the medial condyle (fig. 8.15f) is an oval with its long axis oriented anteroposteriorly (front to back as you view it in this position). The lateral condyle (fig. 8.15g) is smaller and rounder, projecting in a mediolateral axis (side to side) toward the side to which the epiphysis belongs. Another way to side the proximal epiphysis is to place the metaphyseal surface on the table with the little, central notch or indentation away from you. In this orientation, the anterior part

of the epiphysis is now facing you. The raised portion in the middle, the intercondylar eminence (fig. 8.15a), is larger, higher, and thicker on the side to which the bone belongs. In addition, the side of bone that extends farther away from you is on the side from which the bone comes. In this view, the larger articular surface is also on the side to which the bone belongs.

To side the distal epiphysis (fig. 8.15B), place the articular surface on a table with the thicker (medial) side away from you. The side with the larger bump (fig. 8.15h) on the thick part indicates the side from which the bone comes (the bump is anterior and medial). Also, the protruding portion (anterior) of bone that is toward you points to the side from which the epiphysis comes. Alternatively, place the articular surface facing up and the raised edge for the medial malleolus (fig. 8.15c) toward you. On the end facing away from you, the edge protrudes outward on the side to which the bone belongs.

The Fibula

Description at Major Stages. The fibula (figs. 8.16–8.18) is located in the lower leg and is the thinnest of the leg bones. In standard anatomical position, it is lateral to the tibia. It articulates proximally with the tibia, and distally with the tibia and the talus. The growing fibula consists of a shaft (figs. 8.16a and 8.17a) and a proximal and

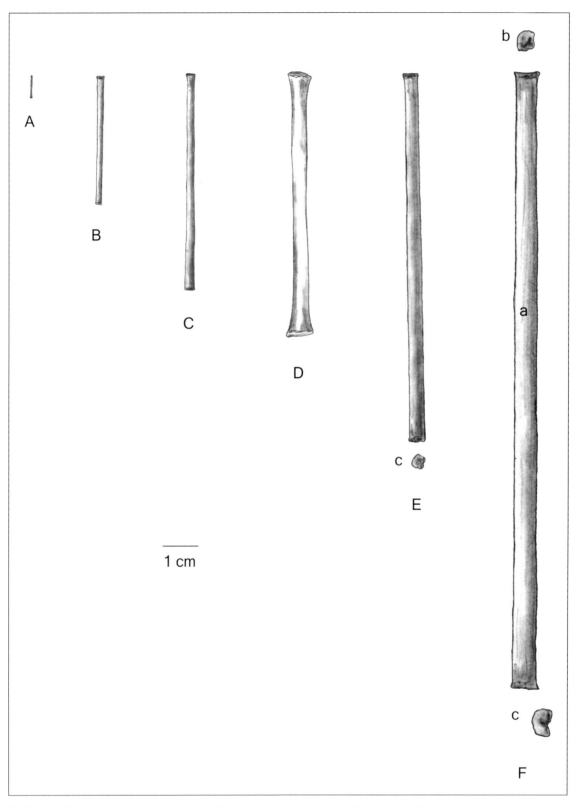

Fig. 8.16 Left fibula, anterior view, shown in actual size at approximate ages, A = first trimester, B = second trimester, C = third trimester, D = perinate, E = 1.5 years, F = 5 years: a, diaphysis; b, proximal epiphysis; c, distal epiphysis.

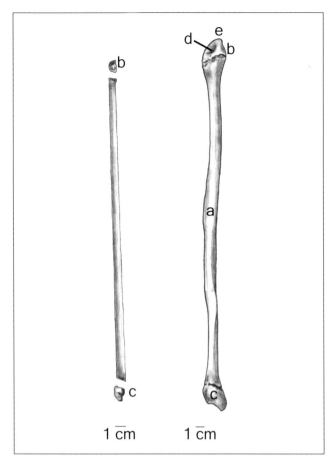

Fig. 8.17 Left fibula, anterior view, at approximate ages, left = 9 years, right = 15 years: *a*, diaphysis; *b*, proximal epiphysis; *c*, distal epiphysis; *d*, articular facet for tibia; *e*, styloid process.

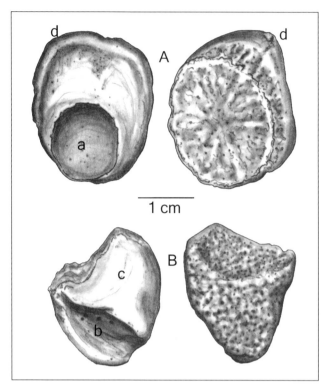

Fig. 8.18 Left fibular epiphyses for the proximal (*A*) and distal (*B*) ends: *a*, articular facet for tibia; *b*, malleolar fossa; *c*, articular facet for talus; *d*, styloid process.

distal epiphysis (figs. 8.16b, c, 8.17b, c, and 8.18). During the first trimester, the fibula begins as a cartilage model and starts to ossify during the eighth week in utero (fig. 8.16A). The proximal epiphysis begins to ossify around 4 years of age in females and around 5 in males. The distal epiphysis typically begins to ossify between the ages of 1 and 2 years.

The fibular diaphysis is distinct from the time of ossification in that it has a minimum of distinguishing features. In other words, a lack of morphological characteristics sets the fibula apart from the other long bones. It is a very straight and narrow bone with a circular cross section from the proximal end toward the midshaft. The distal end displays a more oval cross section. No flaring is present at either end. The nutrient foramen, located in the middle of the diaphysis, enters in a distal direction, away from the knee.

The proximal epiphysis (fig. 8.18A) typically displays a circular, roughened metaphyseal surface bordered by nonarticular areas. The articular facet for the tibia (figs. 8.17d and 8.18a) forms a circle in the middle of the

epiphysis but borders toward the posterior aspect. The proximal epiphysis typically fuses between 12 and 18 years in females and between 15 and 20 in males.

The distal epiphysis (fig. 8.18B) has a flat metaphyseal surface on one end, opposite a more rounded nonarticular surface on the other. A fossa is present by around 6 years of age and is situated below an articular facet. This indentation is the malleolar fossa (fig. 8.18b) and the facet is the articulation for the talus (fig. 8.18c). On the opposite side of these two features, a roughened and convex nonarticular area is present. These features become more distinct as growth continues. The distal epiphysis fuses between 12 and 16 years in females and between 15 and 18 in males.

Differentiation from Other Bones. The radius and ulna are the most likely bones to be confused with the fibula at each stage of development. The fibular shaft is narrower than the bones of the forearm. Its ends are also narrower than the radius in proportion to the shaft and do not flare as much. For fetal and neonatal remains, the proximal end of the ulna is easily distinguishable from the fibula because the ulna possesses the trochlear notch and displays a thickened proximal end, whereas the fibula is straight and narrow throughout its diaphysis. This characteristic straight and narrow shaft also distinguishes the fibula from the radius, which has a bilaterally flared distal end and the radial tuberosity on the proximal end. In more mature juveniles, the fibula is typically irregular in cross section at the midshaft, more circular in cross section near the proximal end, and oval in cross section at the distal end.

The epiphyses are usually not difficult to identify because they begin to ossify later than some of the other epiphyses with which they might be confused. Thus, the initial stages of ossification in which the epiphyses are small, bubbly nodules of bone occur later than those of other leg bone epiphyses. The proximal epiphysis does not attain its characteristic adult shape until late in childhood, when the articular facet for the tibia and the projecting styloid process (fig. 8.17e and 8.18d) distinguish it. The distal epiphysis is recognizable at an earlier age. It is somewhat bulbous in shape with a flat metaphyseal surface. By about age 6, the articular surface and malleolar fossa are well developed and aid in both identification and siding of the epiphysis.

Siding Techniques. The perinatal fibula is the hardest of all the long bones to side. However, several approaches help in this difficult task. First, the proximal metaphysis is distinguishable from the distal metaphysis in that the former is more circular and smaller in diameter than the latter, which is more ovoid. The nutrient foramen most often occurs on the medial aspect of the midshaft. Hold the distal end away from you and the nutrient foramen facing up. In this position, the side of the distal end that has a smooth ligamentous attachment is the side to which the

bone belongs. To double-check, rotate the bone so that the smooth, ligamentous attachment faces down. The distal end also flares toward the side from which the bone comes. These features continue to aid in siding the fibula throughout childhood.

To side the proximal epiphysis (fig. 8.18A), place the metaphyseal surface on a table with the tibial articular facet (fig. 8.18a) facing you. The styloid process (fig. 8.18d) is on the side to which the bone belongs. Alternatively, place the articular surface on the table with the straight edge away from you. The styloid process is again on the side from which the bone comes.

To side the distal epiphysis (fig. 8.18B) hold the metaphyseal surface up and the smooth articular surface (fig. 8.18c) toward you (see fig. 8.18B, left). The indentation for the malleolar fossa (fig. 8.18b) is on the side from which the epiphysis comes. Thus, if the fossa is to the left of the articular facet, the epiphysis is from a left fibula. Alternatively, place the metaphyseal surface on a table with the articular surface facing you. The articular surface is on the side the bone is from (in this view, the fossa is on the opposite side to which the bone belongs).

The Patella

Description at Major Stages. The patella or kneecap (fig. 8.19) is located in the middle of the leg. It articulates only with the distal end of the femur. The patella begins as a cartilage model during the seventh to eighth week in utero. The patella mineralizes from multiple ossification centers, typically between 18 months and 6 years. It is

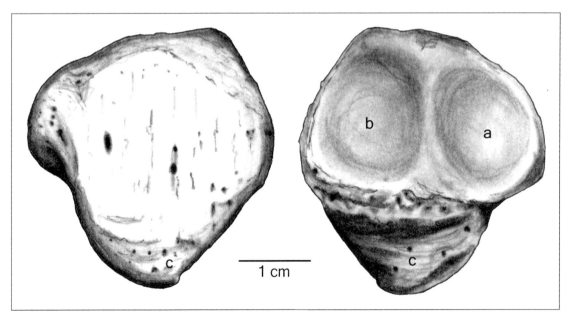

Fig. 8.19 Left patella of an adolescent, left = anterior, right = posterior: *a*, medial articular surface; *b*, lateral articular surface; *c*, apex.

often not present until age 4 or 5. As it first begins to ossify, the patella is an oval disk of bone. As growth progresses, the patella becomes more triangular. It develops a rough, nonarticular surface on its anterior aspect where the quadriceps femoris tendon attaches. On the opposite or posterior surface, two articular facets (fig. 8.19a, b) are separated by a slight rise or convexity, although these may not be distinct until late in childhood. The larger of the two articular facets is located on the lateral side. These surfaces articulate with the distal epiphysis of the femur. Inferior to these articular surfaces is a small, triangular nonarticular area known as the apex (fig. 8.19c) that extends inferiorly. Generally, the patella develops its adult morphology just prior to or during adolescence.

Differentiation from Other Bones. During early development, the patella may be confused with some of the long bone epiphyses such as the forming humeral and femoral heads. Unlike those epiphyses, the patella does not have a metaphyseal surface; instead, it presents a smooth articular surface on one side, while the opposite side displays a roughened, somewhat porous surface. Once the patella develops its adult morphology, it is distinct from all other bones of the skeleton.

Siding Techniques. Siding the patella is difficult until some of the adult morphology is present, which may not occur until late childhood or early adolescence. Identification and labeling of a developing patella during excavation is essential. When the articular facets (fig. 8.19a, b) and the apex (fig. 8.19c) are present, however, siding a patella is relatively simple. Place the articular surfaces of the patella on the table with the apex facing away from you. The patella falls to the side to which the bone belongs.

Chapter 9   The Bones of the Hands and Feet

■ The bones of the hands and feet are treated together in this chapter because of the similarity in their development and in the characteristics of the bones that comprise these appendages. Because hand and foot bones are likely to be confused, this chapter emphasizes their differentiation at various stages. Their indistinct appearance at early phases of development renders it imperative to excavate and bag these small bones in subadult burials very carefully in the field.

The Bones of the Hand

Each human hand consists of twenty-seven separate bones, eight of which form the wrist (the carpals) and nineteen that form the palm (metacarpals) and fingers (phalanges). The five metacarpals are numbered by ray (bones that form each digit). The first ray (which forms the thumb) is the most lateral in standard anatomical position with the palm face up, and the fifth (little finger side) is the most medial. Each finger (rays 2 through 5) has three separate phalanges, the proximal (which articulate with the metacarpals), the intermediate, and the distal, while the thumb (ray 1) only has proximal and distal phalanges. In addition, the hand also possesses additional small bones called sesamoids. These bones are found within tendons. There are typically two sesamoids in each hand, located at the base of the thumb, under the head of the first metacarpal.

In standard anatomical position, the palm of the hand faces forward so that the little finger is toward the leg and the thumb points away from the body. In this position, the bones of the forearm are not crossed. The anterior portion of the hand is known as the palmar or volar aspect, while the back of the hand is the dorsal or posterior aspect. The proximal aspect of each bone is that which is closest to the forearm, while the distal aspect is toward the tips of the fingers.

At birth, only the shafts of the metacarpals and phalanges are present. The wrist is generally cartilaginous until a few months after birth. By age 4, in both males and females, all the epiphyses have formed and centers for at least four carpals have appeared. By age 10, all bones of the hand are present, but fusion of the epiphyses is not complete until about 14 to 17 years, depending on the sex of the individual.

Carpals

The wrist is organized into two rows of four carpals each. The proximal row (from lateral to medial in standard anatomical position) consists of the scaphoid, lunate, triquetral, and pisiform (see figs. 9.1–9.4); the distal row consists of the trapezium, trapezoid, capitate, and hamate (see figs. 9.5–9.8). The proximal and distal rows articulate with each other, forming the midcarpal joint. The proximal surfaces of the scaphoid and lunate contribute to the radiocarpal or wrist joint, while the distal surfaces of the trapezium, trapezoid, capitate, and hamate provide articulations for the carpometacarpal joints.

The carpals all ossify endochondrally from one or two centers and usually do not appear until after birth. Carpals ossify earlier in females than males, initially with only a few months difference in timing, but ending with a gap of 2 years by the time the pisiform ossifies. The capitate and hamate are the first to appear in infancy. These are the only carpals present at 1 year of age. The triquetral begins to ossify in the following year. By age 5, all but the trapezoid, scaphoid, and pisiform are ossified in males, while in females all but the pisiform are present. By age 6, only the pisiform has not begun to ossify in males. Around age 8 or 9 in females and 10 to 11 in males, the center for the pisiform, along with the sesamoids for the thumb, make an appearance. Typically, by puberty, the carpals display their distinct adult features, and they generally reach their adult size by age 12 to 13 in females and 15 in boys.

Scaphoid. The scaphoid (fig. 9.1), sometimes called the navicular of the hand, is the most lateral carpal in the proximal row. It is the second largest carpal. It articulates proximally with the radius, distally with the trapezium, trapezoid, and capitate, and medially with the lunate. The scaphoid does not typically appear until 5 years of age in females and 6 years of age in males, and becomes identifiable by 9 years in females and 11 years in males. Prior to this time, it is an undifferentiated, rounded nodule of bone. In a mature or nearly mature scaphoid, one side is dominated by a large, concave articular facet for the capitate (fig. 9.1a). It is bordered by a slightly convex articulation for the lunate (fig. 9.1b). On the opposite side, there is a convex surface that has two articular facets, one for the radius (fig. 9.1c) and the other for the trapezium and trapezoid (fig. 9.1d, e), divided by a nonarticular groove or indentation (fig. 9.1f). This feature accentuates the shape of one end where the blunt nonarticular projection of the scaphoid tubercle (fig. 9.1g) is located.

Differentiation from Other Bones. Except for its larger size, the immature scaphoid is difficult to distinguish from the trapezium and trapezoid that ossify around the same time. Prior to development of its adult morphology, it can be separated from the carpals that develop earlier by its lack of defined features. The mature scaphoid has very distinct morphology. The only bone that is somewhat similar is the navicular bone of the foot. Although the navicular is similar in form, it is always considerably larger than the scaphoid.

Siding Techniques. To side the scaphoid, hold the concave capitate surface (fig. 9.1a) toward you, with the lunate surface (fig. 9.1b) pointing down and the tubercle (fig. 9.1g) at the top. The scaphoid tubercle points to the side from which the bone comes. Another method is to hold the bone so the long horizontal ridge and groove (fig. 9.1f) face you, with the convex facet up and the facets for the trapezium and trapezoid (fig. 9.1d, e) pointing down. The tubercle is, again, on the side to which the bone belongs (see fig. 9.1, left).

Lunate. The lunate (fig. 9.2) derives its name from its shape like a crescent moon. It articulates laterally with the scaphoid, proximally with the radius, and distally with the capitate, hamate, and triquetral. The lunate appears around age 3 in females and 4 in males, becoming identifiable between 9 and 10 years of age.

The lunate has a distinct half-moon shape because of a large concave surface dominating one side of the bone. The concave articular surface is for the capitate (fig. 9.2a), and it is bordered by a small articular lip for the hamate (fig. 9.2b), adjacent to which is a flat, square to oval articular facet for the triquetral (fig. 9.2c). To one side is the crescent-shaped articulation for the scaphoid (fig. 9.2d). A large, convex articular surface for the radius (fig. 9.2e) is proximal to the concavity.

Differentiation from Other Bones. Before the alar portions of the first sacral vertebra (and sometimes the alar centers for S2) have fused, they look quite similar to a lunate. An unfused ala is usually as large, or larger, than an adult lunate because this component of the sacrum begins to ossify in fetal development. Since it fuses between 2 and 5 years to other sacral elements, it is unlikely to be mistaken for a lunate in its early stages of ossification in a

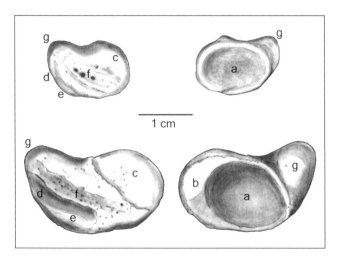

Fig. 9.1 Left scaphoid of an older child (c. 8 years, *top*) and adolescent (c. 15 years, *bottom*): *a*, capitate facet; *b*, lunate facet; *c*, radial facet; *d*, trapezium facet; *e*, trapezoid facet; *f*, nonarticular groove; *g*, tubercle.

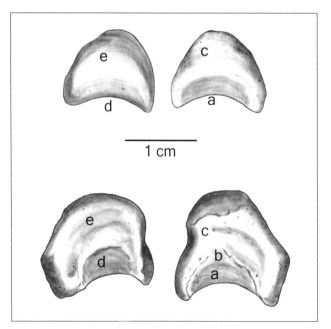

Fig. 9.2 Left lunate of an older child (c. 8 years, *top*) and adolescent (c. 15 years, *bottom*): *a*, capitate facet; *b*, hamate facet; *c*, triquetral facet; *d*, scaphoid facet; *e*, radial facet.

single individual. In situations where subadult remains are commingled, note that the alar elements do not display articular facets that are present on the lunate.

Siding Techniques. To side the lunate, place the rectangular triquetral facet (fig. 9.2c) on a table with the concave capitate surface (fig. 9.2a) away from you. The scaphoid surface (fig. 9.2d) faces up and is mostly on the side to which the bone belongs. Alternatively, place the large, convex radial surface (fig. 9.2e) on the table with the concave capitate surface facing toward you and the rectangular triquetral surface facing up (see fig. 9.2, right). The triquetral surface is displaced toward the side from which the bone comes.

Triquetral. Sometimes called the triangular in older texts, the triquetral (fig. 9.3) articulates proximally with the lunate, laterally with the hamate, and anteriorly (on the palmar aspect) with the pisiform. The timing of the appearance of this bone is somewhat variable, ossifying anywhere from 1 to 3 years of age. It is the third carpal to appear. The bone becomes recognizably triangular shortly after its initial appearance, but it is usually not identifiable in the absence of other carpals until 8 to 10 years of age.

The triquetral has somewhat flattened edges, giving it four to five different sides for a pyramidal shape. One side has a slight convexity and is dominated by a large articular surface for the hamate (fig. 9.3a). This facet is contiguous with the slightly smaller and flat facet for the lunate (fig. 9.3b). A small, ovoid articular surface for the pisiform (fig. 9.3c) may be present on the palmar sur-

face of the bone depending on the stage of development. The triquetral has one surface that is entirely nonarticular (fig. 9.3d).

Differentiation from Other Bones. The triquetral may be confused with the trapezium; however, the trapezium has an identifiable saddle-shaped articular surface for the first metacarpal that the triquetral does not possess. The trapezoid is similar in size and shape as it develops but has distinctive facets and nonarticular areas that give it a shape like a boot. Together, the geometrical straight edges distinguish the triquetral from other carpal bones.

Siding Techniques. To side the triquetral, hold the slightly concave surface for the hamate (fig. 9.3a) toward you with the oval facet for the pisiform (fig. 9.3c) facing up (see fig. 9.3, right). The pisiform articulation is on the side to which the bone belongs. In younger children, the pisiform facet may be poorly developed due to the late ossification of this carpal. Thus, siding the triquetral is more difficult but can be accomplished by holding the flat facet for the lunate (fig. 9.3b) toward you with the tapered part of the bone down and the largely nonarticular surface on which the pisiform facet (fig. 9.3c) develops up. The larger facet for the hamate is on the side from which the bone comes.

Pisiform. The pisiform (fig. 9.4) articulates directly with the triquetral. The pisiform is the last of the carpals to appear, around 8 to 9 years in females and 10 to 11 years in males. It is the smallest of the carpal bones and is named for its resemblance to the shape of a pea.

Differentiation from Other Bones. The pisiform may be confused at different phases of growth with other small, round bones such as the sesamoid bones or the vertebral centra. Because the pisiform ossifies late in childhood, it is unlikely to be mistaken for other bones within the skeleton of a single individual. In the case of commingled subadult remains, the mature pisiform is generally indis-

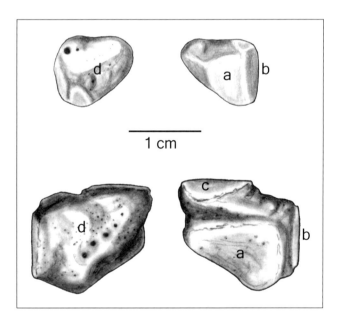

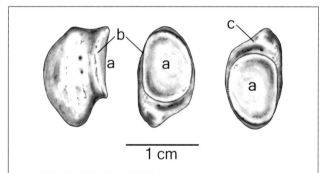

Fig. 9.3 Left triquetral of an older child (c. 8 years, *top*) and adolescent (c. 15 years, *bottom*): *a*, hamate facet; *b*, lunate facet; *c*, pisiform facet; *d*, nonarticular surface.

Fig. 9.4 Left pisiform of an adolescent (c. 15 years): *a*, triquetral facet; *b*, facet tends to hang over; *c*, indentation with vascular foramina.

tinct compared to developing vertebral centra or epiphyses for long bones. It is small in comparison to most epiphyses, lacks a metaphyseal surface, and can be distinguished by the presence of the small, oval articular facet for the triquetral (fig. 9.4a).

Siding Techniques. Siding the pisiform prior to development of adult morphology depends on accurate labeling during excavation. Even when the bone has attained adult morphology, it is difficult to side. To do so, hold the facet toward you and at the top, with the nonarticular area down (see fig. 9.4, middle). The facet points or hangs over toward the side to which the bone belongs (fig. 9.4b). Alternatively, hold the facet toward you with the bulk of the nonarticular area at the top. There is an indentation, which often shows small vascular foramina, in the nonarticular area on the side from which the bone comes (fig. 9.4c). This technique, not highly reliable by itself, provides a good check for the first siding method. It is recommended that both techniques be used together to ensure proper siding.

Trapezium. The trapezium (fig. 9.5) is the most lateral carpal in the distal row. It is often referred to in older texts as the greater multangular. It articulates distally with the first metacarpal, proximally with the scaphoid, and medially with the trapezoid. The trapezium appears around 4 years of age in females and 5 years in males. By 9 years in females and 10 years in males, the trapezium can be identified by its distinctive features.

The trapezium displays a saddle-shaped, concave articular facet for the first metacarpal (fig. 9.5a). Early in

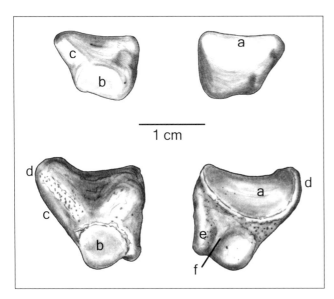

Fig. 9.5 Left trapezium of an older child (c. 8 years, *top*) and adolescent (c. 15 years, *bottom*): *a,* first metacarpal facet; *b,* scaphoid facet; *c,* trapezoid facet; *d,* second metacarpal facet; *e,* tubercle; *f,* groove.

development, the bone appears bulbous, with very little adult morphology. Later, it looks like a cube with a triangle attached. On the opposite side of the saddle facet is a somewhat square surface (on the cube portion) where there is an articular surface for the scaphoid (fig. 9.5b). On the triangular part adjacent to the facet for the scaphoid is another articular surface for the trapezoid (fig. 9.5c). Extending distomedially from the trapezoid surface, another small articular surface may develop for the second metacarpal (fig. 9.5d), but it may not be present until adolescence. A small tubercle (fig. 9.5e) with an adjacent groove for the flexor carpi radialis (fig. 9.5f) is located at the opposite (proximal and lateral) end of the bone. The first metacarpal facet becomes more saddle shaped as development progresses.

Differentiation from Other Bones. The trapezium can be mistaken for the triquetral early in development due to the angularity and multiple articular facets on both bones. The saddle-shaped facet and projecting ridge or tubercle on the trapezium are diagnostic.

Siding Techniques. To side the trapezium, place the large saddle surface (fig. 9.5a) on a table with the square (cube) portion toward you and the triangular portion facing away from you. The trapezoid surface (fig. 9.5c) is on the side to which the bone belongs; the triangular projection also points to that side. Another method is to orient the bone with the tubercle (fig. 9.5e) at the top and facing toward you. The concave facets for the first metacarpal and the trapezoid are on each side. The groove (fig. 9.5f) next to the tubercle is on the side from which the bone comes. Thus, if the groove is to the left of the tubercle, it is a left trapezium.

Trapezoid. The trapezoid (fig. 9.6) articulates distally with the second metacarpal, proximally with the scaphoid, laterally with the trapezium, and medially with the capitate. In older textbooks, this bone is often called the lesser multangular. The trapezoid begins to ossify around the same time as the trapezium (at approximately age 4 in females and age 5 to 6 in males). By age 8 to 10, the bone is identifiable due to the development of the convex facet for the second metacarpal and the concave facet for the scaphoid.

By puberty, the trapezoid has its characteristic adult morphology and is shaped like a boot. There are four distinct articular areas and a large nonarticular area on the dorsal/posterior portion akin to the sole of the boot. Opposite the large nonarticular area on the palmar or volar aspect is a small nonarticular area at the top of the boot (fig. 9.6a) that separates the lateral facet for the trapezium (fig. 9.6b) and distal facet for the second metacarpal (fig. 9.6c). As development progresses, the nonarticular area takes on a V shape (fig. 9.6a) that is diagnostic of this bone and looks like an open zipper on the side of the boot. On the other, proximal, end of the trapezial surface is the articular facet for the scaphoid (fig. 9.6d). Adjacent to the scaphoid surface (toward the top half of the boot on the medial aspect) is a square articular facet for the capitate (fig. 9.6e).

Differentiation from Other Bones. The trapezoid is most often confused with the triquetral due to their similar size and somewhat triangular shape. The triquetral is more angular than the trapezoid and is distinguished at puberty by the round or oval facet for the pisiform. The trapezoid attains its boot shape with distinctive V-shaped nonarticular area by this time and is identifiable before this by its convex facet for the second metacarpal and broad, convex nonarticular area (sole of the boot).

Siding Techniques. To side the trapezoid, the easiest method is to place the V-shaped zipper (fig. 9.6a) toward you with the large, nonarticular surface or sole of the boot down (see fig. 9.6, left). The toe of the boot (fig. 9.6f) points toward the side to which the bone belongs. Note that some of the nonarticular Vs are zipped up farther than others. Alternatively, place the scaphoid surface (fig. 9.6d) on a table with the V-shaped nonarticular area (zipper) facing up, and the trapezium surface (fig. 9.6b) facing toward you. The side that the large nonarticular surface is on (sole of boot) is the side from which the bone comes.

Capitate. The capitate (fig. 9.7) is the largest carpal. It articulates proximally with the scaphoid and the lunate, distally with metacarpals 2, 3 and 4, laterally with the trapezoid, and medially with the hamate. It is the first carpal to ossify. The capitate is occasionally present at birth but usually appears between the second and fourth months after birth. Because it is the largest and the earliest to ossify, the capitate can be distinguished in relation to other developing carpals from the earliest stages of development. By 3 to 4 years of age, the distinctive morphology permits its recognition in the absence of other carpals.

The head (fig. 9.7a) of the capitate is very round and articulates with the scaphoid and lunate. Just distal to the convex and contiguous articular area of the head on the lateral aspect is a small facet for the trapezoid (fig. 9.7b), which is thus positioned between the head and the distal articular areas for the metacarpals. The distal end of the bone is somewhat triangular and displays slightly concave articular facets for the second (fig. 9.7c) and third metacarpals (fig. 9.7d). The facet for the fourth metacarpal (fig. 9.7e) is very small and is located at the dorsomedial edge of the bone, distal to the long, narrow facet for the hamate (fig. 9.7f). This articular area extends down the entire dorsal aspect of the medial side of the bone.

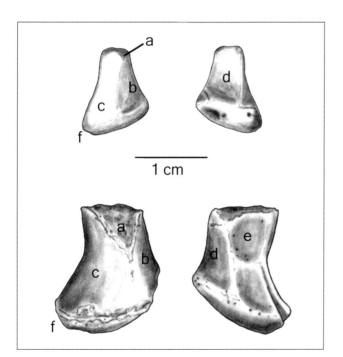

Fig. 9.6 Left trapezoid of an older child (c. 8 years, *top*) and adolescent (c. 15 years, *bottom*): *a,* V-shaped nonarticular area; *b,* trapezium facet; *c,* second metacarpal facet; *d,* scaphoid facet; *e,* capitate facet; *f,* toe of boot.

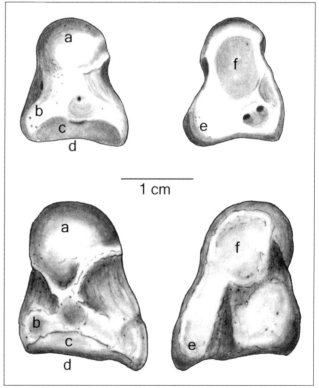

Fig. 9.7 Left capitate of an older child (c. 8 years, *top*) and adolescent (c. 15 years, *bottom*): *a,* head; *b,* trapezoid facet; *c,* second metacarpal facet; *d,* third metacarpal facet; *e,* fourth metacarpal facet; *f,* hamate facet.

The flow of the facet from the smooth head of the bone bears a resemblance to a facial profile with hair (hamate facet) flowing down to the shoulders or Darth Vader's helmet going back and over his head and to his shoulders. Thinking of the bone with Darth Vader in mind assists with siding it.

Differentiation from Other Bones. The capitate should not be confused with other carpals from a single individual at any stage of development because of its large size and distinctive head. It can be confused with other bones that have rounded heads (e.g., the talus) but it is much smaller than a tarsal or the heads and condyles of long bones. Unlike the long bone epiphyses, it has no billowy metaphyseal surface. The distinctive shape and articular facets readily distinguish the capitate from other bones.

Siding Techniques. To side the capitate, place the head (fig. 9.7a) up and the long, narrow articular facet for the hamate (fig. 9.7f) toward you (see fig. 9.7, right). The side on which the hamate articulation is located is the side to which the bone belongs. Thus, Darth Vader's helmet flows down to the shoulders on the side from which the bone comes.

Hamate. The hamate (fig. 9.8) is the most medial bone of the distal row of carpals. It articulates distally with the fourth and fifth metacarpals via a double facet, proximally to medially with the triquetral, and laterally with the capitate. A thin articular area for the lunate is present where the bone is wedged between the triquetral and capitate, giving it a somewhat triangular shape.

The hamate is the second carpal to begin ossification, first appearing at 3 to 4 months postnatally in females and 4 to 5 months in males. At this stage, it is a small, oval nodule like the capitate, though it is smaller. Around age 2, the hamate begins to develop its articular features and it can usually be identified separately by 4 years in females and 5 years in males. The most distinctive attribute of the bone is the projecting hook or hamulus (fig. 9.8a). This feature becomes distinct around age 10 to 11 years in females and 12 to 14 years in males, and the bone attains its adult size within a year or two thereafter.

The hamulus projects in an anterior or palmar direction and is on the medial aspect of the bone. Directly opposite the hamulus is a nonarticular surface that represents the posterior or dorsal aspect. This nonarticular surface is bordered on three sides by the articulations for the fourth and fifth metacarpals (fig. 9.8b, c), the triquetral (fig. 9.8d) and lunate (fig. 9.8e), and the capitate (fig. 9.8f). The capitate articulation is the only one of the three that shares its surface with nonarticular areas. The articular surface for the triquetral is longer and more concave than the articular area for the fourth and fifth metacarpals. A small articular strip at the narrow apex of the bone connects the triquetral and capitate surfaces. The triquetral surface is almost parallel to the capitate surface, while the fourth and fifth metacarpal surface lies between the other two, just under or distal to the hamulus. This articular area forms the short axis of the bone and is characterized by a double concavity because the two small articular facets are contiguous.

Differentiation from Other Bones. Once the hamulus has begun to develop, the hamate is unlikely to be confused with any other bone. Prior to age 10 or 12 (or in the occasional cases where the hamulus fails to develop), the hamate is distinguished by the double concavity for articulation with metacarpals on a short end of the bone, opposite a single, flat facet for the capitate.

Siding Techniques. Most siding techniques rely on the hamulus (fig. 9.8a), so the bone is difficult to side prior to its development. To side the hamate, hold the capitate surface (fig. 9.8f) away from you with the lunatotriquetral surface (fig. 9.8d, e) toward you and the fourth and fifth metacarpal facets (fig. 9.8b, c) facing up. The hamulus points toward the side to which the bone belongs. Another method is to place the large, dorsal nonarticular aspect down and the lunatotriquetral facet away from you (the facet for the capitate is toward you) with the hamulus pointing up. The hamulus and the metacarpal articular area are on the side from which the bone comes. This method can be used in the absence of a defined hamulus by noting that the indentation and small nonarticular area are above the lunatotriquetral facet. When that

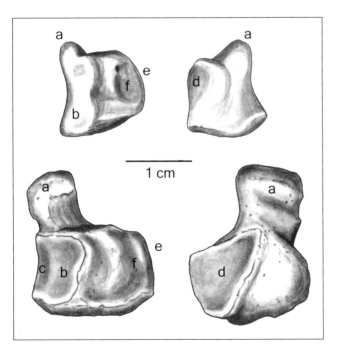

Fig. 9.8 Left hamate of an older child (c. 8 years, *top*) and adolescent (c. 15 years, *bottom*): *a,* hamulus; *b,* fourth metacarpal facet; *c,* fifth metacarpal facet; *d,* triquetral facet; *e,* lunate facet; *f,* capitate facet.

aspect is oriented up and away from you, the facets for the fourth and fifth metacarpals again indicate the side to which the bone belongs. Alternatively, place the dorsal nonarticular area down, the hamulus up, and the metacarpal surfaces toward you. The hamulus is on the side from which the bone comes. This technique also works if a small bump or bubbly area where the hamulus forms is identifiable or if the hamulus is present but not yet well developed.

Metacarpals

The metacarpals (fig. 9.9) are short, tubular bones distal to the carpals and proximal to the phalanges. Five metacarpals make up the palm of each hand. All metacarpal shafts (fig. 9.9a) begin to ossify between 8 and 10 fetal weeks. The metacarpals can be distinguished from each other as early as the fifth fetal month. Each has a concave palmar aspect and a flat dorsal surface, with rounded proximal ends and broader, flatter distal ends. The appearance of each metacarpal at varying stages is described below in detail.

The heads or distal ends (fig. 9.9b) of all but the first metacarpal develop as secondary ossification centers. These initially appear as small, oval elements as early as 10 months in females to as late as 2.5 years in males. These epiphyses are nondescript nodules before age 5 or 6. By this time, they have attained much of the adult morphology and are identifiable as metacarpal heads. The rounded, distal articular surfaces resemble a pillow in shape. The metaphyseal surfaces are lobate and look like the impression of a molar tooth crown (especially the larger second and third heads). These epiphyses fuse to the shaft between 14 and 15 years in females and around 16 to 17 years of age in males according to Scheuer and Black (2000:334), although others indicate that fusion is completed between 18 and 21 years.

Rather than an epiphysis for its head, the first metacarpal forms as a separate secondary epiphysis at the base or proximal end (fig. 9.9c) like a proximal phalanx. The epiphysis appears between 2 and 3 years of age. It is identifiable by age 9 or 10 as a thin, oval disk with a saddle-shaped facet that articulates proximally with the trapezium. The base of the first metacarpal, like the heads of the other metacarpals, completes fusion by 14 years of age in females and around age 16 in males according to Scheuer and Black (2000:334), although others again place complete fusion as late as age 21.

First Metacarpal. This bone (fig. 9.10) is the shortest and most lateral of the metacarpals. It forms the base of the thumb, and articulates proximally with the trapezium and distally with the first proximal phalanx. It resembles the proximal phalanges more than the other metacarpals because it has a proximal (base) epiphysis (fig. 9.10a) rather than a distal (head) epiphysis. It is wider in a medial-lateral direction than in a palmar-dorsal direction, like the other proximal phalanges and unlike the more tubular shape of the other metacarpals.

The dorsal and lateral aspect of the shaft is very straight, while the palmar-medial side is concave and has a nutrient foramen at its distal end. The proximal end is circular and displays an epiphyseal surface prior to the fusion of the proximal epiphysis. The distal end is smooth and rounded for articulation with the first proximal phalanx. Two tubercles are present on each side of the palmar aspect, just at the edge of the distal articular surface. These eminences form the articular aspects for the two small sesamoids that develop around the same time as the pisiform.

Differentiation from Other Bones. The short, squat appearance of the first metacarpal distinguishes it from the other metacarpals at all stages. In fetal and neonatal skeletons, it may be mistaken for a proximal, or even intermediate, phalanx because of its similar size and roughened proximal surface that eventually fuses with an epiphysis. The hand phalanges, however, are much flatter (dorsal to palmar) than the first metacarpal. The distal head of the first metacarpal is broader in relation to the shaft than the distal ends of the phalanges. The first metacarpal is much smaller than the first metatarsal, so these bones are unlikely to be confused in a single individual.

Siding Techniques. To side the first metacarpal in very young individuals, it is best to examine the dorsal surface with the concave palmar surface down, the flatter epiphyseal surface at the base toward you, and the convex head away from you. The straight side of the shaft is lateral, while the more concave side is medial and also displays the nutrient foramen. The concave side of the shaft with the nutrient foramen is on the side to which the bone belongs when viewed dorsally.

In older children, an alternative is to place the epiphyseal surface, or the trapezium articular surface if the epiphysis has fused, toward you with the concave, palmar side up (fig. 9.10b). The tubercle on the distal end that is slightly bigger and more on the palmar aspect is on the side to which the bone belongs (fig. 9.10c). The other tubercle is smaller and extends more toward one side of the bone rather than the palmar aspect. Also, in this orientation a ridge may be present on the proximal half of the shaft and is on the side from which the bone comes. For adolescents in which the base is well developed or has fused, the proximal end is more pointed and projects farther medially, or on the side to which the bone belongs, when viewed dorsally (fig. 9.10d).

Second Metacarpal. The second metacarpal (fig. 9.11) is located at the base of the index finger. It articulates proximally with the trapezium, trapezoid, and capitate. On the

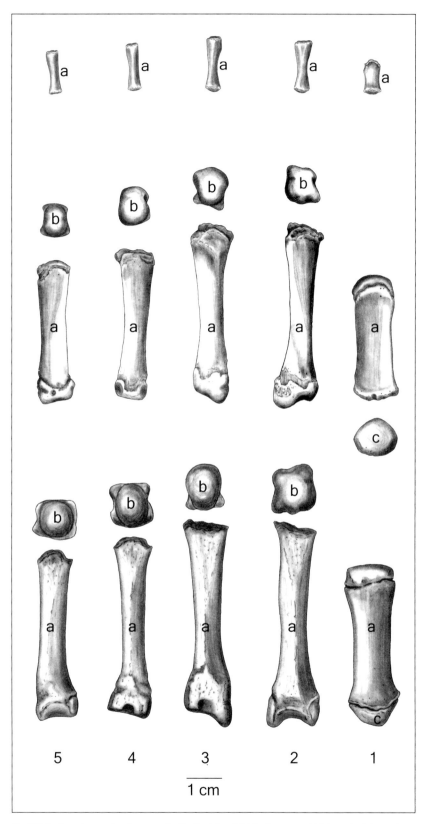

Fig. 9.9 Left metacarpals of a neonate (*top*), older child (c. 8 years, *middle*), and adolescent (c. 15 years, *bottom*). Metacarpal shafts are in dorsal view, unfused heads are in distal view, and unfused base is in proximal view: *a*, shaft; *b*, distal epiphysis; *c*, proximal epiphysis.

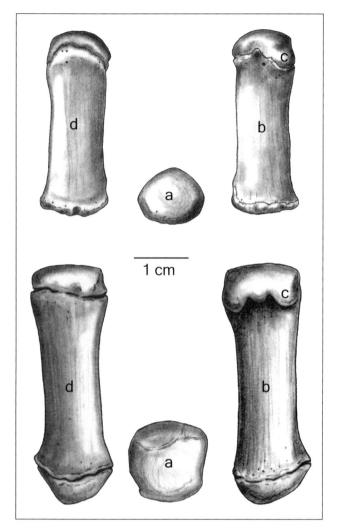

Fig. 9.10 Right first metacarpal of an older child (c. 8 years, *top*) and adolescent (c. 15 years, *bottom*): *a*, base viewed proximally; *b*, palmar view of shaft; *c*, slightly larger, more palmarly placed tubercle; *d*, dorsal view of shaft.

medial side of the base, it articulates with the third meta-carpal. In fetal and infant remains, this bone is distinctive because of its broad proximal and distal ends relative to its length. Furthermore, a ridge runs obliquely along the palmar aspect that sets the distal end off medially and the proximal end off laterally.

By age 3 or 4, the base (fig. 9.11a) begins to develop its distinctive morphology with a medial projection and it attains its characteristic V shape by age 4 or 5. The adult base morphology displays a distinct groove running in a palmar-dorsal orientation, with projections on either side forming the V. The medial side of the V is typically larger than the lateral. The dorsal aspect of the shaft (fig. 9.11b) displays two ridges and is flat between them, while the palmar surface (fig. 9.11c) is concave and marked by a single ridge.

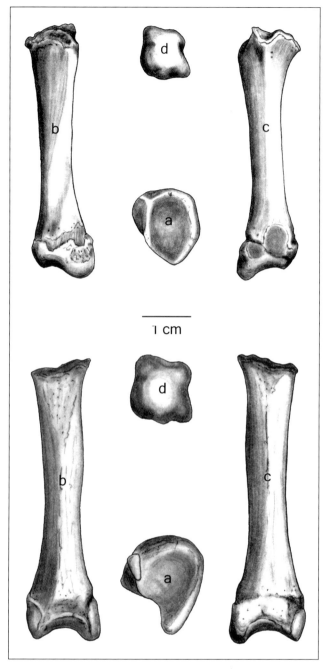

Fig. 9.11 Right second metacarpal of an older child (c. 8 years, *top*) and adolescent (c. 15 years, *bottom*): *a*, base viewed proximally; *b*, dorsal view of shaft; *c*, palmar view of shaft; *d*, head viewed distally.

Differentiation from Other Metacarpals. During all stages of development, the second and third are the two longest of the five metacarpals and are easily distinguished from the others on that basis alone. The second metacar-pal is wider than the third, particularly at its distal end (fig. 9.11d), and has a somewhat twisted appearance even by birth due to oblique ridges on the dorsal and palmar aspects. The early development of the basal projections and its distinctive **V** shape permit the bone to be differentiated from the other metacarpals.

Siding Techniques. In neonates, the nutrient foramen is typically located on the medial side of the shaft. Orient the bone with the straighter dorsal edge toward you and the convex distal end pointing up. The nutrient foramen is on the side from which the bone comes. In children for whom the base has not yet achieved its characteristic shape, orient the bone with the head away from you, the flat dorsal side down, and the concave palmar side up (fig. 9.11c). The head hooks to the lateral side or toward the side to which the bone belongs. Once the base has developed, it permits easy siding of the bone. When oriented as above, with the base toward you, the side that displays the single facet for the trapezium identifies the side from which the bone comes. Alternatively, place the bone with the dorsal surface up, concave palmar surface down, and the head away from you (fig. 9.11b). The largest basal projection is medial, so it is on the side to which the bone belongs in this view.

Third Metacarpal. The third metacarpal (fig. 9.12) is one of the two longest metacarpals. Its base articulates proximally with the capitate (fig. 9.12a), laterally with the second metacarpal, and medially with the fourth metacarpal. In fetal and infant remains, it is straight and narrow with a constriction at midshaft. By puberty, the proximal end has started to develop adult morphology and the styloid process is recognizable on the dorsal and lateral aspect of the base.

Differentiation from Other Metacarpals. The second and third metacarpals can be confused in early stages of development due to their similar length. The third metacarpal is narrower than the second, and its shaft (fig. 9.12b, c) is straighter. The styloid process characterizes the bone after age 11 or 12, but the absence of a well-defined base prior to this age differentiates it from the more developed **V**-shaped base of the second metacarpal.

Siding Techniques. Siding the third metacarpal prior to development of the styloid process is challenging. In neonates, the nutrient foramen is typically located on the medial side of the shaft. Orient the bone with the straighter dorsal edge toward you and the convex distal end pointing up. The nutrient foramen is on the side from which the bone comes. When viewed from the dorsal aspect with the distal head away from you, the edge of the shaft is straighter on the side to which the bone belongs, and that side may also display a stronger muscle marking.

For adolescents, use of the base provides the easiest means of siding. Hold the dorsal surface toward you with the proximal end (base) up. The styloid process is on the side from which the bone comes. Or, orient the

bone with the dorsal surface up and the head away from you (see fig. 9.12b). The side of the base that lacks the styloid process (i.e., the side that projects the least proximally) indicates the side from which the bone comes. Note also that the base angles up and away from you toward that side (a useful tip when the styloid process is not well developed).

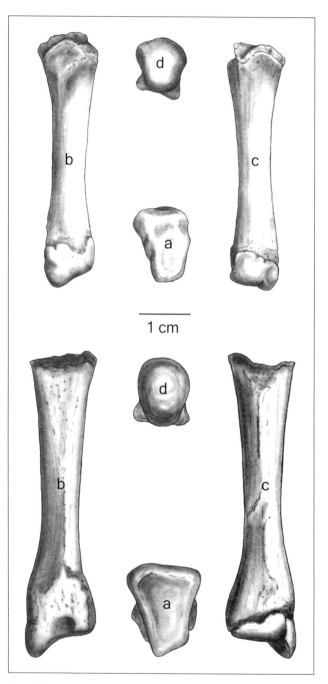

Fig. 9.12 Right third metacarpal of an older child (c. 8 years, *top*) and adolescent (c. 15 years, *bottom*): *a*, base viewed proximally; *b*, dorsal view of shaft; *c*, palmar view of shaft; *d*, head viewed distally.

Fourth Metacarpal. The fourth metacarpal (fig. 9.13) is found at the base of the ring finger and articulates proximally with the capitate and the hamate (fig. 9.13a). On the lateral and medial aspects of its base, the fourth metacarpal articulates with the third and fifth metacarpals, respectively. The bone is much shorter than the second and third metacarpals but slightly longer than the fifth at all stages of development. It does not acquire distinctive features at its base until age 4 or 5. The base is somewhat triangular in shape with the bottom of the triangle on the

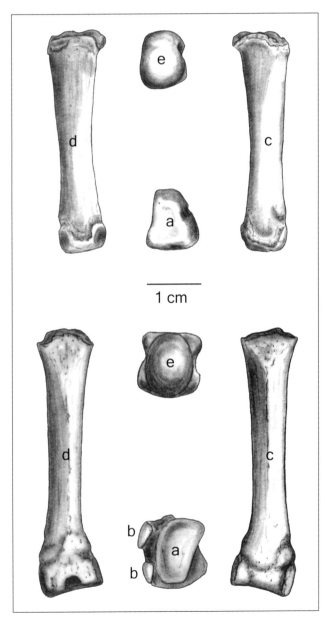

Fig. 9.13 Right fourth metacarpal of an older child (c. 8 years, *top*) and adolescent (c. 15 years, *bottom*): *a,* base viewed proximally; *b,* oval facets for third metacarpal; *c,* palmar view of shaft; *d,* dorsal view of shaft; *e,* head viewed distally.

dorsal surface. The proximal articular facets for the third and fifth metacarpals are diagnostic. There are two small, oval articular facets for the third metacarpal on the lateral side (fig. 9.13b) and a single large facet for the fifth metacarpal on the medial side.

Differentiation from Other Metacarpals. The fourth and fifth metacarpals can be confused in early stages of development due to their similar length. In a single individual, the fourth metacarpal is slightly longer and relatively nondescript in comparison to the fifth. The bulge for the proximal tuberosity of the fifth metacarpal develops by age 5 and permits its distinction from the fourth metacarpal. At this time, the facet pattern on the base of the fourth metacarpal is established.

Siding Techniques. In neonates, the nutrient foramen is typically located on the medial side of the shaft. Orient the bone with the straighter dorsal edge toward you and the convex distal end pointing up. The nutrient foramen is on the side from which the bone comes. After the nutrient foramen is no longer distinct, siding fourth metacarpals is very difficult until the characteristic facet pattern of the base develops around age 4 or 5. Its shaft (fig. 9.13c, d) is straighter on the lateral side and somewhat concave on its medial aspect. When viewed dorsally with the small end (the head) away from you and the larger end (the base) toward you (fig. 9.13d), the side that is more concave toward the base indicates the side from which the bone comes.

In older children, orient the bone with the proximal (base) end facing you and the facet for the fifth metacarpal up. The concave, palmar surface is on the side from which the bone comes. Alternatively, place the flat, dorsal side on a table with the base toward you. The side of the base that displays the two articular facets for the third metacarpal identifies the side to which the bone belongs. If you prefer to view the bone from the dorsal aspect, place the palmar surface down and the head away from you (fig. 9.13d). In this orientation, the large, single facet for the fifth metacarpal is on the side from which the bone comes. The base also appears to be twisted toward the side it is from (i.e., the base angles up and away from you toward the side to which it belongs).

Fifth Metacarpal. The fifth metacarpal (fig. 9.14) is the most medial and second shortest of the metacarpals. It is located at the base of the little finger. The base of the fifth metacarpal articulates proximally with the hamate (fig. 9.14a) and laterally with the fourth metacarpal. It is slightly shorter than the fourth metacarpal at all ages. By age 4 to 5, the nonarticular bulge or tuberosity is identifiable on the medial aspect of the proximal end (fig. 9.14b). The lateral side of the base has a large, single facet for the fourth metacarpal. The proximal end is round to oval with a somewhat saddle shape. In contrast to the palmar aspect (fig. 9.13c), the dorsal aspect (fig. 9.13d) displays a distinct ridge that slopes down the shaft.

Differentiation from Other Metacarpals. Prior to the development of the nonarticular area at the base, the fifth metacarpal is easily confused with the fourth. In subadults under age 4 or 5, the shorter length and the lateral displacement of the base help distinguish it. Although it is the second shortest metacarpal, it is much longer and thinner than the first. Once the nonarticular tubercle develops (fig. 9.14b), the fifth metacarpal is readily identifiable.

Siding Techniques. In neonates, the nutrient foramen is typically located on the medial side of the shaft. Orient the bone with the straighter dorsal edge toward you with the convex distal end pointing upward. The nutrient foramen is on the side from which the bone comes. At all ages, hold the dorsal surface down and the distal end away from you. The base (proximal end) projects farther on the side from which the bone comes.

For older individuals, hold the distal end away from you, with the dorsal or flat aspect of the shaft facing up (fig. 9.14d). The nonarticular tubercle is on the side to which the bone belongs and the base also projects farthest toward you on that side. Alternatively, place the flat, dorsal side on a table with the base toward you (fig. 9.14c). The side of the base that displays the single articulation for the fourth metacarpal (fig. 9.14f) identifies the side from which the bone comes.

Differentiating Metacarpals from Metatarsals. The metacarpals and metatarsals differ in length, with the metacarpals being shorter at all stages of development. They also differ in morphology. In fetuses, neonates, and infants, the distal ends are more circular and convex in metacarpals; metatarsal heads are more oblong and slightly concave. The metacarpal bases display four distinct sides and are rectangular in outline but slightly pinched in the middle. The pinching decreases from the second to the fifth. In contrast, the proximal ends of the metatarsals are rounded in the fourth and fifth metatarsals, and triangular or teardrop shaped in the second and third.

Metatarsal shafts are straighter and narrower than those of metacarpals, even in the very young. Metacarpals clearly have thicker and broader shafts than metatarsals. For example, the relationship between the medial-lateral breadths of the metacarpal shaft, head, and base are similar to one another, whereas metatarsal shaft breadth is considerably narrower compared with head and base breadth. The heads of the metatarsals also tend to be smaller than those of the metacarpals. Metacarpal heads are broader medially to laterally than superiorly to inferiorly (the opposite of metatarsal heads).

Hand Phalanges

Each hand has a total of fourteen phalanges. The fingers of each hand are made up of three phalanges—the proximal, intermediate, and distal phalanges (fig. 9.15). The thumb lacks an intermediate phalanx and is made up of only proximal and distal phalanges.

Proximal Phalanges. The proximal phalanges (fig. 9.15a) articulate proximally with the heads of the metacarpals and distally with the intermediate phalanges for the fingers and with the distal phalanx in the thumb. During juvenile growth, they consist of a shaft and a separate base (proximal end). The shafts first appear between 9 and 11 fetal weeks. Proximal phalanges are the largest of the three rows. In fetal and infant skeletons, they are flat on

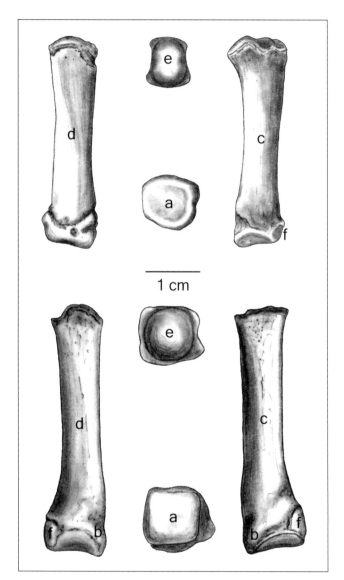

Fig. 9.14 Right fifth metacarpal of an older child (c. 8 years, *top*) and adolescent (c. 15 years, *bottom*): *a*, base viewed proximally; *b*, nonarticular bulge; *c*, palmar view of shaft; *d*, dorsal view of shaft; *e*, head viewed distally; *f*, facet for fourth metacarpal.

1 cm

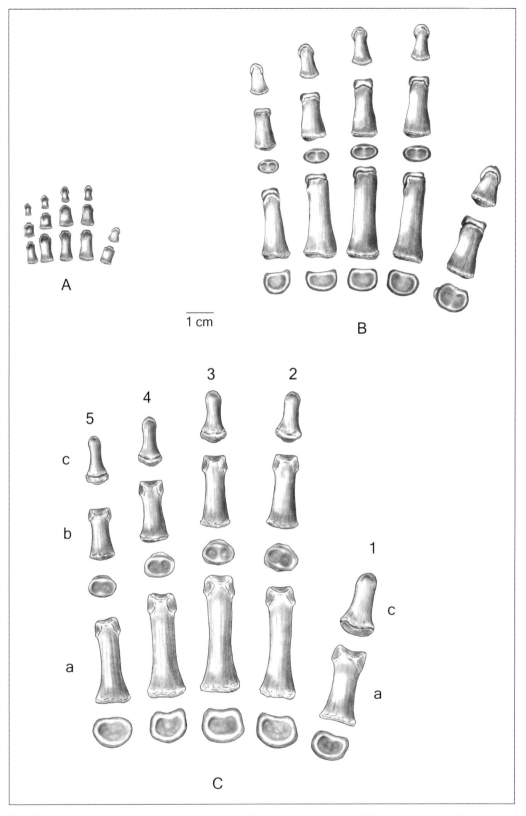

Fig. 9.15 Left hand phalanges of rays 1–5, A = neonate, B = older child (c. 8 years), C = adolescent (c. 15 years): a, proximal row; b, intermediate row; c, distal row. Shafts shown in dorsal view; epiphyses shown in proximal view.

the palmar aspect and very broad at the distal end, giving the midshaft a constricted appearance. The dorsal aspect is rounded, so even at early stages the cross section of these manual phalanges is semicircular. The first proximal phalanx (of the thumb) is much shorter and comparatively broader in relation to length than the others in this row. Its sides are straight, unlike the other proximal phalanges. The fifth proximal phalanx is the next shortest, but is much narrower than the first.

The bases of the proximal phalanges are generally the first epiphyses to appear, between 1 and 2 years of age. They are small, flat disks with a characteristic single, oval, and slightly concave articular surface for the metacarpal heads. These epiphyses are broader medially to laterally than in the palmar to dorsal direction. The palmar edge of the epiphysis is indented at its center, while the dorsal, medial, and lateral borders are all rounded, giving the epiphysis a D shape. Fusion of the bases to the shaft occurs around 14 to 15 years in females and 16 to 17 years in males, with some sources indicating complete fusion takes place as late as age 21.

Intermediate Phalanges. There are four intermediate phalanges (fig. 9.15b) found in the fingers. These are located between the proximal and distal phalanges. The intermediate phalanges are formed from a shaft and a base. The shafts of the second, third, and fourth intermediate phalanges begin to ossify between fetal weeks 10 and 12, but the fifth may not appear until just before birth. The intermediate phalanges are shorter than the proximal phalanges but longer and much wider than those of the distal row, particularly at the base. Because they are relatively short and broad, they lack the midshaft constriction characteristic of the other phalanges. Like the proximal phalanges, they have bilobed distal ends for articulation with the phalanges distal to them. Thus, shape and size distinguish proximal and distal phalanges in early stages of development, whereas the articular ends of both separate them from the pointed ends of the distal phalanges.

The bases of the intermediate phalanges form as secondary epiphyses between 2 and 3 years of age. These epiphyses appear as small, ovoid disks that have an articular surface with two small, concave indentations for articulation with the heads of the proximal epiphyses. The bases are wide medially to laterally but are compressed in the dorsal to palmar direction. With the double indentations separated by a slight ridge on the articular surface, they look like a pig snout. This base form permits the intermediate phalanges to be distinguished from those of the proximal row. The bases fuse to the shafts at approximately 14 to 15 years in females and 16 to 17 years in males, ranging up to age 21 for completion.

Distal Phalanges. There are five distal phalanges (9.15c) in each hand. The distal phalanges are the first bones to ossify in the hand, beginning between 7 and 9 fetal weeks. The base or proximal end forms as a secondary epiphysis, first appearing around 1 to 2 years of age. Of all the phalanges, the bases of the distal row are the first to fuse, beginning around 13.5 years in females and 16 years in males.

Distal phalanges are distinct from proximal and intermediate phalanges at all stages because they are smaller and have a nonarticular distal end. The distal end has a characteristic terminal tuft that resembles a spear point. The only articular surface is located at the proximal end. Like the bases of the intermediate phalanges, the proximal ends of the distal phalanges have two small indentations and resemble pig snouts. They are smaller than the corresponding bases of the intermediate row and more compressed in the dorsal to palmar aspect.

The first distal phalanx is much wider and more robust than the others and can be easily distinguished on that basis. The fifth distal phalanx can also be distinguished in a single individual because it is the smallest of the five and has an attenuated tuft at its distal end. It also has the narrowest shaft.

Siding Hand Phalanges. Mature hand phalanges can be sided, but doing so is very difficult and requires the presence of all phalanges from a given row (D. Troy Case, personal communication, 2002). In children, siding hand phalanges probably is not possible. Thus, it is imperative that all phalanges are bagged and minimally labeled with the side of the body during burial excavation.

Differentiating Hand and Foot Phalanges. Phalanges of either the hands or feet are unlikely to be confused with other bones of the body, even in fetuses. Distinguishing hand and foot phalanges is key and can be accomplished even in early stages of development.

Hand phalanges are longer and the shafts are usually broader than those of the foot. In hands, the palmar surface is flattened, while the dorsal aspect is round, thus giving the shaft a semicircular cross section that looks like the letter D turned on its flat side. The shafts of pedal phalanges, in contrast, are circular in cross section. Manual phalanges are more regular in shape.

When proximal phalanges from the hand and the foot are compared, those of the hand tend to have a head, shaft, and base that are similar in mediolateral breadth. The intermediate and distal phalanges of the hand are longer than those of the foot, with the exception of the first proximal and distal phalanges. The cross section and regular shape of the manual phalanges in the first ray (thumb) help distinguish them. The distal first phalanx is not as rough on its palmar surface as the plantar surface of its counterpart in the foot. The latter has a broader base that becomes squared off on one end as the bone develops.

The Bones of the Foot

Each human foot consists of twenty-six separate bones, or one less than the hand. In all, seven tarsals form the ankle; five metatarsals form the bulk of the foot; and fourteen phalanges form the toes. In addition, two small sesamoid bones are situated under the head of the first metatarsal, and others occasionally develop in tendons elsewhere in the foot. Like the hand, the bones forming each digit are designated as rays, and each ray includes the metatarsal and phalanges. The first ray is the most medial and forms the big toe, while the fifth ray is most lateral in standard anatomical position. All but the first ray are comprised of a metatarsal and proximal, intermediate, and distal phalanges. The first ray, as in the hand, lacks an intermediate phalanx.

In standard anatomical position, the inferior aspect or sole of the foot is referred to as the plantar surface (that aspect which is planted on the ground when one is walking). The top of the foot or superior aspect is known as the dorsal surface. The proximal part of the foot is toward the bones of the lower leg, while the distal aspect is toward the toes.

At birth, the shafts of the metatarsals and phalanges are all present, accompanied by two or three tarsals (the calcaneus, talus, and sometimes the cuboid). By age 2 to 3 in females and 4 to 5 in males, the epiphyses for the metatarsals and phalanges have formed and centers for all seven tarsals have appeared. The calcaneal epiphysis appears as early as age 5 in females and 7 in males. Around age 9 in females and 12 in males, the sesamoids are present. Fusion of the metatarsal and phalangeal epiphyses is complete by age 13 to 15 in females and 16 to 18 in males. The epiphysis of the calcaneus is the last to fuse at approximately 15 to 16 years in females and 18 to 20 years in males.

Tarsals

The tarsals are not as clearly organized into rows as the carpals. The proximal row consists of the calcaneus and talus; the distal row includes the cuboid and the first to third (or medial, intermediate, and lateral) cuneiforms, with the navicular wedged between these and the talus (figs. 9.16–9.22). At birth, only two tarsals, the calcaneus and talus, are typically present. The five other tarsals appear from shortly after birth to about 5 years of age. With the exception of the calcaneus, tarsals usually ossify endochondrally from a single center. In some cases, however, a separate center occurs in other tarsals, producing variations in the form of the bone. By puberty, the tarsals display all the distinct adult features and soon attain adult size.

Calcaneus. The calcaneus (fig. 9.16) is the largest of the tarsal bones, forming the heel. It articulates superiorly with the talus and anteriorly or distally with the cuboid. It is the first tarsal to ossify, beginning as early as 3 to 4 fetal months or as late as 6 to 7 months in utero. It has a unique, identifiable shape at birth, and has recognizable morphology by the end of infancy. It is the only tarsal that consistently has a secondary epiphysis, which develops in childhood and fuses in adolescence to early adulthood.

At birth, the calcaneus is an ovoid nodule with flattened areas on the plantar to medial surfaces that resemble facets, although they are not articular. A small depression and central nutrient foramen are evident on the dorsal side of the nodule. The distal/anterior aspect of the bone is somewhat narrower than the proximal/posterior end of the bone. During infancy (fig. 9.16A), the distal end lengthens and widens as a medial protrusion develops to support the talus. This feature later becomes the sustentaculum tali (fig. 9.16a). Within a few months of birth, the distal portion is broader than the proximal part of the bone. The distal end (fig. 9.16b) flattens for the developing cuboid, while the metaphyseal proximal end develops its rounded calcaneal tuberosity (fig. 9.16c) that has distinct ridges and furrows on its surface. Thus, even in infancy, the calcaneus can be differentiated when found in isolation.

By 3 to 4 years, the calcaneus has the roughly rectangular shape of an adult bone, with a medial shelf, but the articular facets are not well developed until approximately 5 to 6 years of age. At this stage, the bone achieves adult morphology, though not its full adult size.

The articular facets on the calcaneus are variable in number and form. The superior surface has two or three articular facets for the talus. The largest of these is the posterior articular surface (fig. 9.16d), which runs medially to laterally across the middle part of the bone. It is convex and supports the body of the talus. The other articular area is located on the sustentaculum tali on the medial part of the bone for the inferior aspect of the talar head. This facet can be a single, long, thin strip or divided into middle and anterior surfaces (fig. 9.16e, f) that are oval and contiguous. In young children, the anterior facet is the least well defined and often appears quite distant from the middle facet. It is situated at the anterosuperior rim, just above the articular facet for the cuboid at the flat, distal end of the bone. The proximal or posterior end of the calcaneus becomes increasingly defined with its convex tuberosity that displays a large, oval epiphyseal surface. This billowy surface extends inferiorly to the plantar surface of the bone. The lateral side of the calcaneus is rough and relatively flat and featureless compared to the medial aspect of the bone.

The secondary epiphysis (fig. 9.16g) for the calcaneal

tuberosity at the posterior or heel portion of the bone appears anytime between 4 and 12 years of age, beginning earlier in females than in males. It is identifiable in isolation by 8 to 10 years of age, when it looks like a large cornflake that caps the heel. The epiphysis has a roughened, concave metaphyseal surface and a convex nonarticular surface. Its general shape is somewhat oval. It is thicker on the inferior and medial portion, while the superior edge is quite thin. From its center, the epiphysis appears to curve inferiorly and laterally toward a prong at the inferolateral corner that represents the lateral tubercle. This epiphysis generally begins to fuse to the body of the calcaneus between 10 and 12 years in females and 11 to 14 years in males. Fusion is complete by age 16 in females and 20 to 22 in males.

Differentiation from Other Bones. The calcaneus of a perinatal skeleton may be confused with a long bone epiphysis such as that of the distal femur because of its nodular shape. Differentiation is based on the small, flat areas that resemble articular facets opposite the side with an indentation and large nutrient foramen that are evident on a calcaneus at this stage. Long bone epiphyses in neonates lack defined features. By the end of infancy, the calcaneus begins to attain its recognizable shape and is only likely to be confused with the talus, which is smaller and has central depressions on both the superior and inferior surfaces. By age 3, a complete calcaneus is unlikely to be mistaken for any other bone. Fragments, however, must be distinguished primarily from talus fragments because of their complementary facets. The contour of the facets (i.e., the posterior facet is convex on a calcaneus and concave on a talus) is key to differentiating them. Calcaneal fragments in adults are sometimes incorrectly identified as an incomplete patella, but the much later ossification of the patella renders it less likely to be confused with well-defined articular surfaces on the calcaneus of a child.

The calcaneal epiphysis and the fused or unfused calca-

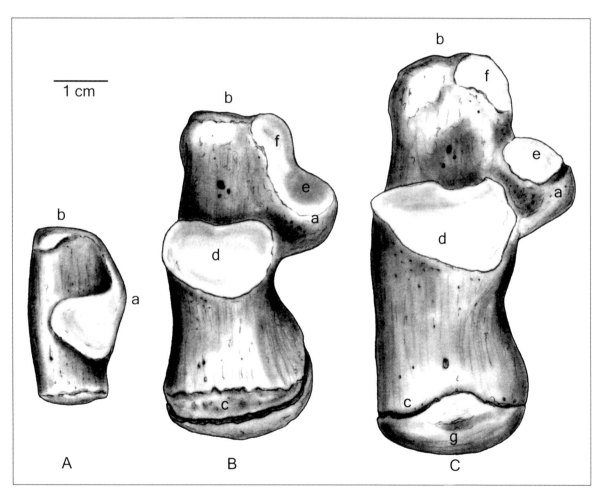

Fig. 9.16 Left calcaneus, superior view, A = young child (c. 2–3 years), B = older child (c. 8 years), C = adolescent (c. 15 years): *a*, sustentaculum tali; *b*, cuboid surface/distal end; *c*, calcaneal tuberosity; *d*, posterior articular facet for talus; *e*, middle articular facet for talus; *f*, anterior articular facet for talus; *g*, epiphysis for calcaneal tuberosity.

neal tuberosity are sometimes misidentified as the greater trochanter of a femur. Both lack articular features, and they are similar in size, but the greater trochanter is much thicker than a calcaneal epiphysis, which is more like a cap. The unfused posterior part of the calcaneus has a well-defined epiphyseal surface on one end and will show breakage at its opposite end, which is blocky. An unfused greater trochanter also displays a billowy metaphyseal surface, but its opposite end is likely to be intact and is more curved than the body of a calcaneus.

Siding Techniques. To side the fetal or neonatal calcaneus, look for the flattened areas that resemble facets and identify the opposite side with the slight indentation and nutrient foramen. Place the indented side down with the flattened surfaces up, and the broader end toward you. One of the flat areas extends downward, along the side to which the bone belongs.

Siding calcanei from older infants and very young children (fig. 9.16A) is easier, although it is still more challenging than siding those from children over about 3 years of age. Hold the bone with the marked indentation up (which is the superior or dorsal surface) and the smoother and slightly convex plantar surface down. Place the distal end (fig. 9.16b) away from you and the rounded proximal end toward you (this is the end immediately behind the indentation). The bone is now in standard anatomical position (see fig. 9.16A). The medial side bulges out (fig. 9.16a), while the lateral side is relatively straight and featureless, and indicates the side from which the bone comes.

In children over 3 years of age and into adulthood (figs. 9.16B, C), the preceding technique can be used with greater ease as the calcaneal tuberosity (fig. 9.16c) develops at the posterior end of the bone and the articular facets become obvious on the superior aspect. As above, orient the bone in anatomical position with the calcaneal tuberosity toward you and the articular surfaces up (fig. 9.16d–f). The straighter lateral side is the side from which the bone comes, while the medial bulge of the sustentaculum tali (fig. 9.16a) is on the opposite side. Thus, if you orient the bone with the calcaneal tuberosity or heel facing away from you with the articular surfaces facing up, the side with the sustentaculum tali is the side to which the bone belongs. A method that is useful if only the proximal part of the bone is present is to place the tuberosity toward you with the narrower apex up. The epiphyseal surface extends down farther on the side from which the bone comes. Alternatively, in older individuals, turn the bone over and examine the plantar surface. The largest tubercle (medial tubercle) lies on the side to which the bone belongs.

Several methods can be used to side the calcaneal epiphysis (fig. 9.16g). Hold the metaphyseal surface away from you with the thin edge up and the thicker, curved edge down. The bone appears to curl under more toward the side it is from due to a small projection for the lateral tubercle. Thus, the small hook or projection indicates the side of the bone. Alternatively, place the thicker, more convex (medial) side toward you with the metaphyseal surface on a table. The bone extends farther away on the side to which it belongs. Another method is to place the metaphyseal surface down, the thin side facing you, with the ridge of the convexity in a parallel line toward you. The thicker side is on the side from which the bone comes.

Talus. The talus (fig. 9.17) is the second largest of the tarsal bones and the second to ossify. It articulates superiorly with the tibia and fibula, inferiorly with the calcaneus, and anteriorly with the navicular. The talus first appears between 6 and 7 fetal months. At birth, it is an ovoid nodule that is compressed superiorly to inferiorly due to depressions on both the plantar and dorsal surfaces. A small ridge is present on the lateral aspect, while the medial side is featureless. By late infancy, the dorsal depression deepens to form a clearly defined neck or constriction (fig. 9.17a). The neck lies posterior to the elongating, rounded head (fig. 9.17b) that articulates with the navicular. The lateral ridge is set off as a thin strip between the depressions, and a small groove is present on the medial side that provides increased definition of the head. The proximal end of the bone is also rounded, but it is broader and more vascularized than the distal head.

By age 2, the talus begins to attain its adult morphology with the further definition of the head and neck and development of the rounded trochlea at the superoposterior aspect of the bone. This surface articulates with the tibia. Later in childhood, the articular surfaces become distinct on the head, trochlea, and on the inferior surface for articulation with the calcaneus.

The bone reaches adult size during adolescence. At this point, it is easily identified by the large, convex, saddle-shaped trochlea on the superior aspect, the constricted nonarticular area of the neck, and its rounded head at the distal end. On the inferior aspect, there are two or three articular facets corresponding to the pattern on the calcaneus, with which they articulate. A deep groove, the sulcus tali (fig. 9.17c), separates the large, concave posterior facet (fig. 9.17d) and the middle calcaneal facet (fig. 9.17e). This facet may be distinct or may be continuous with the anterior calcaneal facet (fig. 9.17f). On either side of the bone, articular surfaces extend from the trochlea. The larger lateral facet is shaped like an inverted triangle that extends to the inferior edge of the bone. This articular surface is for the distal fibula (lateral malleolus). On the medial aspect is a smaller facet, oriented anteroposteriorly, for the medial malleolus of the tibia. The talus may have a small epiphysis that arises between 7 and 11 years, but usually fuses a year or two later. The epiphysis is a very small, triangular bone that fuses to the posterior edge of the talus to form the lateral tubercle. In some cases, the epiphysis does not fuse, forming the separate os trigonum.

Differentiation from Other Bones. Because the talus is a nondescript ovoid until about 2 years of age, it may easily be mistaken for other developing bones or epiphyses. Attention to morphological detail and position during excavation aid in identification. The talus, however, can be distinguished in neonates and infants because of the indentations on both the plantar and dorsal surfaces and its flattened superoinferior height. It is smaller than the developing calcaneal nodule.

By late infancy and early childhood, the talus has a definite neck with rounded proximal (trochlear) and distal (head) ends. At this stage and beyond, a complete talus is unlikely to be confused with any other bone. Fragments are most likely to be mistaken for calcaneal or other tarsal fragments. The complementary facet pattern on the inferior talar surface matches that of the superior calcaneal surface. The large posterior facet of the talus, however, is concave rather than convex. A broken head fragment is much smaller than that of a humeral or femoral head.

Siding Techniques. In fetal and infant remains, siding the talus is problematic because it does not have many identifiable features that permit unambiguous orientation. The depressions on both the plantar and dorsal surfaces of the bone are somewhat distal to the center, but there is no specific landmark to distinguish these surfaces from each other. Thus, the bone can easily be oriented upside down at this stage of development.

Once it has attained some adult morphology (in later infancy and certainly by age 2), the talus can be easily sided. To orient the bone in standard anatomical position, place the head (fig. 9.17b) away from you and the deeper, dorsal depression up. The broad, convex surface of the trochlea is toward you. The head is more medial, while the lateral side of the neck displays a concave curve and, in older infants, a ridge is present toward the plantar edge of the lateral aspect that connects the surfaces of the trochlea and head. The concavity and ridge, therefore, indicate the side from which the bone comes. The articular facets become increasingly defined during childhood and can be used to side the bone. By placing the talus in anatomical position, as above, the side with the large, triangular fibular articular facet is the side to which the bone belongs.

Cuboid. The cuboid (fig. 9.18) is named for its cube shape. It is located on the lateral side of the foot and is the third largest tarsal and the third to ossify. It articulates proximally with the calcaneus, medially with the navicular and the third cuneiform, and distally with the fourth and fifth metatarsals.

The cuboid may begin ossifying as early as the ninth fetal month, but usually appears within 1 to 3 months after birth. It is sometimes present at birth, particularly in

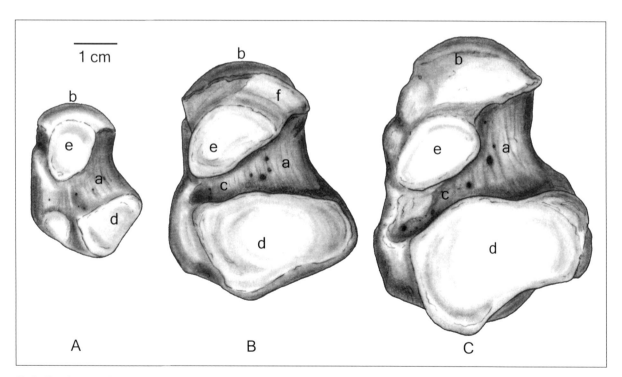

Fig. 9.17 Left talus, inferior view, A = young child (c. 2–3 years), B = older child (c. 8 years), C = adolescent (c. 15 years): *a*, neck; *b*, head; *c*, sulcus tali; *d*, posterior calcaneal facet; *e*, middle calcaneal facet; *f*, anterior calcaneal facet.

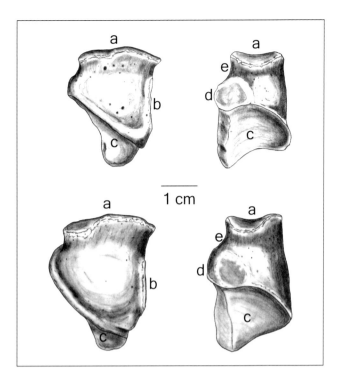

1 cm

Fig. 9.18 Left cuboid of an older child (c. 8 years, *top*) and adolescent (c. 15 years, *bottom*), left = dorsal, right = lateral: *a*, distal aspect; *b*, medial side with facets for third cuneiform and navicular; *c*, articular surface for calcaneus; *d*, peroneal tuberosity; *e*, peroneal sulcus.

females. During its initial formation, the cuboid is a round nodule with no distinguishing features. In infancy and early childhood, its edges flatten so it attains an identifiable cube shape by 3 to 4 years of age. The bone is longer proximally to distally than its medial to lateral breadth. The distal or anterior aspect is completely articular, flat, and somewhat wedge shaped (fig. 9.18a). It angles posteriorly toward the nonarticular, somewhat vascularized (porous), lateral side of the bone. The opposite, medial, side is the longest surface. It is flat or slightly concave with smooth articular surfaces for the third cuneiform and navicular (fig. 9.18b). The proximal (posterior) side is entirely articular and flat or slightly rounded in very young children. This surface becomes increasingly concave throughout childhood for the articulation with the calcaneus (fig. 9.18c). The dorsal and plantar aspects are both nonarticular. The dorsal side is vascularized or porous in appearance, while the plantar surface has a slight bump at the center and a shallow groove just distal (anterior) to it. These features become more defined throughout childhood as the cuboid or peroneal tuberosity and the peroneal sulcus (fig. 9.18d, e). By age 8, the bone is a smaller version of the adult bone.

Differentiation from Other Bones. Until 3 or 4 years of age, the cuboid is not easily identified out of context and may be confused with other developing tarsals or epiphyses. Its recognition depends on the presence of the other tarsals; hence, careful excavation and labeling of each

foot in the field is imperative. After this stage, the bone is identifiable by its characteristic cube shape. Because the bone is blocky, it is usually found intact. By about age 5, the bone is increasingly distinguishable by features such as the peroneal tuberosity and peroneal sulcus, which form a bar of bone and a distinct groove on its plantar surface.

Siding Techniques. Siding a cuboid cannot be done prior to development of some distinctive features at age 3 or 4. To side the cuboid of a young child, it is best to orient the bone in standard anatomical position with the nondescript, nonarticular, dorsal aspect up and the more irregular, plantar surface with the bump and groove down (fig. 9.18d, e). The more challenging task is to distinguish the proximal and distal surfaces for proper positioning. The distal end is flatter, shorter, and more angled than the proximal end in young children. Place this end away from you. In this position, the short nonarticular side is on the side from which the bone comes, opposite the long articular surface of the medial aspect. Alternatively, one can orient the bone with the more irregular plantar surface facing up, the dorsal surface down, and the angled distal end (fig. 9.18a) away from you. The longest side indicates the side to which the bone belongs.

In older children and adolescents, methods used for siding the adult bone are useful. The easiest method involves picturing the bone as an ice cube or a marshmallow that has been squished or pinched on one side. If you place the bone in anatomical position with the irregular plantar surface down and the concave facet for the calcaneus (fig. 9.18c) toward you, the bone is pinched on the side from which it comes (see fig. 9.18, left). You can also orient the bone with the peroneal tuberosity and peroneal sulcus up and the peroneal articular facet toward you. The long articular side with the facet for the third cuneiform (fig. 9.18b) then indicates the side to which the bone belongs. Alternatively, place the long medial facet for the third cuneiform on a table (down) with the flat, wedge-shaped distal articulation away from you. The calcaneal articular surface that faces you flares toward the side from which the bone comes.

Navicular. The navicular (fig. 9.19) is the last tarsal to begin ossification at age 2 to 3 in females and 4 to 5 in males. It is wedged between the head of the talus proximally (posteriorly), and the first to third (medial, intermediate, and lateral) cuneiforms distally (anteriorly). It also articulates laterally with the cuboid. The navicular sometimes has a secondary epiphysis for the tubercle that begins to ossify around 9 years of age in females and 12 years in males. It fuses not long after its appearance.

During the early development of the bone, it is a rounded nodule with a flat side opposite a convex surface. Thus, it resembles a domed coat button. Although it does not attain its full adult morphology until early adolescence, the navicular has a recognizable shape by age 7 or 8, with the development of the large, oval concavity (fig. 9.19a) for articulation with the head of the talus (proximal/posterior). The opposite distal side has a convex kidney-shaped surface exhibiting three articular planes for the three cuneiforms (fig. 9.19b–d). The superior or dorsal aspect of the bone is a thick nonarticular surface that is somewhat convex relative to the thinner, flatter, nonarticular inferior or plantar surface. The lateral aspect angles inferiorly and superiorly to meet at a central point, while the medial aspect is rounded and presents a bubbly surface where the tubercle (fig. 9.19e) eventually develops. Once present, this rounded projection at the inferomedial aspect of the bone is a distinguishing feature. In some instances, the tubercle remains unfused into adulthood and becomes an accessory bone known as the os tibiale externum.

Differentiation from Other Bones. Up to about age 7 or 8, the navicular has few recognizable features and cannot be readily identified in isolation. It can be distinguished within a single individual by its resemblance to a domed button. After 7 or 8 years of age, the bone still resembles a domed disk but is easily identified by the large concavity for the head of the talus and by the three flat, wedge-shaped facets for the cuneiforms on the opposite, convex side. It is easily differentiated from the scaphoid in the wrist because of its greater size. Once the tubercle has developed, the navicular is unlikely to be confused with any other bone.

Siding Techniques. Prior to development of the tubercle, the navicular can be challenging to side. To do so, place the flat or concave proximal side down and the domed distal side up with the long, straight to some-

what concave edge of the plantar surface toward you. The curved side indicates that to which the bone belongs, while the more pointed lateral side is opposite.

Once the tubercle (fig. 9.19e) has developed on the medial side, the bone resembles the body and head of a bear. When positioned as shown on the right side of figure 9.19, the head of the bear points down and to the side from which the bone comes. Alternatively, place the large, concave talar surface (fig. 9.19a) up with the large, superior nonarticular surface toward you. The tubercle points toward the side from which the bone comes. Another option is to hold the bone by the tubercle with the broad, dorsal surface up and the concave facet toward you (see fig. 9.19, left). The body of the bone is toward the side to which the bone belongs.

First or Medial Cuneiform. The first cuneiform (fig. 9.20) is the largest and most medial of the three wedge-shaped cuneiform bones. It articulates proximally with the navicular, laterally with the second or intermediate cuneiform, and distally with the first and second metatarsals. It is most convenient to refer to the bone as the first cuneiform in reference to its position and its primary distal articulation for the first metatarsal.

The first cuneiform is the fifth tarsal to ossify. It typically ossifies from two centers (one superior, one inferior) that appear between the ages of 1 and 3 years. These centers normally coalesce soon after ossification. Unlike the other cuneiforms, which are not easily identified until

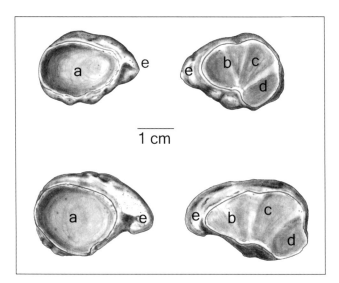

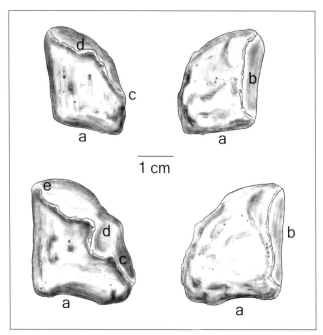

Fig. 9.19 Left navicular of an older child (c. 8 years, *top*) and adolescent (c. 15 years, *bottom*), left = proximal, right = distal: *a,* facet for talus; *b,* facet for first cuneiform; *c,* facet for second cuneiform; *d,* facet for third cuneiform; *e,* tubercle.

Fig. 9.20 Left first cuneiform of an older child (c. 8 years, *top*) and adolescent (c. 15 years, *bottom*), left = lateral, right = medial: *a,* plantar surface; *b,* facet for first metatarsal; *c,* facet for navicular; *d,* facet for second cuneiform; *e,* facet for second metatarsal.

mid-childhood, the first cuneiform has unique morphology by 3 to 4 years of age, and is very similar to its adult form by age 6. At this stage, rather than displaying the characteristic wedge shape of the other cuneiforms, the first cuneiform is more of a crescent shape with five sides. The broadest nonarticular surface (fig. 9.20a) is inferior (plantar surface), while two of its parallel surfaces are completely articular. The larger distal surface is fairly flat with a crescent or kidney-shaped facet for the first metatarsal (fig. 9.20b), while the proximal facet is a smaller, somewhat kite-shaped concavity for the navicular (fig. 9.20c). Only one other surface, the lateral side of the bone, has articular facets. Located at the superolateral aspect, one facet is L shaped and extends from the kite-shaped proximal facet for the navicular. This facet is for the second or intermediate cuneiform (fig. 9.20d) and is contiguous with a small, triangular facet for the second metatarsal (fig. 9.20e) at its distal edge.

Differentiation from Other Bones. The first cuneiform is not readily identifiable until approximately 3 to 4 years of age. It is larger than the other cuneiforms, is less wedge shaped, and develops greater curvature as it rapidly attains its adult morphology. The broad, rounded, nonarticular plantar surface opposite the tapered dorsal surface and its distinguishing articular facets render it unlikely to be mistaken for any other bone.

Siding Techniques. Even in young children, siding the first cuneiform is relatively simple. Orient it with the broadest nonarticular surface down, the tapered point up, and the small, concave facet for the navicular (fig.9.19c) toward you so the bone is in standard anatomical position. The top of the bone curves over toward the side from which it comes, which also bears the L-shaped articular facet for the second cuneiform (fig. 9.20d). Alternatively, place the largest, kidney-shaped facet for the first metatarsal (fig. 9.20b) up and the thin, tapered end toward you. The side that has an articular surface for the second cuneiform and second metatarsal (fig. 9.20d, e) is the side to which the bone belongs.

Second or Intermediate Cuneiform. The second cuneiform (fig. 9.21) is the smallest of the tarsal bones, and the sixth to appear. It articulates proximally with the navicular, medially with the first cuneiform, laterally with the third cuneiform, and distally with the second metatarsal.

The second cuneiform generally appears between 2 and 4 years of age. It is not readily recognizable until approximately age 6, when it has developed most of its adult morphology. At this time, it can be described as being wedge shaped with five sides. The dorsal surface (fig. 9.21a) is nonarticular and somewhat square. The bone tapers inferiorly to a thin plantar aspect that is also nonarticular. The narrow, triangular proximal and distal ends of the bone are completely articular. The smaller,

slightly convex facet is at the distal end for the second metatarsal, while the larger, slightly concave facet is proximal for the navicular (fig. 9.21b). On either side of the proximal facet for the navicular are contiguous facets on the broader sides of the bone for the first and third cuneiforms. The medial edge of the contiguous facets is convex, with a large, somewhat L-shaped articular surface for the first cuneiform. The posterolateral edge is slightly concave and displays an articular surface shaped like a backward B (fig. 9.21c) for the third cuneiform.

Differentiation from Other Bones. The second cuneiform is easily misidentified until it acquires adult morphology at approximately 6 years of age. Before this time, it may be mistaken for any of the other developing tarsal bones or epiphyses. Once it has attained its recognizable shape, it is most easily confused with the third cuneiform because of their similar size and shape. The second cuneiform is the smaller of the two and the dorsal aspect is square rather than rectangular as on the third cuneiform. The facet pattern also assists in differentiating these bones.

Siding Techniques. After about age 6, the second cuneiform can be sided. One method is to hold the bone in standard anatomical position with the broad nonarticular surface (fig. 9.21a) up, the pointed aspect down, and the more concave facet for the navicular (fig. 9.21b) toward you (see fig. 9.21, right). The bone is concave on the side it is from, which also displays the inverted B-shaped facet for the third or lateral cuneiform (see fig. 9.21c). Another option is to place the nonarticular surface on a table with the point of the wedge facing up and the lateral surface with the B-shaped articulation toward you. The facet is on the side from which the bone comes.

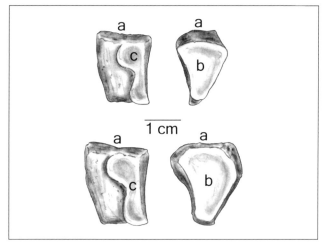

Fig. 9.21 Left second cuneiform of an older child (c. 8 years, *top*) and adolescent (c. 15 years, *bottom*), left = lateral, right = proximal: *a,* dorsal surface; *b,* facet for navicular; *c,* facet for third cuneiform.

Third or Lateral Cuneiform. The third or lateral cuneiform (fig. 9.22) is the fourth tarsal bone to appear. It articulates proximally with the navicular, medially with the intermediate cuneiform, laterally with the cuboid, distally with the second and third metatarsals, and distolaterally with the fourth metatarsal. Because its principal distal articular surface is for the third metatarsal, it is easiest to refer to the bone as the third cuneiform in recognition of this articulation.

The third cuneiform is often present by 6 months of age and generally by the end of the first year after birth. As with the other tarsals, it initially forms as a small, nondescript nodule. It gains some of its characteristic features and becomes identifiable by 4 years of age, and has most of its adult morphology by age 6.

By age 4, the bone retains somewhat rounded edges but has developed the typical wedge shape that identifies it as a cuneiform. The dorsal aspect (fig. 9.22a) is a broad, slightly convex, nonarticular rectangle, with the opposite plantar surface tapering to a narrow ridge of bone. The medial and lateral surfaces are large and have clear articular surfaces, with the lateral side showing a large, round facet for the cuboid (fig. 9.22b) that is a hallmark of this bone. The medial surface shows a long, narrow facet for the second cuneiform (fig. 9.22c) adjacent to a slightly depressed nonarticular area. Although the distal and proximal articular facets are not delimited at this stage, the proximity of the medial and lateral facets to the proximal end of the bone aid in its orientation for proper siding.

After about age 6, when the bone has gained essentially adult features, the third cuneiform is clearly wedge shaped. Only one side (edge) is completely articular and T shaped to form the distal articulation for the third meta-

tarsal. Continuing on one side of this facet (medially) is a small articulation for the second metatarsal (fig. 9.22d) and a small lip on the lateral aspect for articulation with the fourth metatarsal. The opposite or proximal end displays a smaller facet with a nonarticular area extending from it inferiorly, thus giving it a truncated appearance in comparison to the distal articular surface. This somewhat triangular, flat articular facet is for the navicular (fig. 9.22e). Contiguous articular surfaces extend on each side of the bone. The continuation on the medial aspect is the long, narrow B-shaped facet for the second cuneiform (fig. 9.22c). The opposite, lateral aspect bears the large oval facet on the superior or dorsal half for the cuboid (fig. 9.22b).

Differentiation from Other Bones. Differentiating the third cuneiform from other developing tarsals, particularly the other cuneiforms, is very difficult until approximately 4 years of age. Once it has attained its recognizable shape, it is most easily confused with the second cuneiform because of its similar size and shape. The third cuneiform is larger and its dorsal aspect is rectangular, as opposed to the square surface on the second cuneiform. The facet pattern also assists in differentiating these bones. The large, round or oval facet for the cuboid is definitive.

Siding Techniques. To side the third cuneiform at early stages (i.e., between 4 and 6 years), place the side with the large, rounded facet for the cuboid (fig. 9.22b) on a table with the broad nonarticular surface (fig. 9.22a) away from you. The long articular facet for the second cuneiform (fig. 9.22c) is on the side to which the bone belongs. Alternatively, place the broad nonarticular area toward you with the rounded cuboid facet up. The facet is toward the side from which the bone comes.

Once adult morphology is present, other methods can be used for siding the third cuneiform. It can be oriented in standard anatomical position with the broad, nonarticular dorsal surface up, the pointed aspect down, and the smaller facet for the navicular (fig. 9.22e) toward you (see fig. 9.22, right). As an aid in orientation, remember that the facet for the navicular does not extend all the way down the length of the bone. In this position, the large, oval or round facet for the cuboid (fig. 9.22b) indicates the side to which the bone belongs. Also note that the articular surface extends farther along the top edge of the bone on the side it is from and the border of the dorsal surface is also longer on that side. Alternatively, place the large T-shaped facet (for the third metatarsal) toward you with the point of the wedge facing down. The side from which the bone comes displays a very small articular facet for the fourth metatarsal as well as the oval cuboid facet.

Metatarsals

The metatarsals (fig. 9.23) are short, tubular bones distal to the tarsals and proximal to the phalanges. Five

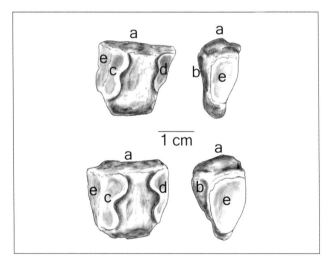

Fig. 9.22 Left third cuneiform of an older child (c. 8 years, *top*) and adolescent (c. 15 years, *bottom*), left = medial, right = proximal: *a,* dorsal surface; *b,* facet for cuboid; *c,* facet for second cuneiform; *d,* facet for second metatarsal; *e,* facet for navicular.

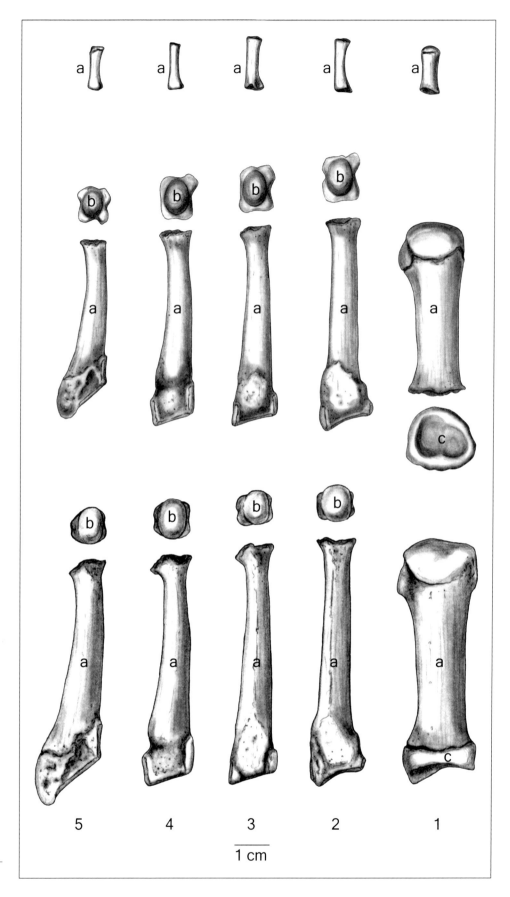

Fig. 9.23 Left metatarsals of a neonate (*top*), older child (c. 8 years, *middle*), and adolescent (c. 15 years, *bottom*). Metatarsal shafts are in dorsal view; unfused heads, in distal view; and unfused base, in proximal view: *a,* shaft; *b,* distal epiphysis; *c,* proximal epiphysis.

1 cm

metatarsals extend from the arch to the ball of each foot. All of the metatarsal shafts (fig. 9.23a) begin to ossify between 8 and 10 fetal weeks, much like the metacarpals. Similar to the metacarpals, the metatarsals have a flat dorsal surface with a concave plantar surface. With the exception of the first metatarsal, which can be differentiated at birth, it is very difficult to distinguish the second through fifth metatarsals until the bases develop their adult morphology in mid-childhood. However, it is possible to side the second through fifth metatarsals even when the specific position of the bone is unknown. Even in infant remains, the base of the metatarsal, when viewed from the dorsal aspect with the distal end away from you, angles toward you (i.e., projects farther proximally) on the side from which the bone comes.

The heads (fig. 9.23b) or distal ends of all but the first metatarsal develop as secondary ossification centers and first appear as small oval elements around 2 to 3 years of age. The heads are recognizable by age 4 or 5, when they develop rounded distal articular surfaces and flat, roughened metaphyseal surfaces on their proximal aspects. The heads are narrow medially to laterally and longer in the dorsal to plantar direction, forming a somewhat rectangular contour with bulges at the corners when viewed from the distal surface. It is very difficult to identify separate, unfused heads, with the possible exception of the fifth. It has a more lobular shape and is much smaller than the other metatarsal heads. If all heads are present, the second is the largest. Without fitting the heads to the metatarsal shafts in older children, any further attempt at identification or siding will be unreliable. The heads begin fusing to the shafts between 11 and 13 years in females and between 14 and 16 years of age in males, with completion generally occurring by age 16 in females and 18 in males.

Like the first metacarpal, the first metatarsal also develops more like a proximal phalanx. It is the only metatarsal to have an epiphysis at its base or proximal end (fig. 9.23c), rather than at the head or distal end of the bone. The epiphysis usually begins to ossify by age 2 or 3 years and it becomes recognizable by 6 to 7 years. Its features are delineated in the first metatarsal section. The base completes its fusion to the shaft at the same time the heads fuse to the other metatarsals (by 15 years of age in females and 18 years in males).

First Metatarsal. This bone (fig. 9.24) is the shortest and most robust of all the metatarsals at all stages of development. It is located at the base of the big toe, and articulates proximally with the first (medial) cuneiform (fig. 9.24a).

The shaft of the bone has a concave plantar surface, while the superior or dorsal surface is convex (fig. 9.24b, c). The lateral side of the bone is also somewhat concave,

while the medial side is much straighter. The proximal end is roughly **D** shaped, with a flat lateral aspect and a convex medial aspect. It is larger in the dorsal to plantar direction than the medial to lateral direction. In contrast, the distal head is rounded and broader mediolaterally. The plantar surface of the head develops two large grooves for the medial and lateral sesamoid bones that begin to ossify around age 9 in females and 12 in males.

Before fusion, the proximal epiphysis is a thin, ovoid to **D**-shaped disk with a billowy metaphyseal surface on one side and a smooth, slightly concave articular surface on the opposite (proximal) side. By age 6 or 7, the articular facet develops its distinctive kidney shape. The lateral aspect of the facet shows a small notch or indentation and is flatter than the convex medial side of the epiphysis. By puberty, the plantar aspect is narrower than the broader dorsal aspect of the epiphysis.

Differentiation from Other Bones. The first metatarsal is unlikely to be confused with the other metatarsals at any stage of development because it is much shorter and

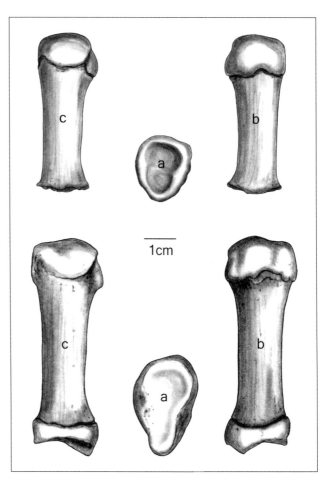

Fig. 9.24 Right first metatarsal of an older child (c. 8 years, *top*) and adolescent (c. 15 years, *bottom*): *a*, base viewed proximally; *b*, palmar view of shaft; *c*, dorsal view of shaft.

broader than the others. Thus, it is most often confused with a first metacarpal, which is also short and broad in comparison to the other metacarpals. A first metatarsal is much larger than a first metacarpal from the same individual. In instances where remains are commingled, noting the differences in the shape of the base and the grooves for the sesamoids on the plantar surface of the head aids in identification of the first metatarsal.

Siding Techniques. To side the first metatarsal, place the concave plantar surface on a table, the rounded dorsal aspect up, and the rounded head away from you (see fig. 9.24c). At all ages, the medial side of the shaft is straighter than the curved, lateral side of the bone (particularly the plantolateral border). Thus, in the dorsal view, the concave side indicates the side to which the bone belongs.

For an unfused proximal epiphysis, orient the disk with the metaphyseal surface away from you and the smooth articular surface toward you (fig. 9.24a). The broader, convex aspect should be up, with the narrower aspect downward. The articular facet has an indentation on the side to which the bone belongs and it is also flatter on that side. In individuals for whom the epiphysis is fused or fusing, this method is also useful and it is much easier to orient the whole bone with the convex dorsal surface up and the concave plantar surface down. When you look directly at the base in this orientation, the flatter side indicates the side to which the bone belongs, and the articular facet is indented on the same side.

Second Metatarsal. The second metatarsal (fig. 9.25) is the longest metatarsal. It articulates distally (fig. 9.25a) with a proximal phalanx, and proximally (fig. 9.25b) with the second cuneiform, as well as first and third metatarsals and cuneiforms on either side of the base. The shaft (fig. 9.25c, d) has a somewhat triangular shape in cross section. The base is shaped like a map of the continent of Africa or South America, depending on its side. On the medial side is a single facet for the first cuneiform that lips over the edge from the base. The lateral side has two small facets for the third metatarsal and third cuneiform.

Differentiation from Other Metatarsals. The second and third metatarsals are similar in length, but the second is longer. The base has a projecting area on one side and the facet patterns distinguish the bones from each other. The second metatarsal has two small facets on the lateral side of the base, whereas the third metatarsal has a single, large, round facet with an oblique groove under it.

Siding Techniques. The second metatarsal can be sided even before the distinctive facet pattern develops on the base. To do so, hold the bone with the dorsal surface up, the concave plantar surface down, and the head away from you (fig. 9.25d). The base slants toward the side to which the bone belongs, so that it projects toward you (proximally) farther on that side. When the articular

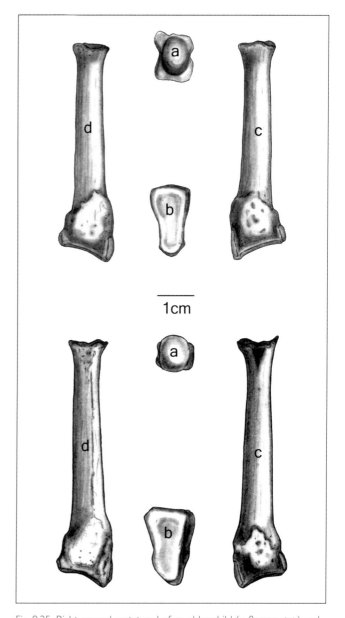

Fig. 9.25 Right second metatarsal of an older child (c. 8 years, *top*) and adolescent (c. 15 years, *bottom*): *a*, head viewed distally; *b*, base viewed proximally; *c*, palmar view of shaft; *d*, dorsal view of shaft.

facets are better developed at about 4 or 5 years of age, the side with the two separate facets is on the side from which the bone comes when oriented in the same manner.

Third Metatarsal. The third metatarsal (fig. 9.26) is the second longest metatarsal. It articulates distally (fig. 9.26a) with the proximal phalanx, proximally (fig. 9.26b) with the third cuneiform, and with the second and fourth metatarsals on either side of the base. The shaft is somewhat twisted (fig. 9.26c, d). The base is shaped like a map of the continent of Africa or South America, depending on its side. The medial side of the base normally has two small, separate, round facets for articulation with the second metatarsal. The lateral side of the base has a single, large, round facet for articulation with the fourth metatarsal with an oblique groove just inferior to it.

Differentiation from Other Metatarsals. The second and third metatarsals are similar in length, but the third is slightly shorter. The base is flatter than that of the second, which is slightly convex due to the more proximal projection on one side. The facet pattern of the third metatarsal is distinctive with the single, round facet and oblique groove on the lateral aspect of the base. Note that the groove separating the two small facets on the lateral side of a second metatarsal is straight up and down rather than angled.

Siding Techniques. Even in neonates, the base of the metatarsal projects farther proximally toward the side

from which the bone comes. Thus, with the dorsal aspect up and the head away from you, the base angles toward you on the side from which it comes (fig. 9.26d). In older individuals, that side of the base also shows the large, round facet and oblique groove. Another method is to place the dorsal edge on a table with the concave plantar surface up and the proximal base facing you (fig. 9.26c). The side of the base that displays the two smaller articulations for the second metatarsal identifies the side from which the bone comes.

Fourth Metatarsal. The fourth metatarsal articulates distally (fig. 9.27a) with a proximal phalanx, proximally (fig. 9.27b) with the cuboid, and with the third metatarsal and third cuneiform and the fifth metatarsal on

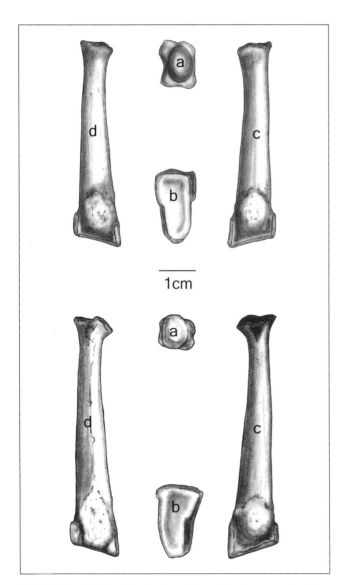

Fig. 9.26 Right third metatarsal of an older child (c. 8 years, *top*) and adolescent (c. 15 years, *bottom*): *a*, head viewed distally; *b*, base viewed proximally; *c*, palmar view of shaft; *d*, dorsal view of shaft.

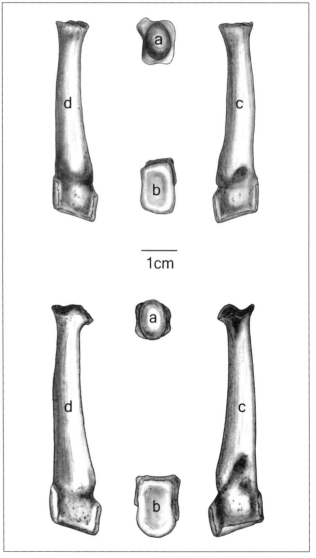

Fig. 9.27 Right fourth metatarsal of an older child (c. 8 years, *top*) and adolescent (c. 15 years, *bottom*): *a*, head viewed distally; *b*, base viewed proximally; *c*, palmar view of shaft; *d*, dorsal view of shaft.

either side of the base. The shaft (fig. 9.27c, d) is some-what twisted like that of the third metatarsal, and the base is roughly square or rectangular. The medial side of the base has one articular facet for the third metatarsal, and the lateral side has a single, large, ovoid to almost triangular facet for articulation with the fifth metatarsal.

Differentiation from Other Metatarsals. The fourth metatarsal has single facets on both sides of its base. The large, single facet on the lateral side has a groove under it like the third metatarsal, which makes these two metatarsals the easiest to confuse. The fourth is shorter than the third and the much squarer base distinguishes it.

Siding Techniques. Even at the earliest stages of development, the base slants toward you or projects more proximally on the side from which the bone comes when viewed with the dorsal surface up, the concave plantar aspect down, and the base toward you (fig. 9.27d). In this position, older subadults exhibit a large facet with an oblique groove on the lateral side, indicating the side to which the bone belongs. Another method is to view the concave plantar surface with the proximal base toward you (fig. 9.27c). The side of the base with the more vertically oriented facet for the third metatarsal, and lacking the groove, identifies the side from which the bone comes.

Fifth Metatarsal. The fifth metatarsal articulates distally (fig. 9.28a) with a proximal phalanx, proximally (fig. 9.28b) with the cuboid, and with the fourth metatarsal on the medial side of the base. In fetal and infant remains, the shaft is shorter and more robust than all but the first metatarsal. In older individuals, the shaft (fig. 9.28c, d) has a well-defined ridge on the dorsal surface, and the base is unique in that it has a large non-articular protuberance or styloid process (fig. 9.28e) on the lateral side that develops in childhood. The plantar aspect of the proximal end is marked by a medial prominence opposite the styloid process and the head also displays a groove on the plantar surface. A single articular facet is present on the medial side of the base for the fourth metatarsal, while the proximal articular facet for the cuboid is somewhat triangular and slightly convex.

Differentiation from Other Metatarsals. In fetal and neonatal remains, the fifth metatarsal is shorter than all but the robust first metatarsal. It is similar in size to the fourth metatarsal, with which it shares a rounded base. The fifth, however, is more robust than a fourth metatarsal in the same individual, with a broader base and head. As the styloid process develops, this bone is unlikely to be mistaken for any other metatarsal.

Siding Techniques. Until the styloid process is recognizable, the easiest way to side a fifth metatarsal is to note that, like the second through fourth, the base projects proximally or angles toward you on the side it is from when viewed dorsally with the base facing you

(fig. 9.28d). In older children and adults, the more difficult aspect of orientation is determining which side is dorsal. The plantar aspect is more rounded, while the dorsal surface has a sharp ridge on the medial aspect of the shaft. It is more obvious in larger individuals.

Once the styloid process (fig. 9.28e) is apparent, hold it toward the floor with the articular surface for the fourth metatarsal facing you. The articular facet is shaped like a right triangle and the 90-degree angle is on the side to which the bone belongs. Also in this position, the flatter side of the midshaft is on the side from which the bone comes. Another technique is to hold the bone with the dorsal aspect (and ridge) up, plantar surface down, and

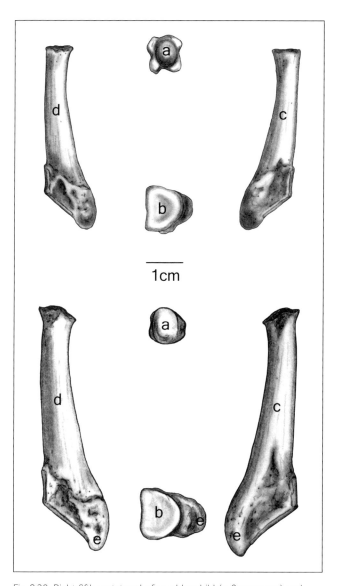

Fig. 9.28 Right fifth metatarsal of an older child (c. 8 years, *top*) and adolescent (c. 15 years, *bottom*): *a,* head viewed distally; *b,* base viewed proximally; *c,* palmar view of shaft; *d,* dorsal view of shaft; *e,* styloid process.

base toward you (see fig. 9.28d). In this position, the styloid process indicates the side to which the bone belongs.

Differentiating Metatarsals from Metacarpals. The metatarsals and metacarpals differ in length, with the metatarsals being longer. They also have substantial differences in morphology. Metatarsals have straighter, narrower, and more rounded shafts, even in fetal development. Metatarsal shaft breadth is considerably narrower compared with head and base breadth than in metacarpals because the metatarsal heads and shafts are compressed in the mediolateral direction. Metatarsal heads are smaller than those of the metacarpals.

In fetuses, neonates, and infants, the distal ends of the shafts are oblong and slightly concave in metatarsals; metacarpal heads are more circular and convex. The proximal ends are rounder in the fourth and fifth metatarsals, and more triangular or teardrop shaped in the seconds and thirds. In contrast, metacarpal bases display four distinct sides and are rectangular in outline but slightly pinched in the middle.

The Foot Phalanges

Each foot has a total of fourteen phalanges; however, fusion of the distal and intermediate phalanges in the fourth and fifth rays is not uncommon. Each toe (except the first ray or big toe) is typically comprised of three phalanges: the proximal, intermediate, and distal phalanges (fig. 9.29). The first ray has only proximal and distal phalanges. Throughout development, the proximal and intermediate phalanges of the foot can be sided, although it is not possible to side the distal phalanges, with the exception of the first. It is very difficult to distinguish the ray to which each row of phalanges belongs, with the exception of the first or big toe.

Proximal Phalanges. The proximal phalanges (fig. 9.29a) articulate proximally with the metatarsal heads and distally with the intermediate phalanges, except in the first ray where the proximal phalanx articulates directly with the distal phalanx. They form from a shaft and a base (proximal end). The shafts first appear between 14 and 16 fetal weeks.

The proximal phalanges are the largest of the three rows of phalanges, and display a circular, concave base. The distal end is bilobed or somewhat spool shaped. The first proximal phalanx is much larger than the others and can be distinguished at all stages of development by its robusticity. The proximal phalanges decrease in size from the first through the fifth rays.

Epiphyses for the bases appear between about 1 and 2 years of age. These epiphyses are small, oval disks with a slightly concave surface for articulation with the head

of the metatarsals. Fusion of the bases to the shaft occurs between 13 and 15 years in females and 16 to 18 years in males.

Intermediate Phalanges. There are four intermediate phalanges (fig. 9.29b) found in rays 2 through 5 that articulate at their bases with the proximal phalanges and at their heads with the distal phalanges. Each is formed from a shaft and a base. The shafts begin to ossify between fetal weeks 16 and 20. In fetal and neonatal skeletons, these bones are much smaller and squarer than the proximal phalanges but lack the pointed ends of the distal phalanges. The heads of the intermediate phalanges become increasingly bilobate or spool shaped through childhood.

Epiphyses for the bases form between 1 and 2 years. Like those of the proximal phalanges, they are small, ovoid disks. In contrast, they have an articular surface with two small, concave indentations for articulation with the heads of the proximal epiphyses. Like the intermediate phalanges of the hands, the proximal facets resemble a pig snout. The bases fuse to the shafts at approximately 11 to 13 years in females and 14 to 16 years in males.

Distal Phalanges. The distal phalanges (fig. 9.29c) on rays 2 through 5 are distinct from the proximal and intermediate phalanges because they are very small and have only one articular surface on the proximal end, while the distal end has a terminal tuft or spear-point shape like the distal hand phalanges. This feature is known as the distal phalangeal tubercle. The proximal end has a double articular facet that resembles a pig snout, like those of the intermediate phalanges. The distal phalanx for the first ray is very distinct because of its large size. It is the only distal phalanx that can be easily differentiated and sided.

The distal foot phalanges are formed from a small shaft and a base. They first appear between 9 and 12 fetal weeks. The base or proximal end forms as a secondary epiphysis, and the appearance varies by ray. The base of the distal phalanx on the first toe appears around 9 months of age in females and 14 months in males. The epiphyses for rays 2 through 5 appear between 2 and 3 years in females and 4 to 5 years in males. Fusion of the bases to the shafts occurs between 11 and 13 years in females and 14 and 16 years in males.

Siding Foot Phalanges. Unlike the hand phalanges, the proximal and intermediate foot phalanges can generally be sided. To do so, place the flatter plantar aspect down, the rounded dorsal side up, and the distal head away from you (see fig. 9.29). The bilobate head slants down toward the side from which the bone comes. In other words, the lower lobe is the side to which the bone belongs because the head projects farther distally on the medial aspect. In some phalanges, this distinction may be very slight and

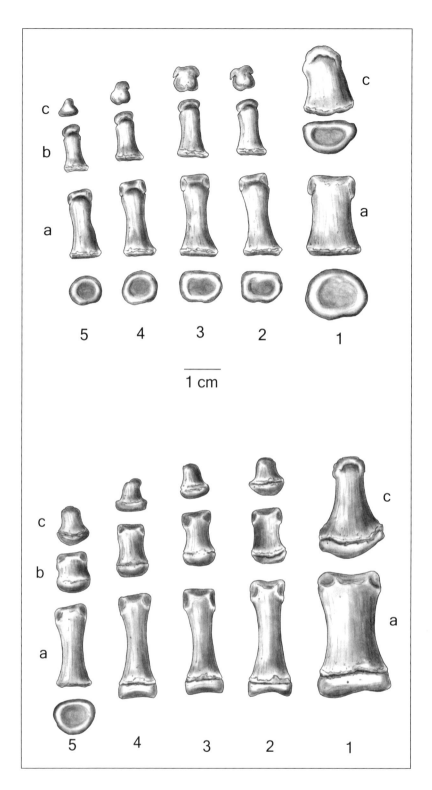

Fig. 9.29 Left foot phalanges of an older child
(c. 8 years, *top*) and adolescent (c. 15 years, *bottom*),
with shafts in dorsal view and bases in proximal view:
a, proximal row; *b*, intermediate row; *c*, distal row.

those bones may not be readily sided. The first distal phalanx is the only one in the distal row that can be sided re-
liably. It has a projecting area on the medial side of its
proximal end. Thus, the side of the base that protrudes
the least indicates the side to which the bone belongs.

Differentiating Hand and Foot Phalanges. Foot phalanges
are much shorter than hand phalanges. Their shafts are
round in cross section, while those of the hand phalanges are flat on the palmar surface and semicircular or
D shaped. On proximal and intermediate foot phalanges,

a fossa is usually present on the plantar surface near the base. The foot phalanges also tend to be irregular in shape.

When proximal phalanges of the hand and foot are compared, those of the foot tend to have larger bases and heads, and the shafts are constricted in a mediolateral direction. The intermediate and distal phalanges of the foot tend to be short, with shafts that are concave on both the anterior (plantar) and dorsal surfaces, while those of the hand are only concave on the anterior (palmar) surface. The distal foot phalanges look stunted in comparison to the distal hand phalanges and appear to have no constriction or neck. Distal hand phalanges are long and slender in comparison. An easy way to remember this difference is to note that a *foot* phalanx looks like a *foot*ball player who has a head and broad shoulders, but no discernible neck.

PART FOUR
Quick Reference

The last part of this book is designed to provide the investigator with rapid means of identifying human subadult bones and teeth and estimating the stage of development. Chapter 10, therefore, includes tables indicating the timing of appearance and fusion of various ossification centers, as well as illustrations of long bones at several stages of development. Additional templates of other bones at various ages are included to assist in identification. These figures may be useful complements to skeletal inventory forms.

Chapter 10 Age Estimation and Templates for Identification

■ The major focus of this book is to provide the excavator or student with techniques to identify the skeletal remains of fetuses, infants, and children in archaeological and forensic contexts. Once all excavated skeletal elements have been identified, the following tables and templates can be used to determine the age category to which the individual belongs. These tables and templates act as a basic summary of subadult skeletal and dental aging techniques and also help the reader better understand which elements should be present at various stages of development.

Generally accepted methods for estimating age at death rely on dental and skeletal evidence. Dental evidence typically includes the sequence of tooth eruption and the pattern of tooth formation. Dental formation is the preferred aging method because it is the best approximation of chronological or "true" age (Garn et al., 1958; Moorrees et al., 1963; Smith, 1991).

Skeletal age indicators, such as long bone diaphysis lengths and epiphyseal fusion times, are more variable than dental indicators. Dental remains may not always be present and, therefore, skeletal age indicators play an important role in subadult age estimation. Researchers often correlate skeletal age indicators with dental ages when both dental and skeletal evidence are present. This approach attempts to provide population-specific skeletal growth profiles that can be used to age skeletal remains when dental evidence is lacking (Hoppa, 1992).

The development and testing of subadult aging methods is an active area of research in physical anthropology. These methods, however, are often population and sample specific. Thus, a particular aging method appropriate for some samples may not be appropriate for others. Measurements of skeletal elements, particularly long bone diaphysis lengths, are frequently used to estimate subadult age at death and are available in several publications (e.g., Fazekas and Kósa, 1978; Kósa, 1989; Scheuer and Black, 2000; Ubelaker, 1989, 1999). In this chapter, we provide general aging templates for limb bone length and epiphyseal appearance and fusion. However, the reader should consult the references listed above when conducting more detailed analyses of subadult age estimation.

Appearance and Fusion of Skeletal Elements

The presence and fusion of certain bones and epiphyses are very useful in determining the approximate age of an individual, while also indicating which other elements are likely to be forming or fusing. Summary appearance and fusion data are provided in the following tables for the epiphyses of the long bones (table 10.1); flat and irregular bones, including the scapula, os coxa, ribs, and patella (table 10.2); vertebral column (table 10.3); and bones of the hands (table 10.4) and feet (table 10.5).

Age-Related Templates

The templates in figures 10.1–10.12 permit rapid visual assessment of the size and appearance of representative skeletal and dental elements at varying stages of development. These templates are designed to enable the reader to make general age assessments from subadult remains while also serving to identify those elements that should be present at general stages of development. The templates, therefore, can assist in recovery and identification of subadult skeletal remains. Figures 10.1 and 10.2 can be used as a visual inventory or documentation sheet for an infant skeleton. All of these visual reference guides should be used in conjunction with data presented in tables 10.1–10.5.

Table 10.1. Approximate Ages for Appearance and Fusion of Long Bone Epiphyses

Long Bone Epiphysis	Fetal Trimester			Infant		Young Child		Older Child		Adolescent		Young Adult	
	1st	2nd	3rd	0–0.5	0.5–1	1–3	3–6	6–9	9–12	12–15	15–20	20–25	25–30
Femur, distal	—	—	P	U	U	U	U	U	U	U	F/C	C	C
Femur, proximal	—	—	—	P	P	U	U	U	U	F/C	F/C	C	C
Tibia, proximal	—	—	—	P	U	U	U	U	U	F/C	F/C	C	C
Tibia, distal	—	—	—	P	P	U	U	U	U	F/C	F/C	C	C
Humerus, proximal	—	—	—	P	U	U	U	U	U	F/C	F/C	C	C
Fibula, distal	—	—	—	—	P	P	U	U	U	F/C	F/C	C	C
Femur, greater trochanter	—	—	—	—	—	P	P	U	U	F/C	F/C	C	C
Radius, distal	—	—	—	—	—	P	U	U	U	F/C	F/C	C	C
Humerus, capitulum	—	—	—	—	—	P	U	U	U	F/C	C	C	C
Humerus, greater tubercle	—	—	—	—	—	P/F/C	F/C	C	C	C	C	C	C
Ulna, distal	—	—	—	—	—	—	P	P	U	U	F/C	C	C
Radius, proximal	—	—	—	—	—	—	P	U	F/C	F/C	F/C	C	C
Fibula, proximal	—	—	—	—	—	—	P	U	U	F/C	F/C	C	C
Humerus, medial epicondyle	—	—	—	—	—	—	—	P	U	U	F/C	F/C	C
Humerus, lesser tubercle	—	—	—	—	—	—	P/F/C	C	C	C	C	C	C
Tibia, tuberosity	—	—	—	—	—	—	—	P	P	F/C	C	C	C
Ulna, proximal	—	—	—	—	—	—	—	P	P	F/C	F/C	C	C
Humerus, trochlea	—	—	—	—	—	—	—	P	F/C	C	C	C	C
Femur, lesser trochanter	—	—	—	—	—	—	—	—	P	U	F/C	C	C
Humerus, lateral epicondyle	—	—	—	—	—	—	—	—	—	P	F/C	C	C
Clavicle, medial	—	—	—	—	—	—	—	—	—	P	U	F/C	F/C
Clavicle, lateral	—	—	—	—	—	—	—	—	—	—	P/F/C	C	C

P = first present; U = unfused; F = fusing; C = complete fusion

Table 10.2. Approximate Ages for Appearance and Fusion of Irregular and Flat Bones and Epiphyses

Irregular & Flat Bone or Epiphysis	Fetal Trimester			Infant		Young Child		Older Child		Adolescent		Young Adult	
	1st	2nd	3rd	0–0.5	0.5–1	1–3	3–6	6–9	9–12	12–15	15–20	20–25	25–30
Manubrium	—	P	U	U	U	U	U	U	U	U	U	U	U
Sternebra 1	—	P	U	U	U	U	U	U	U	U	F/C	C	C
Sternebra 2	—	—	P	U	U	U	U	U	F/C	F/C	F/C	C	C
Sternebra 3	—	—	P	U	U	F/C	F/C	F/C	C	C	C	C	C
Sternebra 4	—	—	—	P	P	F/C	F/C	F/C	C	C	C	C	C
Xiphoid process	—	—	—	—	—	—	P	U	U	U	U	U	U
Patella	—	—	—	—	—	P	P	C	C	C	C	C	C
Scapula, coracoid	—	—	—	—	P	U	U	U	U	F/C	F/C	C	C
Ilium, iliac crest	—	—	—	—	—	—	—	—	P	P	F/C	C	C
Ishium, ischial tuberosity	—	—	—	—	—	—	—	—	—	P	P	F/C	C
Scapula, acromion	—	—	—	—	—	—	—	—	—	P	P/C	C	C
Rib, tubercle	—	—	—	—	—	—	—	—	—	—	P/F/C	C	C
Scapula, medial border	—	—	—	—	—	—	—	—	—	—	P/F/C	F/C	C
Rib, head	—	—	—	—	—	—	—	—	—	—	P/F/C	P/F/C	C

P = first present; U = unfused; F = fusing; C = complete fusion

Table 10.3. Approximate Ages for Appearance and Fusion of Vertebral Elements

Vertebral Element	Fetal Trimester			Infant		Young Child		Older Child		Adolescent		Young Adult	
	1st	2nd	3rd	0–0.5	0.5–1	1–3	3–6	6–9	9–12	12–15	15–20	20–25	25–30
Cervical/thoracic neural arches	P	U	U	U	U	F/C	C	C	C	C	C	C	C
Cervical/lumbar centra	P	P	U	U	U	U	F/C	C	C	C	C	C	C
Thoracic centra	P	U	U	U	U	U	F/C	C	C	C	C	C	C
Lumbar neural arches	—	P	U	U	U	F/C	C	C	C	C	C	C	C
Sacrum 1-2 alae, lateral parts	—	P	P	U	U	F/C	F/C	C	C	C	C	C	C
Sacrum 1 and 2 centra	P	U	U	U	U	F/C	F/C	C	C	C	C	C	C
Sacrum 1 and 2 neural arches	—	P	U	U	U	U	U	F/C	F/C	F/C	C	C	C
Sacrum 3 and 4 centra	—	P	U	U	U	F/C	F/C	C	C	C	C	C	C
Sacrum 3 neural arches	—	P	P	U	U	U	U	F/C	F/C	F/C	C	C	C
Sacrum 4 and 5 centra	—	P	U	U	U	F/C	F/C	C	C	C	C	C	C
S5 and S4 elements	—	—	—	—	—	—	—	—	—	—	F/C	C	C
S5-S4 and S3 elements	—	—	—	—	—	—	—	—	—	—	F/C	F/C	C
S5-S3 and S2 elements	—	—	—	—	—	—	—	—	—	—	—	F/C	F/C
S5-S2 and S1 elements	—	—	—	—	—	—	—	—	—	—	—	—	F/C
Coccyx 1, body and cornua	—	—	—	P	U	U	F	F/C	C	C	C	C	C
Coccyx 2	—	—	—	—	—	—	P	U/F	U/F	U/F	U/F	U/F	U/F
Coccyx 3	—	—	—	—	—	—	—	—	P	U/F	U/F	U/F	U/F
Coccyx 4	—	—	—	—	—	—	—	—	—	P	U/F	U/F	U/F
Annular rings	—	—	—	—	—	—	—	—	—	P	F/C	F/C	C

P = first present; U = unfused; F = fusing; C = complete fusion

Table 10.4. Approximate Ages for Appearance and Fusion of Hand and Wrist Bones

Hand and Wrist Bones	Fetal Trimester			Infant		Young Child		Older Child		Adolescent		Young Adult	
	1st	2nd	3rd	0–0.5	0.5–1	1–3	3–6	6–9	9–12	12–15	15–20	20–25	25–30
1st metacarpal, base	—	—	—	—	—	P	P	U	U	F/C	F/C	C	C
Proximal/distal phalanges 1-5, base	—	—	—	—	—	P	U	U	U	F/C	F/C	C	C
Intermediate phalanges 2-5, base	—	—	—	—	—	P	U	U	U	F/C	F/C	C	C
Metacarpals 2-5, heads	—	—	—	—	—	—	P	U	U	F/C	F/C	C	C
Capitate and hamate	—	—	—	P	P	—	—	—	—	—	—	—	—
Triquetral	—	—	—	—	—	P	—	—	—	—	—	—	—
Scaphoid and lunate	—	—	—	—	—	—	P	P	—	—	—	—	—
Trapezium and trapezoid	—	—	—	—	—	—	P	P	—	—	—	—	—
Pisiform	—	—	—	—	—	—	—	P	P	—	—	—	—

P = first present; U = unfused; F = fusing; C = complete fusion

Table 10.5. Approximate Ages for Appearance and Fusion of Foot and Ankle Bones

Foot and Ankle Bones	Fetal Trimester			Infant		Young Child		Older Child		Adolescent		Young Adult	
	1st	2nd	3rd	0–0.5	0.5–1	1–3	3–6	6–9	9–12	12–15	15–20	20–25	25–30
1st distal phalanx, base	—	—	—	P	U	U	U	F/C	F/C	F/C	C	C	C
Metatarsals 2-5, head	—	—	—	—	P	U	U	F/C	F/C	F/C	C	C	C
Intermediate phalanges 2-5, base	—	—	—	—	P	U	U	F/C	F/C	F/C	C	C	C
Proximal phalanges 1-5, base	—	—	—	—	P	U	U	U	F/C	F/C	C	C	C
Distal phalanges 2-5, base	—	—	—	—	P	P	U	F/C	F/C	F/C	C	C	C
Metatarsal 1, base	—	—	—	—	—	—	P	U	F/C	F/C	C	C	C
Calcaneus	—	P	P	—	—	—	—	—	—	—	—	—	—
Talus	—	—	P	—	—	—	—	—	—	—	—	—	—
Cuboid	—	—	—	P	—	—	—	—	—	—	—	—	—
3rd cuneiform	—	—	—	—	P	—	—	—	—	—	—	—	—
1st cuneiform	—	—	—	—	—	P	—	—	—	—	—	—	—
2nd cuneiform and navicular	—	—	—	—	—	P	P	—	—	—	—	—	—
Calcaneus, epiphysis	—	—	—	—	—	—	P	P	P	F/C	C	C	C

P = first present; U = unfused; F = fusing; C = complete fusion

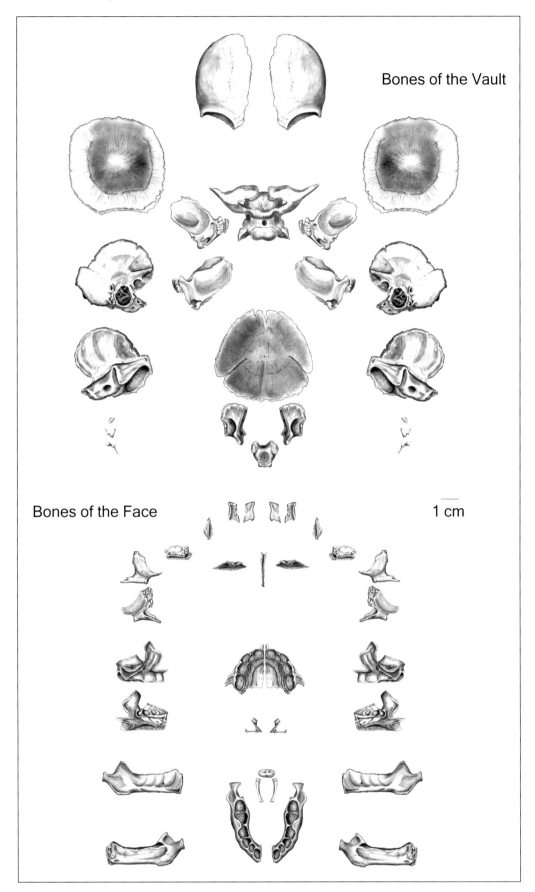

Bones of the Vault

Bones of the Face

1 cm

Fig. 10.1 Infant skull inventory sheet with bones of the cranial vault and face.

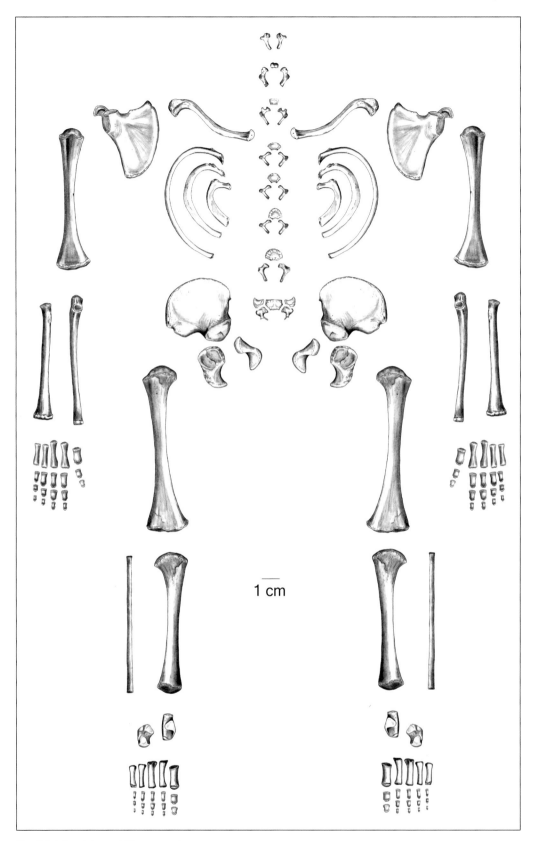

Fig. 10.2 Infant infracranial inventory sheet.

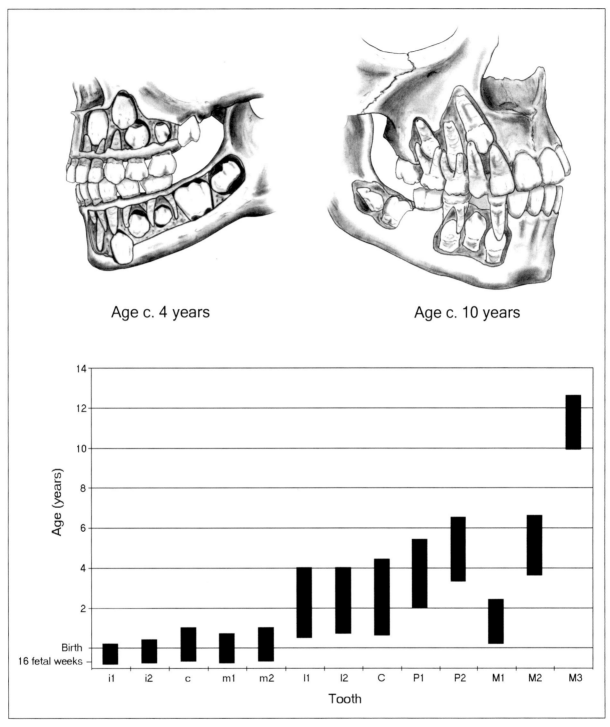

Age c. 4 years   Age c. 10 years

Fig. 10.3 Dental aging template. A chart showing the approximate range of crown calcification is useful for estimating the age of subadults. Illustrations show children at different stages of crown and root formation, as well as tooth eruption.

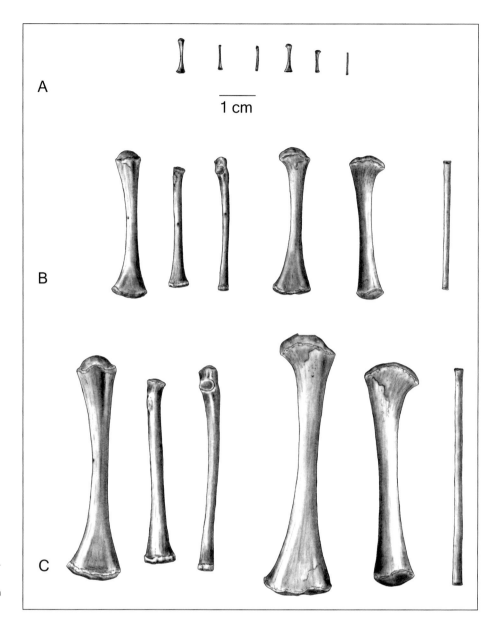

Fig. 10.4 The left long bones of a developing fetus at actual size: A, first trimester; B, second trimester; C, third trimester. Views are same as shown in chapter 8 figures.

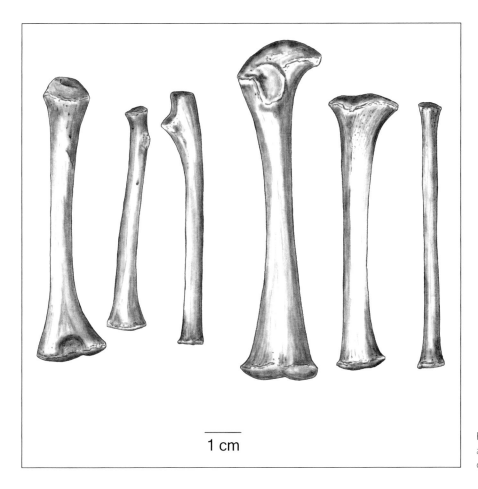

1 cm

Fig. 10.5 The left long bones of a neonate at actual size. Views are same as shown in chapter 8 figures.

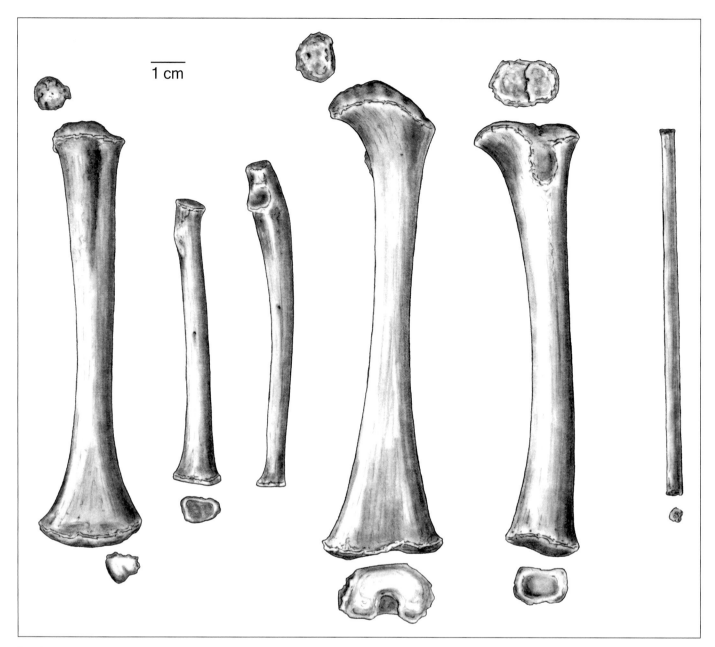

Fig. 10.6 The left long bones of a young child (c. 1.5 years) at actual size. Views are same as shown in chapter 8 figures.

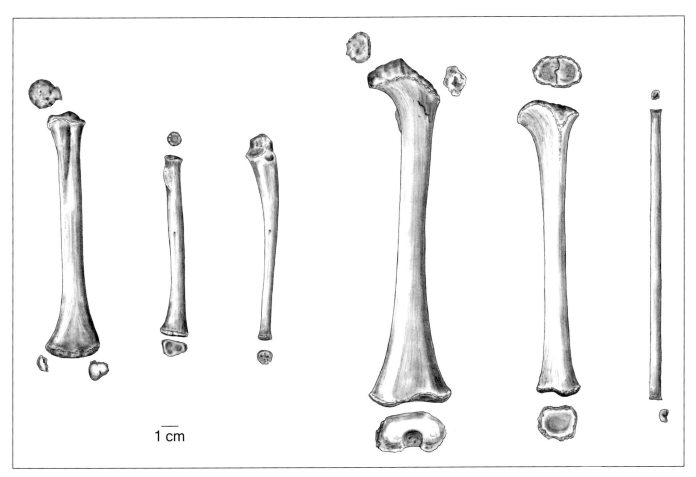

Fig. 10.7 The left long bones of a young child (c. 3 years) at approximately half actual size. Views are same as shown in chapter 8 figures.

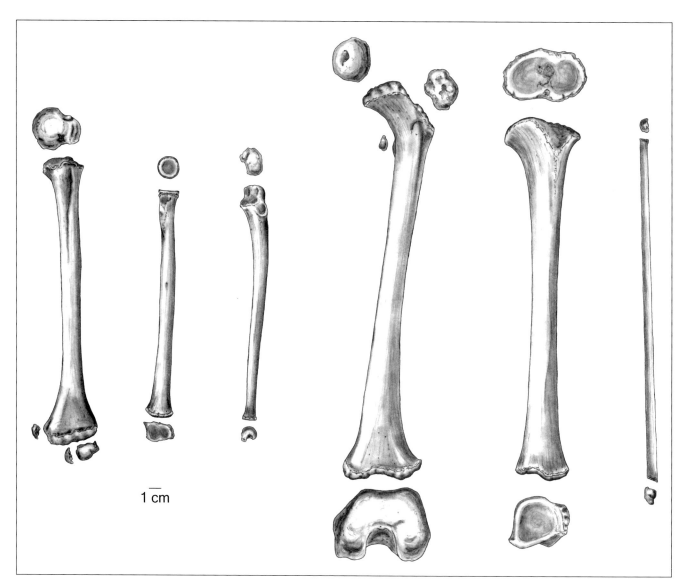

Fig. 10.8 The left long bones of an older child (c. 9 years), shown at approximately 40% actual size. Views are same as shown in chapter 8 figures.

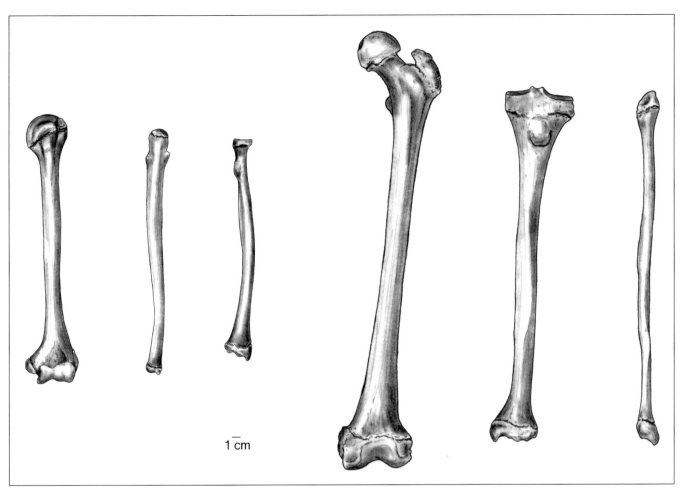

1 cm

Fig. 10.9 The left long bones of an adolescent (c. 15 years), shown at approximately 20% actual size. Views are same as shown in chapter 8 figures.

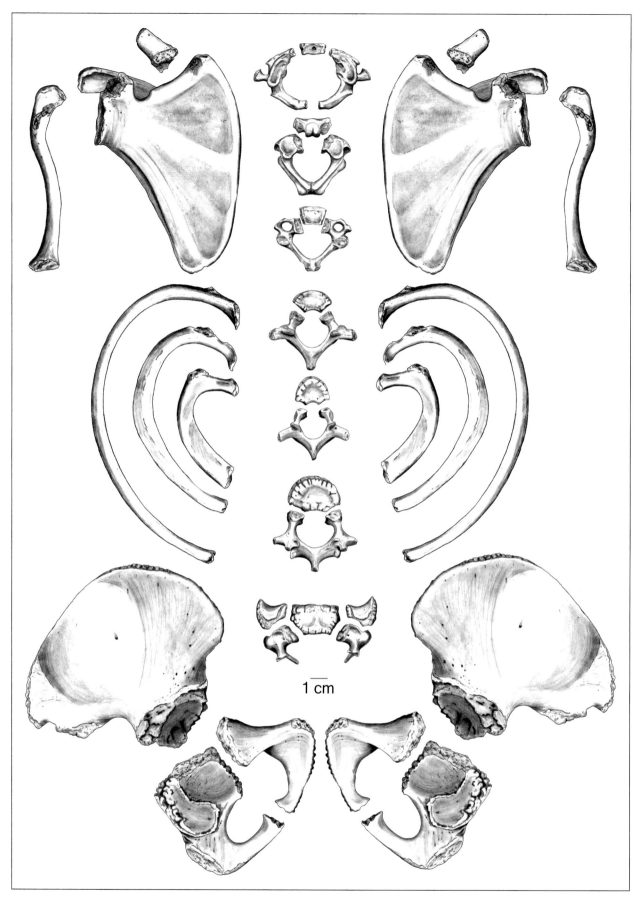

Fig. 10.10 Elements from the axial skeleton are shown to represent children age 3 to 9 years, and can be used in conjunction with appropriate long bone templates for skeletal inventory. Bones are shown in roughly anatomical position but left and right sides are reversed (i.e., bones from the left are on the right and vice versa).

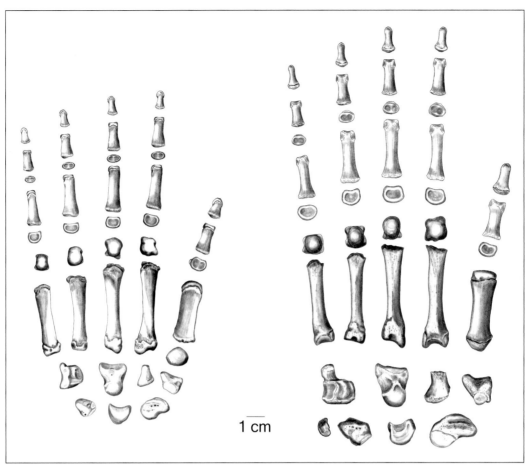

Fig. 10.11 The left hand and wrist of an older child (c. 8 years, *left*) and adolescent (c. 15 years, *right*), shown at approximately half the actual size. Metacarpals and phalanges are in dorsal view with reflected epiphyses. Carpals are in approximate anatomical position showing distinctive features of each bone.

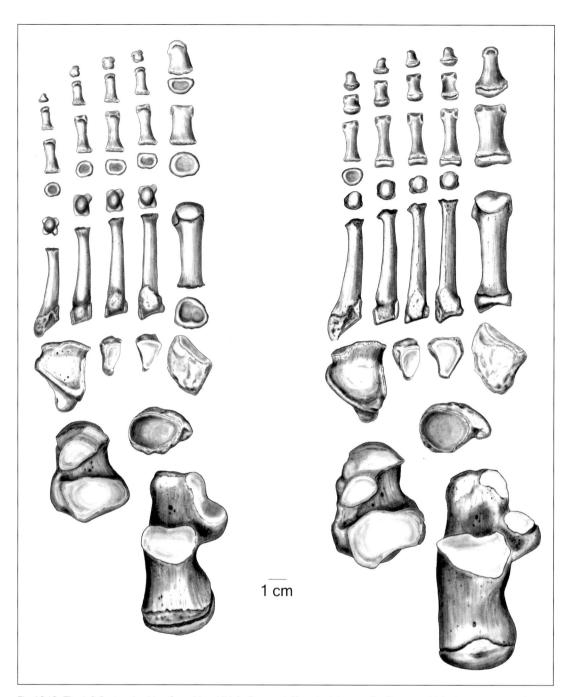

Fig. 10.12 The left foot and ankle of an older child (c. 8 years, *left*) and adolescent (c. 15 years, *right*), shown at approximately half the actual size. Metatarsals and phalanges are in dorsal view with reflected epiphyses. Tarsals are in approximate anatomical position showing distinctive features of each bone.

References Cited

Anderson JE. 1962. The human skeleton: A manual for archaeologists. Ottawa: National Museum of Canada.

Aufderheide AC, Rodríguez-Martín C. 1998. The Cambridge encyclopedia of human paleopathology. Cambridge: Cambridge University Press.

Baker BJ. 1992. Collagen composition in human skeletal remains from the NAX cemetery (A.D. 350–550) in Lower Nubia [dissertation]. University of Massachusetts, Amherst. Ann Arbor: University Microfilms International.

Bass WM. 1995. Human osteology: A laboratory and field manual. 4th ed. Columbia: Missouri Archaeological Society.

Black T. 1978. Sexual dimorphism in the tooth crown diameters of the deciduous teeth. American Journal of Physical Anthropology 48:77–82.

Boucher BJ. 1955. Sex differences in the foetal sciatic notch. Journal of Forensic Medicine 2:51–54.

Boucher BJ. 1957. Sex differences in the foetal pelvis. American Journal of Physical Anthropology 15:581–600.

Brothwell DR. 1981. Digging up bones. 3rd ed. Ithaca: Cornell University Press.

Buikstra JE, Ubelaker DH, editors. 1994. Standards for data collection from human skeletal remains. Research Series No. 44. Fayetteville: Arkansas Archeological Survey.

Cooper A, Fleischer R, James H, Tuross N. 1994. Studies of the effects of bone consolidants on endogenous DNA. Ancient DNA Newsletter 2:15–16.

DeVito C, Saunders SR. 1990. A discriminant function analysis of deciduous teeth to determine sex. Journal of Forensic Sciences 35:845–58.

Elder A, Madsen S, Brown G, Herbel C, Collins C, Whelan S, Wenz C, Alderson S, Kronthal L. 1997. Adhesives and consolidants in geological and paleontological conservation: A wall chart. SPNHC Leaflets 1(2). Society for the Preservation of Natural History Collections.

Fazekas I, Kósa F. 1978. Forensic fetal osteology. Budapest: Akadémiai Kiadó.

Garn SM, Lewis AB, Koski K, Polacheck DL. 1958. The sex difference in tooth calcification. Journal of Dental Research 37:561–67.

Garn SM, Rohmann CG, Silverman FN. 1967. Radiographic standards for postnatal ossification and tooth calcification. Medical Radiography and Photography 43:45–66.

Gordon CG, Buikstra JE. 1981. Soil pH, bone preservation, and sampling bias at mortuary sites. American Antiquity 46:566–71.

Gowland RL, Chamberlain AT. 2002. A Bayesian approach to ageing perinatal skeletal material from archaeological sites: Implications for the evidence for infanticide in Roman Britain. Journal of Archaeological Science 29:677–85.

Gray H. 1977. Gray's anatomy: The classic collector's edition. New York: Bounty Books.

Greiner TM, Walker RA. 1999. Morphometric variation of the human auditory ossicles. Presented at the 69th annual meeting of the American Association of Physical Anthropologists, Columbus, Ohio.

Greulich WW, Pyle SI. 1959. Radiographic atlas of skeletal development of the hand and wrist. 2nd ed. Stanford, CA: Stanford University Press.

Gustafson G, Koch G. 1974. Age estimation up to 16 years of age based on dental development. Odontologisk Revy 25:297–306.

Guy H, Masset C, Baud CA. 1997. Infant taphonomy. International Journal of Osteoarchaeology 7:221–29.

Hillson S. 1996. Dental anthropology. Cambridge: Cambridge University Press.

Holcomb SMC, Konigsberg LW. 1995. Statistical study of sexual dimorphism in the human fetal sciatic notch. American Journal of Physical Anthropology 97:113–25.

Hoppa RD. 1992. Evaluating human skeletal growth: An Anglo-Saxon example. International Journal of Osteoarchaeology 2:275–88.

Hoppa RD, Vaupel JW, editors. 2002. Paleodemography: Age distributions from skeletal samples. Cambridge: Cambridge University Press.

Horie CV. 1987. Materials for conservation. Oxford: Butterworth-Heinemann.

Humphrey L. 2000. Growth studies of past populations: An overview and an example. In: Cox M, Mays S, editors. Human osteology in archaeology and forensic science. London: Greenwich Medical Media. p 23–38.

Hunt DR. 1990. Sex determination in the subadult ilia: An indirect test of Weaver's nonmetric sexing method. Journal of Forensic Sciences 35:881–85.

Hunt EE, Gleiser I. 1955. The estimation of age and sex of preadolescent children from bones and teeth. American Journal of Physical Anthropology 13:479–87.

Johansson L. 1987. Bone and related materials. In: Hodges HWM, editor. In situ archaeological conservation. Mexico: Instituto Nacional de Antropología e Historia, and Century City, CA.: J. Paul Getty Trust. p 132–36.

Johnson J. 1994. Consolidation of archaeological bone: A conservation perspective. Journal of Field Archaeology 21:221–33.

Johnston FE, Zimmer LO. 1989. Assessment of growth and age in the immature skeleton. In: İşcan MY, Kennedy KAR, editors.

Reconstruction of life from the skeleton. New York: Alan R. Liss. p 11–21.

Konigsberg LW, Frankenberg SR. 1994. Paleodemography: "Not quite dead." Evolutionary Anthropology 3:92–105.

Kósa F. 1989. Age estimation from the fetal skeleton. In: İşcan MY, editor. Age markers in the human skeleton. Springfield, IL: Charles C. Thomas. p 21–54.

Kres L, Lovell N. 1995. Comparison of consolidants for archaeological bone. Journal of Field Archaeology 22:508–15.

Larsen CS. 1997. Bioarchaeology: Interpreting behavior from the human skeleton. Cambridge: Cambridge University Press.

Lewis M. 2000. Non-adult palaeopathology: Current status and future potential. In: Cox M, Mays S, editors. Human osteology in archaeology and forensic science. London: Greenwich Medical Media. p 39–57.

Liversidge HM, Herdeg B, and Rösing FW. 1998. Dental age estimation of non-adults. In: Alt KW, Rösing FW, Teschler-Nicola M, editors. Dental anthropology, fundamentals, limits, and prospects. Vienna: Springer-Verlag. p 419–22.

Logan WHG, Kronfeld R. 1933. Development of the human jaws and surrounding structures from birth to the age of fifteen years. Journal of the American Dental Association 20:379–427.

Loth SR, Henneberg M. 2001. Sexually dimorphic mandibular morphology in the first few years of life. American Journal of Physical Anthropology 115:179–86.

MacKay RH. 1961. Skeletal maturation (chart). Rochester, NY: Eastman Kodak.

Mays S. 1993. Infanticide in Roman Britain. Antiquity 67:883–88.

Mays S. 1998. The archaeology of human bones. London: Routledge.

McGowan GA, LaRoche CJ. 1996. The ethical dilemma facing conservation: Care and treatment of human skeletal remains and mortuary objects. Journal of the American Institute of Conservation 35:109–21.

Milner GR, Wood JW, Boldsen JL. 2000. Paleodemography. In: Katzenberg MA, Saunders SR, editors. Biological anthropology of the human skeleton. New York: Wiley-Liss. p 467–97.

Mittler DM, Sheridan SG. 1992. Sex determination in subadults using auricular surface morphology: A forensic science perspective. Journal of Forensic Sciences 37:1068–75.

Liversidge HM, Molleson T. 2004. Variation in crown and root formation and eruption of human deciduous teeth. American Journal of Physical Anthropology 123:172–80.

Moorrees CFA, Fanning EA, Hunt EE. 1963. Formation and resorption of three deciduous teeth in children. American Journal of Physical Anthropology 21:205–13.

Nicholson GJ, Tomiuk J, Czarnetzki A, Bachmann L, Pusch CM. 2002. Detection of bone glue treatment as a major source of contamination in ancient DNA analyses. American Journal of Physical Anthropology 118:117–20.

Ortner DJ. 2003. Identification of pathological conditions in human skeletal remains. 2nd ed. San Diego: Academic Press.

Paine RR, editor. 1997. Integrating archaeological demography: Multidisciplinary approaches to prehistoric population. Occasional Paper No. 24. Carbondale: Center for Archaeological Investigations, Southern Illinois University.

Rogers T, Saunders S. 1994. Accuracy of sex determination using morphological traits of the human pelvis. Journal of Forensic Medicine 39:1047–56.

Saunders SR. 2000. Subadult skeletons and growth-related studies.

In: Katzenberg MA, Saunders SR, editors. Biological anthropology of the human skeleton. New York: Wiley-Liss. p 135–61.

Saunders SR, Hoppa RD. 1993. Growth deficit in survivors and non-survivors: Biological mortality bias in subadult skeletal samples. Yearbook of Physical Anthropology 36:127–51.

Scheuer L. 2002. Brief communication: A blind test of mandibular morphology for sexing mandibles in the first few years of life. American Journal of Physical Anthropology 119:189–91.

Scheuer L, Black S. 2000. Developmental juvenile osteology. San Diego: Academic Press.

Scheuer L, Black S. 2004. The juvenile skeleton. San Diego: Academic Press.

Schour I, Massler M. 1940. Studies in tooth development: The growth pattern of human teeth, part II. Journal of the American Dental Association 27:1918–31.

Schutkowski H. 1987. Sex determination of fetal and neonate skeletons by means of discriminant analysis. International Journal of Osteoarchaeology 2:347–52.

Schutkowski H. 1993. Sex determination of infant and juvenile skeletons: I. Morphognostic features. American Journal of Physical Anthropology 90:199–205.

Schwartz JH. 1995. Skeleton keys: An introduction to human skeletal morphology, development, and analysis. New York: Oxford University Press.

Sease C. 1994. A conservation manual for the field archaeologist. Los Angeles: University of California.

Smith BH. 1991. Standards of human tooth formation and dental age assessment. In: Kelley MA, Larsen CS, editors. Advances in dental anthropology. New York: Wiley-Liss. p 143–68.

Smith CW. 2002. Archaeological conservation using polymers. College Station: Texas A&M University Press.

Smith P, Kahila G. 1992. Identification of infanticide in archaeological sites: A case study from the Late Roman–Byzantine periods at Ashkelom, Israel. Journal of Archaeological Science 19:667–75.

Steele DG, Bramblett CA. 1988. The anatomy and biology of the human skeleton. College Station: Texas A&M University Press.

Sutter, RC. 2003. Nonmetric subadult skeletal sexing traits: I. A blind test of the accuracy of eight previously proposed methods using prehistoric known-sex mummies from Northern Chile. Journal of Forensic Sciences 48:927–35.

Tanner JM, Whitehouse RH. 1959. Standards for skeletal maturity based on a study of 3000 British children. London: Institute of Child Health.

Tocheri MW, Dupras TL, Sheldrick P, Molto JE. 2005. Roman period fetal skeletons from the east cemetery (Kellis 2) of Kellis, Egypt. International Journal of Osteoarchaeology.

Ubelaker DH. 1989. The estimation of age at death from immature human bone. In: İşcan MY, editor. Age markers in the human skeleton. Springfield, IL: Charles C. Thomas. p 55–70.

Ubelaker DH. 1999. Human skeletal remains: Excavation, analysis, interpretation. 3rd ed. Washington, DC: Taraxacum.

Walker PL, Cook DC, Lambert PM. 1997. Skeletal evidence of child abuse: A physical anthropological perspective. Journal of Forensic Sciences 42:196–207.

Weaver DS. 1980. Sex differences in the ilia of a known-sex and age sample of fetal and infant skeletons. American Journal of Physical Anthropology 52:191–96.

White TD. 2000. Human osteology. 2nd ed. San Diego: Academic Press.

Index

Page numbers in *italics* refer to figures.